A Psychological Inquiry into the Meaning and Concept of Forgiveness

This book explores the psychological nature of forgiveness for both the subjective ego and what C.G. Jung called the objective psyche, or soul. Utilizing analytical, archetypal, and dialectical psychological approaches, the notion of forgiveness is traced from its archetypal and philosophical origins in Greek and Roman mythology through its birth and development in Judaic and Christian theology, to its modern functional character as self-help commodity, relationship remedy, and global necessity. Offering a deeper understanding of the concept of "true" forgiveness as a soul event, Sandoval reveals the transformative nature of forgiveness and the implications this notion has on the self and analytical psychology.

Jennifer M. Sandoval is a practicing psychologist in southern California, USA.

Researching Social Psychology Series

1. **Addressing Loneliness**
   Coping, Prevention and Clinical Interventions
   Edited by Ami Sha'ked & Ami Rokach

2. **Qualitative Research Methods in Consumer Psychology**
   Ethnography and Culture
   Edited by Paul M. W. Hackett

3. **Detection and Prevention of Identity-Based Bullying**
   Social Justice Perspectives
   Britney G Brinkman

4. **Psychology of Fear, Crime and the Media**
   International Perspectives
   Derek Chadee

5. **Sexual Assault Prevention on College Campuses**
   Matt J. Gray, Christina M. Hassija, and Sarah E. Steinmetz

6. **A Psychological Inquiry into the Meaning and Concept of Forgiveness**
   Jennifer M. Sandoval

A Psychological Inquiry into the Meaning and Concept of Forgiveness

Jennifer M. Sandoval

LONDON AND NEW YORK

First published 2017
by Routledge

2 Park Square, Milton Park, Abingdon, Oxfordshire OX14 4RN
52 Vanderbilt Avenue, New York, NY 10017

Routledge is an imprint of the Taylor & Francis Group, an informa business

First issued in paperback 2018

Library of Congress Cataloging-in-Publication Data
Names: Sandoval, Jennifer M., author.
Title: A psychological inquiry into the meaning and concept of forgiveness / Jennifer M. Sandoval.
Description: New York : Routledge, 2017. | Series: Researching social psychology series ; 6 | Includes index.
Identifiers: LCCN 2016045288 | ISBN 9781138671355 (hardcover)
Subjects: LCSH: Forgiveness—Psychological aspects.
Classification: LCC BF637.F67 S36 2017 | DDC 155.9/2—dc23
LC record available at https://lccn.loc.gov/2016045288

ISBN: 978-1-138-67135-5 (hbk)
ISBN: 978-0-367-19577-9 (pbk)

Typeset in Sabon
by ApexCoVantage, LLC

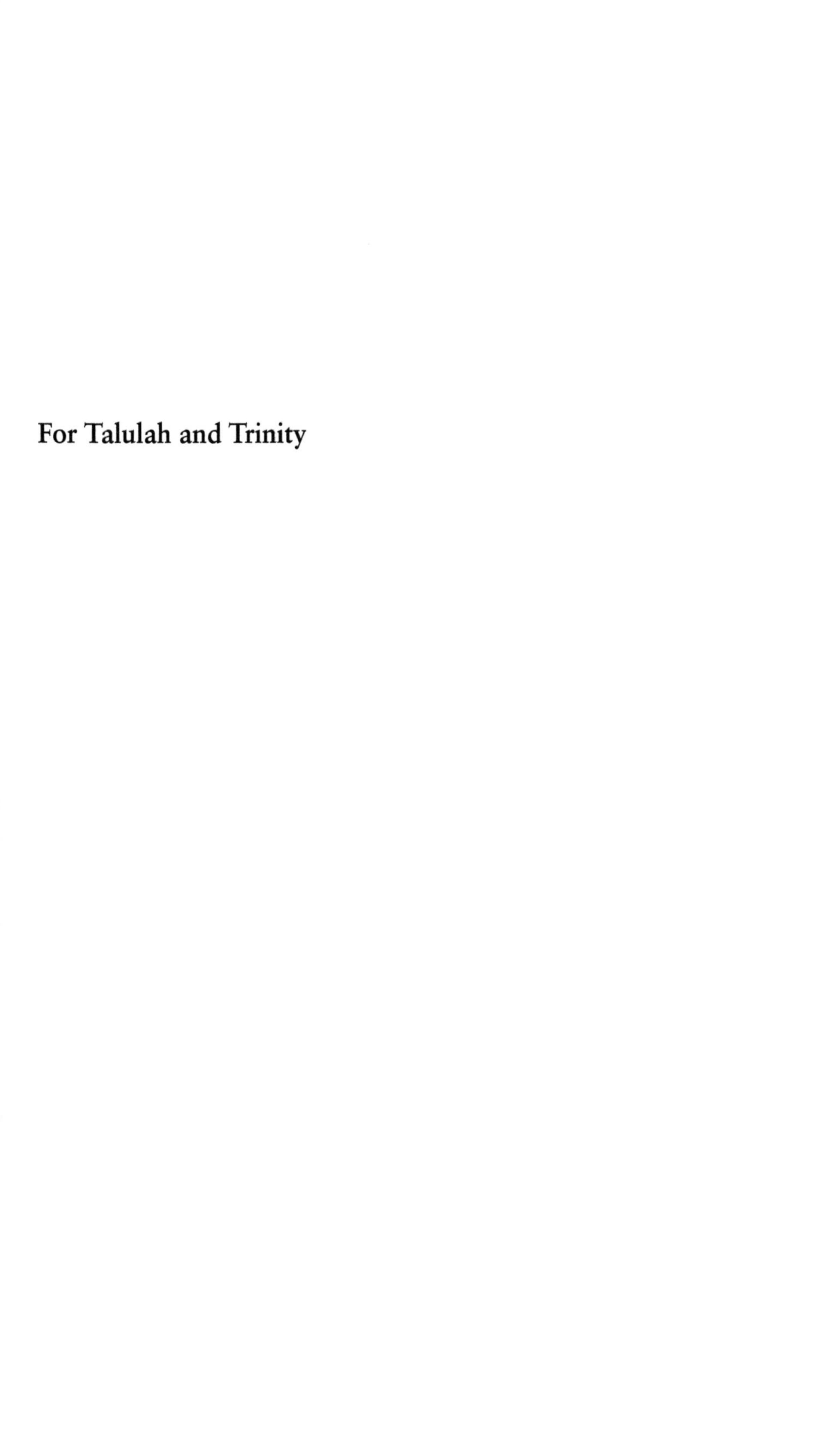

For Talulah and Trinity

Contents

1 Introduction

A Psychological Inquiry into the Meaning and Concept of Forgiveness

The holiest of all the spots on earth is where an ancient hatred has become a present love.[1]

While it was long ago when I first read these words, I am still moved by their beauty. In my imagination, the holy spot is a grassy flat area on the top of a small hill, or in a green meadow. Two people walk toward one another, arms outstretched, and surrender into a warm embrace. Maybe they are enemy kings who have laid down their arms and come to make peace after centuries of war, or siblings who have been estranged for years, finally ready to love again. To me, the image evokes the miraculous reunion of souls who, until the moment of communion, had been utterly lost to one another. Here is revealed an entirely new state of relating that had formerly been unimaginable to consciousness. In the extraordinary transformation from hatred to love, an image of the soul's truth is revealed. Such a profound shift in perspective, which we call *forgiveness*, reveals the enormous power and possibility of psyche and reflects psychological transformation of the highest order.[2]

One's first observation of the opening statement may well be the *rarity* of such an event. Why is true forgiveness so singular? The act of forgiving is simple. In its apparent sense, forgiveness would merely wipe the slate clean, clearing any past offending action between parties. Now there is nothing to avenge, no wrong to right, no debt to pay. Forgiveness would lay down a new perspective in which future relating is conditioned by something *other* than past suffering and grievances, offering an entirely new possibility for relationship. Whether it happens within oneself, between two people, extending to groups, races, religions, cultures, and nations—given what could be gained, especially in light of the stakes[3]—forgiveness would seem a very small thing to ask. Why, then, is forgiveness so rare? What makes forgiveness "impossible"?

James Hillman writes,

> We must be quite clear that forgiveness is no easy matter. If the ego has been wronged, the ego cannot forgive just because it 'should' . . . The ego

> is kept vital by its *amour-propre*, its pride and honor. Even where one wants to forgive, one finds one simply can't, because forgiveness doesn't come from the ego.[4]

Ultimately, true forgiveness often proves an impossible task—a miracle. We can see this reality in centuries-old violence and enmity between cultures and religions. The miracle here is not the parting of the sea or the turning of water into wine. It is the miraculous *transformation* of enemy to brother, the astonishing journey from war to peace. This is the miracle of forgiveness, and it is an honest miracle to the ego, which has no access to such transformation on its own.

The act of forgiveness, while 'simple,' is simultaneously a remarkably complex and sophisticated notion. Forgiving bears the mark of a consciousness capable of what C. G. Jung often referred to as an *opus contra naturam*—a work against [its own] nature. True forgiveness asks the forgiving mind to willingly give up familiar and comfortable strongholds, such as justice, power, and future guarantees, forever denying recourse to the reality of a past inside of which the offense occurred. Such disarming demands are not only unnatural, but highly threatening to an ego whose primary aim is its own self-protection and survival.[5] Because of this, forgiving is perverted into a manipulation, negotiated or refused altogether for the ego's own advantage. True forgiving is inherently "aneconomic," undertaken with no aim of gain for the forgiver.[6] The ego by definition can have no real interest in, capacity for, or relationship to genuine forgiveness.

So, already, we arrive at the first of many deadlocks. After all, contradiction lies at the very *heart* of forgiveness. As Lucy Allais observes, "Forgiving seems to mean ceasing to blame, but if blaming means holding the perpetrator responsible, then forgiveness requires *not* ceasing to blame, or else there will be nothing to forgive."[7] Such 'impossible' moments of contradiction and deadlock are crucial for the dialectical expansion of consciousness to occur. Slavoj Zizek writes, "The awareness that the power of a proper act is to retroactively create its own conditions of possibility should not make us afraid to embrace what, prior to the act, appears as impossible: only in this way does our act touch the Real."[8] The 'impossible' act of forgiveness is imbued with this dialectical sensibility; when it occurs, it retroactively 'punches a hole' through the presiding construct of reality and reveals a moment of the Real—reflected in the phrase above as "the holiest spot on earth." Forgiveness's dialectical aspect is revealed in the sublated presence of its opposite ("enmity") as a necessary condition for psychological truth ("holiness"); without prior 'ancient hatred,' the 'present love' would not be designated as 'the holiest.' A meaningful inquiry into a dialectical phenomenon such as forgiveness necessitates a truly *psychological* perspective, one that sees through the apparent (empirical or semantic) reality to the inherent logical form giving rise to it.

The Psychological Difference

The main concern of a psychological inquiry into any subject matter is the nature of the subject matter's relation to consciousness at large, or what Jung called the objective psyche, or "soul." The surprise here may be that psychology is not primarily concerned with *people's* thoughts and behavior (i.e., psychology is not to be confused with anthropology, sociology, or behavioral science). Rather, psychology is concerned with consciousness *per se*—which happens to make its appearance *via* individuals' thoughts and behavior. The seemingly subtle shift in focus is the defining feature of a non-ego or depth psychology. The difference between the subjective psyche or ego on the one hand and the objective psyche or soul on the other is what Wolfgang Giegerich calls *the psychological difference*. It is the awareness of this difference that characterizes a perspective as "psychological" in nature. A truly psychological inquiry takes into account consciousness in its objective, abstract, or "soul" form. When the psychological difference goes unrecognized, ignored, or neglected in favor of a strictly localized,[9] empirical, or subjective view, the inquiry veers into unpsychological territory. Psychology must be, as Jung put it, psychology "with soul"—or it fails to be psychology at all.

At once we are faced with the crucial question, what is soul?[10] As the intangible essence of consciousness itself, a concrete definition of soul by its nature is elusive. Hillman, the founder of archetypal psychology, describes it in this way:

> [Soul is] a perspective rather than a substance, a viewpoint toward things rather than a thing itself. This perspective is reflective; it mediates events and makes differences between ourselves and everything that happens. Between us and events, between the doer and the deed, there is a reflective moment—and soul-making means differentiating this middle ground.[11]

For Hillman, soul is what makes meaning possible and deepens events into experiences that move us. Soul is communicated in love and is the aspect of human imagination that expands consciousness. We *feel* soul in the delight of a child, in our lover's eyes, and in the depths of our sorrow. Individuation is given by a life in which we become who we are, in alignment with soul. Forgiveness, as imagined from this perspective, occurs in the "gap" recognized between doer and deed, in the middle ground. Forgiveness enables the 'dis-lodging' so to speak of identicalness with the position of doer or deed; forgiveness occurs in the domain of pure reflected consciousness, thereby qualifying as an act of "soul-making."

Taking into consideration the profound and undeniable historical movements in consciousness from Plato to Descartes to Hegel, we are obliged to acknowledge that the soul no longer holds to its classical ideal as a metaphysical entity that a person *has*, nor does it exist as a substantial mystical essence found in nature, gods, or God. While still referred to in religious terms or popularized in new-age spiritual circles, to speak of a substantive "soul" as a *reality* in the twenty-first century is dismissed as antiquated or sentimental; it is fair to say that "the soul" has become obsolete, if not disappeared altogether.[12] Soul no longer appears to us in substantiated form *in any sense* and in effect "vanishes" in our attempts to concretize or materialize it.[13] The modern soul has "released" all literal form, in a sense shedding "the mythical garments in which [it] had hitherto been cloaked,"[14] having returned to itself in its unmediated logical form as absolute negativity, or that which human subjectivity *is*. This movement of "disrobing" or releasing consciousness from constrictive semantic signifiers into its emancipated form as pure process aligns with forgiving as a liberating movement, a release and freeing of both forgiver and forgiven into an experience in which a deeper 'truth' of the relationship, which was there along, is yet newly acquired.

One may correctly argue that the underlying truth of a phenomenon such as forgiveness is *not* apparent in its abstract or universal notion as such but rather in its very real expression as an intimate act between two human beings. Psychologically, what we are witnessing in the act of forgiveness is an extraordinary moment of unity between the objective and subjective domains of consciousness, what Hegel called "concrete universality." Such a moment does not merely depict the relationship of the particular to the universal, but rather is a moment in which *the soul relates directly to itself*. This self-actualization of the soul occurs vis-à-vis human beings. As Hegel observed, "it is in the *finite consciousness* that the process of knowing spirit's essence takes place and that the divine self-consciousness thus arises. Out of the foaming ferment of finitude, spirit rises up fragrantly."[15] It is from mortal and ordinary life that the divine fragrance of forgiveness arises.

Why Study Forgiveness?

Much has been written about forgiveness. Bookstores are flooded with self-help books advocating the practice, offering testimonials, and giving various step-by-step methods of how to forgive others and oneself. The phenomenon has received increasing attention in the field of psychology, with numerous studies devoted to analyzing how forgiveness happens, testing differing theoretical models of how to achieve forgiveness, and measuring predictive, co-occurring, and resulting physiological, emotional, behavioral changes in those who forgive. However, the elusive question of *how* forgiveness is achieved, much less what forgiveness actually *is*, has yet to be definitively answered.[16]

While there appears to be a renewed interest in forgiveness in certain arenas, we must also acknowledge that in contemporary culture at large, forgiveness is dismissed as passé, a sentimental or merely political and empty gesture. Forgiving adds a layer of unnecessary subjectivity to what otherwise would be a simple mistake to be righted. No "forgiveness" needed, only adjustment: a mere course correction. For example, what would have formerly been a stunning plea of Pope Francis to the gay community—"We Christians should ask forgiveness from them"—now rings somewhat hollow.[17] Of *course they should.* Everyone "knows" that, and has known (albeit unconsciously) for quite some time. However, it is an inherent feature of forgiveness that it is by nature "obsolete." If it is offered "on time," is it usually rejected in astonishment and outrage by the ego. Rather, time must pass, justice must be served or the injury reduced to a faded memory before forgiveness—always offered or requested too late—be allowed. This, however, is the ego-mediated form of forgiving. (One of the few "timely" acts of forgiveness may have been Jesus's plea for forgiveness, *during his crucifixion*, on behalf of his persecutors.[18]) The primary assertion of this book is that the process of unmediated or "true" forgiveness mirrors the unfolding of consciousness itself—which is already always *catching up* to its former status. Gaining an understanding of the notion of forgiveness is of tremendous and timely relevance to the study of and by psychology.

With regard to the transformative nature of forgiveness, we can see that by definition, true and lasting forgiveness involves a *metanoia*, or a change of attitude, by the forgiver toward the forgiven. Depth psychology has long concerned itself with this kind of profound shift in awareness. Relevant here is Jung's conception of the *transcendent function* and the new attitude emergent upon the union of the opposites, or the joining of conscious and unconscious psychic elements, out of which a reconciling symbol is born. While analytical psychology imagines the transformative character of the transcendent function as a creative synthesis out of the tension of the opposites, Giegerich's dialectic (following Hegel's dialectical model) describes the source of transcendence or *insight* as dissolution or *decomposition* (as in the alchemical process of dissolution of the *unio naturalis*) or as *negation* and a "going under."[19] According to Giegerich et al., such a deepening process opens up a "totally new and unexpected dimension . . . the intentional space of interiority or 'the soul.'"[20]

The encounter with the *offense* to be forgiven and many of its felt aspects, including its often concrete and positivistic nature, along with an experience of its having its source in an offending "other," is of major psychological significance. The implications here evoke several applications of depth psychological theory, including the fundamental conception of the unconscious as being experienced first as external phenomena;[21] unwanted or rejected parts of the self (or one's "shadow" characteristics) are unconsciously projected and seen as belonging to external objects (such as the offending other). Depth psychological explorations of shadow integration as put forward by von Franz,[22] Giegerich,[23] and Hillman[24] are relevant. We are reminded again of Jung's transcendent function, in which the integration of opposites held in awareness become "me" and "not me." The question of relating to the world and one another in the absence of projection then arises.[25] The concrete and positivistic nature of the offense finds response in both Hillman's archetypal psychology, in which emphasis is placed upon *psychologizing* or seeing through literal events (the "offense" to be forgiven) to possible deeper or archetypal meaning, and again inside the notion of the dialectical approach,[26] in which the "relentless absolute-negative interiorizing of positivity"[27] is thought to result in the transformative alchemical process of soul-making.

According to Hillman, the primary concern with depth psychology is with such deeper meanings of the soul. "Psychology's one obligation is to see through, to think and feel psychologically."[28] Archetypal psychology is particularly attuned to forgiveness insofar as forgiving resides within a moral context in the sense that one "should" offer forgiveness, or upon committing a wrong should beg pardon. According to Hillman, "Archetypal reflection of each psychic movement returns the morality of actions to the gods from whom all morality supposedly comes. Reverting moral issues to their archetypal base deepens one's moral sense by recalling that moralities are transpersonal."[29] Already we can see a shift in perspective away from a literal guilty ego, which must forgive or beg forgiveness to a broader, symbolic space in which to situate the phenomenon of forgiving, recognizing that while the ego may carry forgiveness fantasies to assuage its burdens, forgiveness itself does not come from the ego.

With regard to the desire and longing for the experience of forgiveness, psychoanalytic research offers insights into the many ego defense mechanisms behind the wish to forgive, to receive forgiveness, or to avoid forgiving altogether. Insofar as the urge toward forgiveness remains in the realm of ego fantasy, true forgiveness may remain elusive. However, such deep yearning for reconciliation with the other appears also to transcend ego dynamics, entering into the realm of the Self, or the objective psyche. In this case, might teleological or archetypal elements be at work in forgiveness? As Jung might have asked, what is psyche engaging in forgiveness *for*? This is the underlying question guiding this book.

Organization of the Book

While acknowledging and exploring the profound implications of forgiving, this book does not explicitly advocate for forgiveness (as we shall see, the active *intention* to forgive can readily serve as an obstacle to its accomplishment). Nor does this study offer a "how-to" primer on forgiving, as do so many contemporary self-help and pop psychology books in which forgiveness is often operationalized and commodified under an assumption of unquestioned benefits. Rather, the aim is simply to offer an exploration of the notion of forgiveness from a depth psychological perspective, guided by several psychological images.

To that end, Chapter 2 examines the historical origins of forgiveness, inspired by Hillman's reminder that "the Gods rarely forgave." Chapter 3 provides a foundation by exploring various existing psychological and philosophical definitions of forgiveness. Chapter 4 explores the question of evil, repentance, and forgiving the unforgivable as taken up in Simon Wiesenthal's landmark consideration of forgiveness in relation to the Holocaust in his classic book, *The Sunflower*. In Chapter 5, the figure of Jesus, as both a symbol of the Self and the originator of the modern notion of forgiveness, will be considered in terms of analytical, alchemical, and archetypal psychology. The final chapter investigates the underlying dialectical logic of forgiveness (and redemption) through interiorizing forgiveness into itself.

Notes

1. Helen Schucman (ed.), *A Course in Miracles: Combined Volume* (3rd ed.) (Mill Valley, CA: Foundation for Inner Peace, 2007) (Original work published 1976), 562.
2. James Hillman, "Betrayal," in *Senex and Puer* (1st ed., Vol. 3, pp. 193–213) (Putnam, CT: Spring Publications, 2005) (Original work published 1964).
3. Bishop Desmond Tutu has observed that without forgiveness, there is no future (*No future without forgiveness*, London: Random House, 1999) reminding us of the profoundly violent cycle of attack, revenge, and counter-attack that characterizes much of human relations throughout modern history. With the development of nuclear and chemical weapons, this cycle threatens to annihilate the existence of humanity altogether. Indeed, both Freud and Jung lamented, "'*Homo homini lupus*' [man is to man a wolf] is a sad, yet eternal truism." (C.G. Jung, 1946/1970, p. 231 [CW 10, para. 463]) Yet Bishop Tutu's observation imbues the psychological act of forgiveness with the power to interrupt a millennia-old catastrophic pattern of human violence and save us from the destruction seemingly inherent in our own nature. One must wonder whether such faith in forgiveness to rescue the future is well placed or an illusory and costly mistake.
4. Hillman, "Betrayal," 209.
5. (Freud, 1923/1961) Per Giegerich: "I am ego as long as I am defined as an existing being and consequently have as my prime interest my self-preservation—not only literal physical self-preservation, not only emotional self-preservation, but also *logical* self-preservation, i.e., the preservation of the very definition of me as existing entity or being." (2001/2005, 184–185).
6. Jacques Derrida, *On Cosmopolitanism and Forgiveness* (Oxford: Taylor & Francis, 2007).
7. Lucy Allais, "Wiping the Slate Clean: The Heart of Forgiveness," *Philosophy & Public Affairs*, 36, no. 1 (January 2008): 33–68, doi:10.1111/j.1088-4963.2008.00123.x, 32.
8. Slavoj Žižek, *Less Than Nothing: Hegel and the Shadow of Dialectical Materialism* (London; Brooklyn, NY: Verso Books, 2012), 223.
9. By "localized" I mean considering a phenomenon split off from its given context. This should not be confused with "eachness," a perspective that is committed to viewing each particular phenomenon or matter at hand completely in terms of itself, a necessity for reaching the interiority of the phenomenon.
10. Wolfgang Giegerich wrote an entire book devoted to this question, titled, *What Is Soul?*
11. James Hillman, *Re-Visioning Psychology*, (New York: HarperCollins, 1975), x.
12. In modern academic discourse or the clinical setting, for example, one rarely makes use of the term "soul."
13. The common resistance of accepting the modern form of soul as absolutely negative, or the ego's insistence upon "having a soul experience" or presencing the Absolute, is considered by Giegerich to be neurotic. See *Neurosis*.

14. Wolfgang Giegerich, "Jung's Thought of the Self in the Light of Its Underlying Experiences," in *The Neurosis of Psychology* (Vol. 1, pp. 171–190) (New Orleans, LA: Spring Journal Books, 2005), 187.
15. G.W.F. Hegel, *Lectures on the Philosophy of Religion Vol. III: The Consummate Religion*, ed. by Peter Hodgson (Berkeley, CA; London: University of California Press, 1998), 233.
16. A consistent definition in psychological literature of what it means to forgive has yet to be determined.
17. "Visiting Auschwitz, Pope Francis Asks God To Forgive 'So Much Cruelty.'" *The Forward.* Accessed August 31, 2016. http://forward.com/news/breaking-news/346392/visiting-auschwitz-pope-francis-asks-god-to-forgive-so-much-cruelty/.
18. For two thousand years, consciousness has been struggling to "catch up" to Jesus's call for forgiveness of his Jewish captors, which Pope John II and Pope Francis's multitude of apologies in recent years reflects.
19. Wolfgang Giegerich, David L. Miller, and Greg Mogenson, *Dialectics & Analytical Psychology*: (New Orleans, LA: Spring Journal Books, 2005), p. 5.
20. Giegerich et al. (2005), p. 16.
21. C.G. Jung, *Two Essays on Analytical Psychology (Collected Works of C.G. Jung, Vol. 7)*, trans. Gerhard Adler and R. F. C. Hull, 2nd ed. (Princeton, NJ: Princeton University Press, 1972).
22. Marie-Louise von Franz, *Projection and R-e-Collection in Jungian Psychology* (London: Open Court, 1978/1980).
23. Wolfgang Giegerich, "First Shadow then Anima" in *Soul Violence* (New Orleans, LA: Spring Journal Books, 1988/2008), 77–109.
24. James Hillman, *The Thought of the Heart and the Soul of the World* (New York: Spring, 1979/1992).
25. Hillman, *The Thought of the Heart*; Veronica Goodchild, *Eros and Chaos* (Lake Worth, FL: Nicholas Hays, 2001).
26. Giegerich et al., *Dialectics & Analytical Psychology*; Wolfgang Giegerich, *The Soul Always Thinks (Collected English Papers, Vol. IV)* (Woodstock, CT; Lancaster: Spring Journal, Inc., 2010).
27. Giegerich, *The Soul Always Thinks*, 366.
28. Hillman, *Re-Visioning Psychology*, 180.
29. Hillman, *Re-Visioning Psychology*, 180.

2 A Brief History of Forgiveness

Modern forgiveness can take a multitude of forms, from the public request of a world leader for centuries of mistreatment,[1] to a redemptive experience of self-forgiveness, to a private interpersonal intimacy that can be granted or refused in a quiet glance. While forgiveness is inherently relational, modern forgiveness is particularly *interpersonal*; a pope begs forgiveness from Jews,[2] an addict from oneself, lovers from one to another. Indeed, interpersonal relationships often teem with subtle micro-moments of negotiations that communicate the withholding and offering of 'forgiveness.'

While interpersonal forgiveness will be explored at length in later chapters, with particular attention paid to the question of the ego-personality's access to true forgiveness, the context of this study of forgiveness is not sociological but rather *psychological* in nature. It examines the phenomenon of forgiving in relation to consciousness at large, or what C.G. Jung called the "soul."[3] With the notion of soul, we are immediately faced with the question of what qualifies as soul phenomena and what does not. The distinction between the two, or what is referred to as the *psychological difference*, will help guide our inquiry with an eye toward personal and interpersonal relations on the one hand, and objective or soul consciousness on the other. To take a psychological approach in examining a phenomenon, in our case forgiveness, would mean to pay *particular* attention to the "soul side" of the psychological difference.

Our best teacher in understanding the evolution of objective consciousness is history; psychology recognizes the soul as fundamentally *historical* (i.e., the soul changes and develops through time as it gains further self-determination and self-awareness). Thus, we begin our psychological study by examining the historical emergence of the concept of forgiveness in the Western world. Such an investigation, while in no way comprehensive, can nevertheless be helpful in providing historical context and illuminating different cultural, moral, political, and spiritual influences on the development of the concept. In wandering through the vast mythic landscape given by the topic, I will use as a guidepost a brief quote from James Hillman that aptly sums up the ancients' take on forgiveness, all the while keeping in mind the underlying question of the psychological presence, relevance, and meaning of forgiveness.

Part 1: Forgiveness and Myth

"The Gods forgive little and rarely."[4]

There is scarcely room for argument concerning Hillman's assertion. When the gods are crossed, one imagines their terrible wrath, predictable impulse to brutal vengeance, and shocking lack of compassion or inner reflection—fittingly described as the "impossible litany of outrage, rape and desecration which constitutes Greek mythology."[5] Indeed, the archaic Greek world was not familiar with empathy or forgiveness.[6]

Our guiding statement describes an aspect of the relationship between "the Gods" and those who have offended them. The idea of forgiveness inherently requires relationship: two entities are involved, the forgiver and the forgiven (even in the case of self-forgiveness, the self forgives that inner aspect that has caused offense). The statement, "The Gods forgive little and rarely" thus describes a mythic relationship that includes unforgiving gods on one side of the equation and both gods and/or mortals on the other side. Our study begins with examining the nature of the relationship between gods and mortals.

As mentioned above, the gods were not apt to practice forgiveness in general. Early on, however, we find the Olympians harboring a rather fraternal relation with mortals. Tantalus, for example, who is the wealthy king of Lydia, is also a regular guest on Mount Olympus. Though he develops a reputation for drinking too much ambrosia and dropping divine secrets and names, as Ovid explains, the gods tolerate him and even grace him with their presence one evening for a feast in his castle. However, when the plates are uncovered, to their horror they realize that Tantalus has cut up and cooked his own son, Pelops, as a sacrificial offering to the gods in the style of Titan worship. Unfortunate Demeter, still devastated by the abduction of her daughter Persephone, distractedly takes a bite of Pelops's shoulder before noticing what she has done.

In a similar move, the Arcadian king Lycaon offers the flesh of his son to the gods as a test of Zeus's omniscience:

> Zeus, of course, passed the test, and promptly killed all fifty of Lycaon's other sons in retribution—but that he was so tested speaks volumes about the nature of the Olympians. As Roberto Calasso (1993) points out, "Of the Olympians, the first thing we can say is that they were *new* gods."[7] They ruled, but in the background of everything they did there lurked an older, darker order—that of the Titans, the Fates and the Furies, faceless, impersonal and terrifying beings. When he approaches cannibalism, Zeus himself approaches a realm in which he does not rule.[8]

The Olympian gods were scandalized by Tantalus's act; cannibalism and infanticide belonged to the Titans' older, less civilized generation. While the gods resurrected Pelops by boiling his bones and flesh in a cauldron and calling on the Fates to restore him, Tantalus, guilty of the unforgivable sin of tempting the gods to transgression, was administered his well-known punishment in the darkest corner of Hades—perpetually on the brink of starvation, left straining for ripe fruit that is always just out of reach, neck deep in a pool of water that recedes just as he attempts to drink. From a psychological perspective, that the appalling "sin" of cannibalism occurs as "foreign" reveals it as a projected inner unconscious element—a requirement of the beginning stages of consciousness,[9] and the Olympians' reaction of horror and rage exposes hostility toward remnants of the old, darker Titan consciousness. While the Olympians are "new" gods—symbolic of a more "modern" consciousness—they remain defined by their savagery, the "impossible litany of outrage, rape and desecration which constitutes Greek mythology." In the way "civilized" governments administer the death penalty to "uncivilized" killers, the question lingers as to whether the Olympians are *different* gods of a higher order, or whether their attitude reflects the well-known tendency of consciousness to distance itself from its shadowy origin, from its shameful and chthonic roots in the unconscious.

Tantalus's outrageous act marks the end of the social exchange between gods and mortals. Several generations later, keeping company with the gods will be unimaginable. "In Tantalus' time, the line which divides men from gods remained permeable; after him it will become a terrifying borderland, the unthinkable limit of the mortal world."[10] Yet the gods and mortals would certainly maintain contact. Indeed, Greek mythology is the graphic documentation of the relationship between gods and humanity; our legends depict those moments in which the boundary between worlds is transgressed.

What, then, is the nature of this newly distant relationship? Kinnucan notes two primary modes of relating: the frequent rape and kidnapping of mortals by the gods, and mortals' sacrificial offerings to the gods. I would also add to this the administration of punishment upon mortals by the gods. While these ways of relating each have relevance to our topic of forgiveness, the mode of *sacrifice* is of particular interest; as a means of atonement, alleviation of guilt, restoration of ruptured relations with the deity, and purification, sacrifice is fundamental to the notion of forgiveness. For this reason I would like to explore the topic more broadly than the other avenues of divine-mortal relations.

Sacrifice and Its Relation to Sin, Guilt, and Restoration

"Greek tragedy tells us that behind our institutions of home and court lies a need for sacrifice as a connection with the divine".[11] Indeed, a primary mode of relating between the ancient gods and man continues along the lines of Pelops's offering with the ritual of human and animal sacrifice, a practice occurring on all continents and in all epochs.[12] Practiced continuously for nearly one hundred thousand years, ritual sacrifice was the bedrock of human existence and is considered to be the earliest form of religious act.[13] The basic functional understanding of cultic sacrifice is the destruction of a victim to bring about positive relations with a deity.[14] Some underlying psychological reasons for how this was accomplished are relevant to the study of forgiveness.

Sacrifice was typically practiced as a rite of purification and atonement and a means of removing evil, sin, and guilt. Perera notes that the original Judaic sacrificial scapegoat ritual required two goats—one for the removal of sins, and the other for the removal of guilt. "The blood of the immolated victim atones and purifies"[15] while the second wandering exiled goat "will bear all their faults away with it to a desert place" (Leviticus 16:22, Jerusalem Bible), thereby literally removing "the taint of guilt."

The removal of sin and guilt achieved by sacrifice paved the way for restored relations with the offended deity. Freud made the observation that ritual sacrifice served two simultaneous functions; the (sinful) appropriation of the father's (the god's) attributes, and the restorative undoing of guilt generated by such an act. "The [sacrificial] victim was killed (re-enjoying the hostile destructiveness towards the god-father), eaten (consummating the incorporative urges toward the god-father) and offered to the god (replenishing the harmed god-father)."[16] It is worth noting that the "having one's cake and eating it too" dual nature of sacrifice described by Freud is also present when forgiveness is employed as the psychological defense of denial to avoid unpleasant experiences or consequences, for example in cases where undesired behavior is repeatedly denied or "forgiven"—and thereby collusively allowed—by the victim. Sacrifice's dual function of recommitting the "sin" while overriding its consequences is reflected in versions of forgiveness in which the offense, though not explicitly punished, is kept and fostered in memory.[17]

The motif of sacrifice as restoration was operative in the event of the infringement of a taboo. "One who violates a taboo must seek atonement through a renunciation of some possession or freedom, for restoration of the bond to some important power requires such a sacrifice."[18] The "restoration" of a ruptured bond implies a reestablishment of a relationship to its original pristine condition, a "bringing back into existence" or "back to an original condition." Similar to the way in which the successful restoration of a work of art evokes the presence of the original piece, restoration is an experience that presences a new version of an old reality, a version in which the rupture has disappeared, is undetectable, yet still exists within the reality of having been ruptured. Forgiveness, too, would excuse or pardon the offense causing the rupture, thereby bringing back into existence the originating bond. Forgiveness, with its root *gifan* meaning "to give," also strives for restoration, as "restore" means to "give back." Forgiveness as restoration suggests a "giving [oneself] back" to the fullest extent, such that the rupture of "an ancient hatred" has restored the originating bond and "become a present love." The contradiction inherent in the idea of forgiveness as restoration—insofar as both the original bond between parties *and* its rupture co-exist—is identified in the dialectical notion of *sublation*, explored in Chapter 6.[19]

Sacrifice as Remembrance

For James Hillman, sacrifice was not about purification or restoration, but remembrance. What the Greek gods asked for "was not blood; it was not to be forgotten" (Hillman 1994, 5). (The theme of remembrance runs through another avenue of the gods' relationship with mortals, which is their brutal and astonishing punishment of mortals, a topic to be visited below.) For Hillman, rites of sacrifice were rituals that served as mental tools to prevent our forgetting; "Rituals help remembering; that's all, but that's plenty" (13). To the extent that forgiveness equates with "forgetting" or "overlooking," is it no wonder that "The Gods forgive little and rarely." Soul, as symbolized by the ancient gods, *wants to be remembered*—to stay in existence—not to forgive and be forgotten.

Sacrificial killing not only reminds us of the gods but also that we are *not* gods; unlike the deities, we are mortal and must die, thereby producing "between gods and mortals a connection which is also a separation." The separation results from the way a sacrificial offering amplifies the power differential between mortals and gods, preventing hubris and inflation by reminding us that we are not gods, but merely human. In our humanity, our failures and sin, we are forced to confront our mortality and their divinity accordingly.

Yet from the perspective of Freud, the act of sacrifice was not an intentional act of remembrance, as could be inferred from Hillman's description. It was instead an inevitable outcome of the trauma given by the very first psychological act of sacrifice—the Oedipal murder of the father, or of God:

> The memory of the first great act of sacrifice [the murder of the father] . . . proved indestructible, in spite of every effort to forget it; and at the very point at which men sought to be at the farthest distance from the motives that led to it, its undistorted reproduction emerged in the form of the sacrifice of the god.[20]

The "indestructible memory" carries with it associated "indestructible guilt"; Wapnick (1998) describes the psychological impact of such guilt as inherent to the structure of the modern ego.

> The ego's foundation is based on sin, guilt, and fear. Our belief that we are inherently sinful, a state of separation and alienation that seems beyond correction from Heaven or earth, causes us to experience guilt over what we believe we have done and even more basically, who we believe we are. As a result of this sense of basic wrongness and wrongdoing, we will fear the punishment we are sure is forthcoming as our just

> desserts. We are seemingly helpless in the face of the basic anxiety and terror that inevitably accompany the belief in our own guilt.[21]

Whereas the primary method to assuage profound guilt in early history was ritual sacrifice, Freud identified the contemporary method to be the *psychological projection* of such guilt. The profound connection between projection and forgiveness is explored in depth in Chapter 3.

Giegerich too notes a major *historical* change in the psychological significance of sacrifice, the watershed moment being discernible with God's demand of Abraham to sacrifice his son Isaac. Giegerich describes the story as "edited" back from the brink of sacred and ultimate *molk* or child sacrifice as apotheosis[22] and instead reduced to a mere "test" of Abraham by God. This historical shift in attitude from ritual sacrifice as a profound and sacred act to one that is resisted and ultimately rejected is referred to by scholars as the "spiritualization" of sacrifice. Daly[23] notes that with spiritualization, emphasis shifts away from the literal *act* of the sacrifice to the *disposition of the sacrificer* as a measure of "effective" sacrifice. Finlan (2005) puts forward multiple classifications of spiritualization, beginning with substitution, moralization, interiorization, and metaphorical appropriation of sacrificial images to the total rejection of literal sacrifice and its replacement by spiritual values.[24]

Spiritualization refers to a process of symbolization, or the concentration on the *notion* of sacrifice rather than on sacrifices themselves.[25] The *ritualistic* or pre-spiritualized mode of being-in-the-world is still in full practice during the era of ancient Greek and Roman culture, although the Greek philosophers and Old Testament prophets were heading the trend toward spiritualization of sacrifice (for example, Plato objected to the idea that the gods could be "bribed" with sacrifices[26]). For sacrificing cultures in the ritualistic mode, the literal, bloody sacrificial killing "was an event of the highest purpose and meaning."[27]

Sacrifice as the Birth of the Soul

In his important essay, "Killings," Giegerich explicates the notion of ritual sacrifice as the very origin of the soul's coming into being. "In a kind of self-bootstrapping, the soul first made itself through killing, it killed itself into being, and this is why I consider sacrificial killings as the primordial soul-making."[28] Distinct from the biological function of killing and eating small animals for survival, the organized hunt with its sacrificial act of killing large game signifies the first "insurrection"—or *opus contra naturam*—of the soul away from natural biological life and instinct.

> [T]he deed of killing is the sole point at which the breakthrough into consciousness could in fact be successful: only one's own act of a deathblow into the intactness of life, an act ruthlessly violating one's own life interests, has the power to logically (not ontologically!) burst open one's

> logical envelopment in natural life and thus to achieve a distance from one's own being and the emancipation from instinctual drives. Ritual acts are the first human acts not caused by instincts nor conditioned by circumstances, they are freely and fully posited for the soul's own intents and purposes.[29]

Deliberate killing as the cessation of biological life forces the end of one's total identification with the physical body and ushers in the *realm of meaning* and a breakthrough into consciousness. As Giegerich explains:

> [S]oul and consciousness are nothing natural. They are *contra naturam*. They owe their existence to a revolution, to the logical negation of life, to the intrusion of death, which violently disrupts the continuity and intactness of the sphere of biological life and displaces human existence from biology as its primary basis of life and instead installs it in mind (mindedness) or soul as its new true ground of life. Of course, that death that is capable of truly intruding into life's intactness and thus has the power to shock life *out of* the "innocence of becoming" (Nietzsche) and *into* consciousness could in no way have been that innocent death that merely happens to a living being as a natural life event to be passively endured. No, it must be a death in the active sense, as the unnatural, outrageous, deliberate act of killing.[30]

In addition to the birth of consciousness, Giegerich asserts a fundamental relationship between sacrifice and primordial, *a priori* image, wherein sacrifice is, in fact, *the source of image itself*. He states, "In the sacrificial blow, the soul knocked its natural instincts out of itself and *ipso facto* knocked them into itself as (no longer natural, but human-cultural) images of gods or as archetypes. The blow . . . *is* the origin of the images."[31] And the sacrificial act is not only the origin of image, but functioned as the image itself:

> It was the sacrificial blow itself that generated the image "for the first time," or more correctly, *was* the image. It was the image by being the blow that within the dullness of life, blew open that clearing or opening that we call image or meaning. It starts from the blow.[32]

Why is this important? Because through the sacrificial act, man participates and "has his part here in the generation of [primordial] images; he is needed for them and must make his active contribution."[33] *The sacrificial act becomes a generative and creative act in the most profound sense.* Ultimately, "The blow with the sacrificial ax is a manifestation of the soul's power to give itself its own origin."[34] With each sacrifice, the soul experiences a rebirth of itself. Giegerich states,

> The blow, inasmuch as it is in fact "commencement," is capable of having a retroactive effect on the past (even its own past). It can create the

> past anew and along with it "the world"; it can replace (sublate, reduce to a mere moment in the new "world") any previously existing "beginning." Sacrifice is a cosmogonic act.[35]

If the act of sacrifice "can create the past anew" and "replace any previously existing beginning" then it holds the key to forgiveness; the soul is able to renew and restore itself, generating the "self-renewal intrinsic to forgiveness."[36] The soul becomes reborn through the act of sacrifice.

With the spiritualization of sacrifice, the sacrificial acts as literal death blows are no longer needed. Yet the self-renewing and creative elements of sacrifice still remain. "[Sacrificial acts] are (one form of) the fantasy activity by which the psyche *creates* (not just remembers) reality every day."[37] The spiritualization of sacrifice does not blunt its power to be used for the *creation of reality* itself.

Forgiveness has a fundamental relationship with the past, as its object is an occurrence or state that has *already* happened or demonstrated itself. Asking to be forgiven is akin to asking for one's past to be overlooked, improved, atoned for, and restored in the eyes of the forgiver. As philosopher Lucy Allais asserts, "in forgiving, we allow the wrongdoer to make a genuinely fresh start; the slate is wiped clean."[38] Moreover, "this change is a central part of what the person who wants to be forgiven wants: when you want the wrongdoing to be 'put behind us', you want it no longer to play a role in the way the victim feels about you as a person."[39] As forgiveness "wipes clean" the slate of the past, both sacrifice and forgiveness are concerned with a present and future unconditioned by an undesirable past. As explained by Giegerich,[40] sacrifice is a means for the soul to re-make itself or override the past, thereby becoming "born again" to itself, to God and to the world. A soul reborn is once again innocent. We find in sacrifice the soul's means of rebirth, renewal, and restoration, which is why sacrifice is inextricably bound to forgiveness.

The Wrath of the Gods

From the perspective of mortals, ritual sacrifice served as a form of connection and communion with the ancient gods. From the gods' side, the first manner of transgression of the borderland between worlds is brutal and sexual, consisting of

> an endless series of rapes and abductions, along with the mortals produced by these couplings and the ensuing entanglement of divine with mortal affairs. (The Trojan War itself is the aftermath of Zeus's love for Leda; Helen the all-too-beautiful is the grim consequence of this union.)[41]

Keuls states, "In no other mythology of which I am aware does rape play a more prominent part."[42] While arguably "erotic" from the divine perspective, it would seem likely that the mortal perspective of these encounters was predominantly experienced as traumatic—aggressive, terrifying, and numinous. Rape has little with pleasure or procreation, being primarily a violent act intent on establishing male power over his female victim[43] and is a manifestation of "the principle of domination by means of sex."[44] Groth finds that "in all cases of forcible rape, three components are present: power, anger, and sexuality. . . . Rape is always and foremost an aggressive act."[45] Masculine aggression toward the feminine is reflected in Neumann's assertion that "Greek mythology is largely the dragon-fight mythology of a consciousness struggling for independence from the mother image."[46] While incidences of rape and abduction in Greek mythology are often metaphorically interpreted by psychologists as symbolic of initiation encounters,[47] as phenomenologically experienced within the historical epoch of ancient Greece and Rome, the high incidences of rape and abduction in the mythology serve to psychologically intimidate, establishing the power of gods over mortals.

On the other hand, Lefkowitz[48] argues that referring to sexual liaisons between gods and mortals as "rapes" is inaccurate; we should instead refer to them primarily as abductions or seductions because "the gods see to it that the experience, however transient, is pleasant for the mortals."[49] She notes that the "seductions" of women happen outside their fathers' or husbands' homes, which is an important detail because abduction or seduction occurring within the home was equivalent to murder under Greek law. Lefkowitz notes also that "the women give their consent, at least initially,"[50] and mortals who are "seduced" by the gods are rarely ashamed of the encounter. Moreover, the consequences of the unions usually bring fame and glory to the families of the mortals involved, despite and even because the suffering endured. According to Lefkowitz,

> violence is not a characteristic of female mortals' encounters with the gods, at least in the heroic age; nor do gods tend to violate the laws of hospitality of a male relative's home; nor do they concern themselves with married women. Instead, the encounters between gods and mortal women usually take place in beautiful settings, outside of the woman's home, while she is unmarried. Even though the encounters between gods and mortal women are almost always of short duration, they have lasting consequences, not only for the females involved, but for civilization generally, since the children born from such unions are invariably remarkable, famous for their strength or intelligence or both. Whether we moderns choose to approve of it or not, most women in archaic Greek epic, perhaps because they believed that their gods existed and did not question the historicity of their mythology, tended to cooperate in their seduction.[51]

Whether the encounters with the gods were viewed as welcome or traumatic, they served to reinforce the remembrance and power of the gods in the minds of mortals, both emotionally through erotic or violent encounter, and literally through their resulting legendary progeny.

This leads us to a third mode of contact between gods and mortals: the dynamic consisting of divine vengeance. Examples in Greek myth abound of the powerful gods' fierce and traumatic punishments upon powerless mortals, from Artemis's dismembering curse upon Actaeon to Apollo's flaying of Marsyas. Images of traumatic punishment and violence (including rape and abduction) likely enforced upon mortals a profound psychological and emotional intimacy with the gods. The theory of *traumatic bonding* elaborated by Dutton and Painter (1993) describes the "paradoxical attachment" that arises in relationships exhibiting power imbalances and intermittent punishment, as can be found in the dynamic in which powerful gods enact harsh vengeance on mortals.

> As the power imbalance magnifies, the subjugated person feels more negative in their self-appraisal, more incapable of fending for themselves, and is, thus, increasingly more in need of the dominator. . . . Concomitantly, the person in the high power position develops an inflated sense of their own power (just as the low power person develops an exaggerated sense of their own powerlessness) which masks the extent to which they are dependent on the low power person to maintain their feeling of, as Fromm (1973) put it, "the transformation of impotence into omnipotence."
>
> (p. 322)[52]

Let us take, for example, Ovid's rendition of the story of Niobe, queen of Thebes, which begins by her boasting of her fourteen beautiful children. Upon publicly mocking the goddess Leto at her own ceremony, describing her mere two children (Apollo and Artemis) as a "scanty breed, scarce fit to name," serving only Leto's "just escape [from] the childless woman's shame," Leto immediately sends both to brutally murder Niobe's seven sons. Incredulously, while mourning their deaths, Niobe *continues* to boast that at least she still has seven daughters left—far more than Leto! Of course within minutes, Apollo and Artemis kill her remaining daughters right in front of her. Upon witnessing the massacre, Niobe's husband commits suicide, and Niobe herself, overcome with grief, transforms to stone, eternal tears falling from her marble face.

One can imagine the satisfaction and renewal of omnipotent power that the goddess Leto enjoyed when her progeny Artemis and Apollo savagely struck down that of the proud and mortal queen. Niobe's inexplicable defiance after her sons were murdered makes more sense when viewed in the context of paradoxical attachment and its inherent mechanism of masochism.[53] The unforgiving brutality of the gods toward humankind both compelled humanity's need for them and betrayed their need for humanity. The fact that the gods *noticed* the actions of mere mortals meant that what they did was of consequence. Leto's supreme humiliation by Niobe's boasting reveals her desire for mortals' favor. What we thought of the gods *mattered* to them, thereby validating the meaning and potential of our own lives.

What does this have to do with the question of forgiveness? What we have seen so far would indeed support Hillman's assertion that "The gods forgive little and rarely." Seen psychologically, or from the perspective of the soul, the gods' *lack* of forgiveness yielded a passionate engagement with mortals and maintained a psychological and emotional bond, serving as a connection between worlds. In this context, forgiveness by the gods would blunt "the transformation of impotence into omnipotence" experienced by the gods, and from the standpoint of mortals, the gods would disappear and be forgotten.

As noted earlier, what the Greek gods asked for "was not blood; it was not to be forgotten." Hillman cites the unforgiving attitude of Aphrodite, whose love, Hillman observes, does not forget:

> She lays claim on those who forget her, she retaliates through her relatives, the Furies, who—like the return of the repressed, as they are called in psychoanalysis—forget nothing. The Gods want to be remembered, and they do not ask forgiveness for their havoc, so that their havoc is also remembered.[54]

Hillman emphasizes the preservation of memory, of lasting legacy, of the gods' wish to make a permanent mark upon those who offend them. *Remember the gods!* the myths say. *We are not to be forgotten*. In the same way that sacrificial rituals "help remembering," the punishments of the gods served as signposts of remembrance.

Where our myths are concerned, if vengeance means remembrance, it would follow that forgiving means forgetting. And what if we had been allowed to forget Aphrodite? What if the Furies had ignored us? The mythical image that the gods rarely *forget* becomes the psychological statement that not only do the gods want our remembrance of *them*, neither do they forget *us*. The brutal and vengeful acts of the gods were markers, cues that shocked us into remembering the existence of the gods and our debt to them, because without them we would forget, and through our forgetting be forgotten.

Might also the gods through their vengeance have protected us in some way? Might Zeus's prohibition against fire also include prudence, in the way of withholding scissors from a small child? Is it possible humanity was not yet ready to receive the gifts Prometheus stole? Niobe exposed the mortal's love of glory above that of her own children. It would seem that we could not yet be trusted. And the myths reminded us of this.

The Unforgivable Sin of Hubris

The gods' indelible mark often finds its expression in the literal transformation of the offender, so that it cannot be forgotten. Think of Zeus's conversion of poor, beautiful Io into a white heifer, driven mad by a gadfly sent by Hera, or jealous Athena's spidery revenge upon the talented but boastful weaver Arachne. While psychologically violent, these penalties are mild in comparison to many others, a startling number of which punish the ancient and unforgivable sin of hubris, or the appropriation of what is the gods' for oneself. Hubris, signifying the human aspiration to be equal with God, is the "self-elevation of man into the sphere of the divine."[55] Tillich explains,

> If man does not acknowledge . . . the fact that he is excluded from the infinity of the gods . . . he falls into hubris. He elevates himself beyond the limits of his finite being and provokes the divine wrath which destroys him. This is the main subject of Greek tragedy.[56]

Those who commit acts of hubris neglect or deny the power and authority of the gods. In Greek mythology we find examples of hubris in the form of trickery, such as Sisyphus's cunning imprisonment of Hades and eventual exit from the underworld on the pretense of properly performing his own burial rights with no intention of returning, theft—as in Prometheus's unauthorized sharing of fire with humankind—or glorification (Niobe's dismissal of Leto's divinity and flagrant bragging about her own children, for example). In these cases and many more, divine retribution for mortal hubris wrought gruesome outcomes for the offenders. In Greek mythology, no mercy was shown toward the boastful, and sanctions against hubris included harrowing and creative punishments enthusiastically administered by the offended gods.

Even in the rare case that divine "mercy" showed itself, the grace given was somewhat dubious. We can see this in the story of Arachne, a young and extraordinarily talented weaver of intricate tapestries. Her embroidered masterpieces rivaled those of the goddess Pallas Athena herself, a fact Arachne flaunted, denying any debt owed to the goddess for her mortal skill. Ovid explains:

> Pallas her mistress shone in every line.
> This the proud maid with scornful air denies,
> And ev'n the Goddess at her work defies;
> Disowns her heav'nly mistress ev'ry hour,
> Nor asks her aid, nor deprecates her pow'r.
> Let us, she cries, but to a trial come,
> And, if she conquers, let her fix my doom.[57]

At this invitation, Pallas disguises herself as an old woman and warns Arachne to recant the challenge and humble herself with an apology before the goddess:

> Young maid attend, nor stubbornly despise
> The admonitions of the old, and wise;

For age, tho' scorn'd, a ripe experience bears,
That golden fruit, unknown to blooming years:
Still may remotest fame your labours crown,
And mortals your superior genius own;
But to the Goddess yield, and humbly meek
A pardon for your bold presumption seek;
The Goddess will forgive.[58]

It is interesting to note the allowance of mortal pride and offer of forgiveness *if only the young Arachne would forsake her hubris and submit to the goddess*. Unfortunately for Arachne, she remains defiant, engaging in a literal contest with Pallas, which, of course, she cannot win on principle. The punishment of violent blows to the head Arachne tries to avoid by hanging herself, but Pallas "mercifully" intervenes, instead condemning her to a worse fate:

When Pallas, pitying her wretched state,
At once prevented, and pronounced her fate:
Live; but depend, vile wretch, the Goddess cried,
Doomed in suspense for ever to be tied;
That all your race, to utmost date of time,
May feel the vengeance, and detest the crime.

Then, going off, she sprinkled her with juice,
Which leaves of baneful aconite produce.
Touched with the poisonous drug, her flowing hair
Fell to the ground, and left her temples bare;
Her usual features vanish'd from their place,
Her body lessened all, but most her face.
Her slender fingers, hanging on each side
With many joints, the use of legs supplied:
A spider's bag the rest, from which she gives
A thread, and still by constant weaving lives.[59]

Arachne's tragic tale portrays hubris as the refusal to acknowledge the contribution of the gods (or one's debt to them) and the mortal assertion of *self*-creation. Tillich (1975) notes that hubris as "sin in its total form" is, "man's turning away from the divine center to which he belongs. It is turning toward one's self as the center of one's self and one's world."[60] In so doing, man fails to acknowledge his finitude and "identifies partial truth with ultimate truth," resulting in "tragic self destruction"[61] following in hubris's wake. In imagining her tapestries as rivaling those of the goddess, Arachne exemplifies the case in which "man identifies his cultural creativity with divine creativity . . . [and] attributes infinite significance to his finite cultural creations, making idols of them, elevating them into matters of ultimate concern."[62] Such a mistake of hubris has catastrophic implications, according to Tillich: "The divine answer to man's cultural hubris comes in the disintegration and decay of every great culture in the course of history."[63]

Other celebrated stories of the unfortunate cost of hubris are found in the well-known myths of high-flying Icarus and Phaeton—Icarus's wax wings melt when he foolishly flies too close to the sun and plunges into the sea, and Helios's mortal son unwisely insists he can control the chariot of the sun (just like his father) and is shot down by Zeus to save the earth. Both sons' tragic fates might have been avoided had they remembered the warnings of their fathers. Both myths serve to warn against the dangers of inflation, of failing to yield to the wisdom of authority, and the hazards of youthful adventure. It is interesting to consider the myths from the point of view of the young men. A young poet offers the following reflection on the experience of Icarus:

> Oh Father, I am in flight again,
> That last incarnation on the horizon
> (I see it in my dim side-vision
> Like a ruffle of swans);
> And though I planted my wandering feet,
> My leaping feet,
> And refused to look upward or outward for weeks on end
> For fear of the beckoning;
> And though I thought only of vultures as birds,
> With their plucked necks, where plumage
> Should hide the natural deformity;
> And though I focused my heart on night
> And the walls of the hut
> I arose in my sleep, saved candle-ends
> And feathers from dead things the cat brought in
> And awoke, melting gaily
> In the face of the sun.[64]

This poem poignantly conveys the *humanity* of Icarus. His genuine attempt to suppress his natural *puer* enthusiasm—by "planting my wandering feet, My leaping feet" and focusing his "heart on night and the walls of the hut"—was of no use. The human spirit will soar, and continue to soar despite the cost. A clinical patient, suffering through infertility, miscarriage, and loss, exclaimed, "How amazing it is that we know we will die, that we will lose everything, yet we continue to yearn and to love with all our hearts. There is such an *innocence* in that!" Icarus's heartbreaking longing for the sun was unflappable and unyielding to consequence. Paradoxically, the "sin" of relentless yearning for admittance into the "sphere of the divine" also suggests in human frailty a beauty and innocence. Forgiveness here may involve a remembrance, acceptance, and embrace of our humanity, such that it is overcome, sublated, and released into its truth as innocence.

Informing a more grounded interpretation is the fact that the above poem was written in 1987, well into our modern age of consciousness. The author reinterprets the myth through a contemporary lens, ascribing a modern neurotic subjectivity to the character of Icarus, who cannot seem to help himself, sleep-walking through the neurotic motions of flight—even at the cost of his very life. Giegerich would argue here that retroactively attributing a modern neurosis to a character of ancient Greek mythology is a mistake.[65] We have no indication that Icarus was possessed by a neurotic compulsion and "couldn't help himself" in flying too close to the sun. Nor for Giegerich is neurosis idealized or fetishized but rather seen as a baseless enterprise perpetrated by the "neurotic" or sick soul of modernity that insists upon the concrete presence of The Absolute once again—in stubborn resistance and resolute denial of its own truth and the truth of modern life, which is that God, and the gods, are dead.[66] Accordingly, in modernity, those seeking forgiveness no longer appeal to the divine, but to one another, as we shall see below.

Part 2: Forgiveness and Classical Civilization

Forgiveness in Literature

If their gods did not forgive, it would follow that neither did the ancient Greeks and Romans. Classical scholars argue this is generally the case.[67] While they employed other strategies of reconciliation, "forgiveness in the full moral (and modern) sense of the word was not among them; for where we are inclined to seek confession and apology, they looked rather to excuse or exculpation."[68]

Scholars argue that the archaic Greek world was not familiar with empathy or forgiveness as evidenced by literary works. Braund, a scholar of the ancient works of Seneca, observes: "When we take a global look at Greco-Roman literature, we cannot fail to be struck by the prominence of anger, resentment, and vengefulness. . . . Overall, in the Greek epic and tragic world . . . forgiveness is a rarity."[69] Braund notes that this is also true in Roman poetry and Latin tragedy, in which anger is central.

DuBois takes into particular consideration the *Iliad* and examines the question of whether Priam "forgives" Achilles for the killing of his son Hektor, or likewise if Achilles forgives Priam for fathering Hektor, the man who killed his beloved Patroklos.[70] She asks whether the powerful scene in the *Iliad* in which Achilles foregoes killing Priam when he comes into Achilles's camp and asks for the body of his son, and Achilles's rather remarkable agreement to honor Priam's request, is a scene of "tolerance and reconciliation" or "one of true forgiveness." She argues effectively for the former, citing the literal Greek translation and correcting the popular *Iliad* translations of Lattimore (2011) and Fagles (1990), which employ the word *forgiveness*. DuBois argues that translators tend to project from a modern world and postmodern perspective, using a vocabulary of compassion and empathy, thereby apt to employ a "forgiveness" that betrays earlier Greek meaning.

DuBois cites specific evidence in the Iliad to support her argument. For example, just before he kills Hektor, Achilles addresses the Trojan hero who has asked that the two swear an oath not to defile the other's corpse, if one succeeds in killing the other: "[A]fter I have stripped your glorious armour, Achilleus,/I will give your corpse back to the Achaians. Do you do likewise?" (22.258–59). Achilles answers:

> Hektor, argue me no agreements, I cannot forgive you.
> As there are no trustworthy oaths between men and lions,
> nor wolves and lambs have spirit that can be brought to agreement
> but forever these hold feelings of hate for each other,
> so there can be no love between you and me, nor shall there be
> oaths between us, but one or the other must fall before then
> to glut with his blood Ares the god who fights under the shield's guard.
> (22.261–67)

DuBois points out that the first line translated here is *Hektor mê moi alaste sunêmosunas agoreue*, which literally means, "Hector, speak to me not, wretch, about *covenants, agreements.*" DuBois states:

> Lattimore imports a foreign notion when he translates "forgive," as does Fagles, when he gives us: "You unforgivable, you . . ." (1990, p. 550). The Greek says nothing of the sort, as Achilles naturalizes their enmity: there are no oaths between men and lions, between wolves and lambs.[71]

Concluding that the Greeks "did not know empathy and that translations effacing the difference between our language and theirs transfer our emotional landscape back in time"[72] DuBois continues:

> Belief in a universal, inborn forgiveness might be a serious error in a world in which there are those who still prize warrior skills and an undying commitment to avenging the dead. Some may value forgiveness and wish it were an innate, universal human quality, but the example of the Homeric Achilles demonstrates its fragility and its precarious status as a product of centuries of cultural labor.[73]

DuBois cautions against the assumption that forgiveness is a "natural, hard-wired aspect of human behavior or consciousness," or looking for evidence of forgiveness as a universal feature (of psyche) when we imagine Achilles "forgiving" Priam for example, when in fact the most that was going on emotionally at that point was pity, pride, and fear. Forgiveness, argues duBois, is a *learned* behavior, one in which modern-day presence is evidence for the evolution of humanity:

> I fear a colonizing of the past and of other cultures that not only erases their difference from our own but also suggests that there will be no change for the better in human beings. Did not the Enlightenment argue for the abolition of slavery, for example, on the basis of a newly developed sense of shared humanity and sympathy for the oppressed, itself something new in human history?[74]

The expanded interest in forgiveness in current culture marks a definite change from ancient Greek and Roman culture, but whether it is "a product of centuries of cultural labor" and evidence for humanity's evolution is uncertain. Indeed, while the organized argument for the abolition of slavery may have been sourced from of "a newly developed sense of shared humanity and sympathy for the oppressed, itself something new in human history," it must be noted that in our current epoch, according to the U.S. State Department's annual reports on trafficking in persons, an estimated 27 million men, women, and children are trafficked for commercial sex or forced labor around the world today.[75]

In addition to the assertion that forgiveness is not an innate human behavior but rather an accomplished behavior, duBois concludes that another possible cause of forgiveness's later emergence is theological. She states:

> It may be that a polytheism is less likely to exhibit and prize the practice of forgiveness. In monotheistic, Abrahamic religions, especially in the Hebrew Bible, the personality of the divinity often appears prickly, jealous, punitive and judgmental. He, emphatically masculine, is seen as overlooking the faults of his chosen people (the Israelites) and their many transgressions, and for a time at least, offering them new chances to win his favor. A polytheistic system has no single source of redemption, cleansing, or forgiveness; if one of the gods were to spare the perpetrator of an injury, this is less a metaphysical event that a private arrangement between that one god and one of her many worshipers.[76]

In other words, the lack of a "single source of redemption, cleansing, or forgiveness" may have prevented the practice of forgiveness from gaining universal visibility or stature in a polytheistic culture.

Early Greek Philosophers

Ancient philosophers focused on goals of moral perfection and seemed to have little use for or interest in the concept of forgiveness. For Plato, forgiveness was insignificant because "a good person is invulnerable to harm and so has nothing to forgive; and because he will himself not hurt others voluntarily, neither will he be in need of forgiveness."[77] With nothing to forgive or be forgiven for, the question of forgiveness was immaterial to classical philosophers and writers.

Where the opportunity for forgiveness might normally present itself, for example in the case of a personal slight, a measured response of anger was seen as most appropriate. According to Aristotle,

> A person is praised who is angry for the right reasons, with the right people, and also in the right way, at the right time and for the right length of time . . . [I]t is a slavish nature that will submit to being insulted or let a friend be insulted unresistingly.[78]

The practice of forgiveness would not be of explicit concern to Aristotle, as forgiveness in the sense of ceasing to be resentful is assumed to happen as a matter of course after "the right length of time" in the case of justified anger. To be overly consumed with anger would mean a show of weakness and "submission" to the insult. For, as Jacobs notes, "The Aristotelian great-souled man would regard himself as above forgiveness, seeing himself as largely above the slights and the disrespect that many people feel it is gracious to forgive."[79] The Stoics, like Plato and Aristotle, considered forgiveness unbecoming of a sage; a man of perfect character was thought to be immune to the slights of others, nor would his moral perfection ever cause offense to them. In this sense the Stoic view of forgiveness is compatible with that of philosopher Minas (1975), who makes the case that forgiveness has no connection to the divine, for the possession of (morally perfect) divine attributes precludes taking offense in the first place. Only a thoroughly *human* (imperfect) being can truly feel hurt by another.

These early philosophical perspectives are in contrast to the Judaic and Christian faith traditions, in which forgiveness

> ultimately has a ground in the fact that no one is so virtuous—or even so *capable* of perfect virtue—that he or she will not sin and not *need* to be forgiven. Also, no one is above forgiving in the way that a Platonic or Aristotelian perfectly virtuous agent would be.[80]

The Christian tradition asserts a need for divine assistance for human beings, without which mortals would "go astray" due to their "fallen" nature. Aristotle sees no such need as mortals are not considered to be fallen or wounded in that way. "Aristotle's virtuous agent is immune to the 'need' for radical ethical self-correction while the faith traditions do not understand human nature to be capable of that immunity" (Jacobs, p. 230). For Aristotle, the extent to which man has *understanding* guarantees moral action. "The person whose activity accords with understanding . . . would seem to be in the best condition, and most loved by the gods" (1999, p. 167).

However, there are factors that may prohibit a man's understanding, in which case he is literally unable to act morally, and in this sense he cannot be held responsible for his actions. In other words, his behavior is not an appropriate candidate for forgiveness because he could not have acted otherwise, nor could he change his behavior in the future. This is in stark contrast to the Jewish and Christian faith traditions, which claim that all humans have access to right moral knowledge through divine revelation and therefore have the corresponding ability and responsibility to change their actions and their character according to the given laws. "Even the very bad person can know what is required"[81] and is thus accountable before God for his or her behavior. Medieval Jewish scholar Moses Maimonides writes "whoever is bad is so by his own choice. If he wishes to be virtuous, he can be so; there is nothing preventing him."[82] However, Aristotle's conception of the "bad" or "vicious" agent is one whose character has become fixed

> in bad habits, wrong values, and a disfigured sensibility. All of that can render the person unable to attain a correct grasp of ethical considerations. The plasticity of his character may be substantially exhausted, and his judgment and disposition irremediably corrupted, so that he cannot bring himself to act rightly. Even if he somehow manages to achieve a correct ethical awareness, his second nature may be an impediment to changing his character and acquiring virtuous dispositions. Some very bad people may be confined to painful regret of their vices, unable to overcome them.[83]

Indeed, these "vicious agents," even when made aware of their failings, are often condemned to rather miserable lives of self-loathing, for such people "have nothing lovable about them, and so have no friendly feelings for themselves."[84] As forgiveness is inapplicable, so too the notion of self-forgiveness would likely be inexplicable to Aristotle, as any kind of acceptance of what is unjust or imperfect would utterly violate the ideal. Ironically, in Aristotle's perspective of the vicious agent as a "hopeless" case we find acknowledgment of the enormous and often overwhelming influences of the psyche (or unconscious forces) upon the personality, to the extent that even after having achieved "correct ethical awareness," the conscious will cannot overcome them.

Justice and Power vs. Clementia

Not only was forgiveness considered unnecessary to a highly moral person, but it was also deemed incompatible with justice. Stoic wise men "do not experience pity or have forgiveness for anyone; they do not relax the penalties fixed by the laws, since indulgence and pity and even leniency are psychological incapacity, pretending kindness in place of punishment."[85]

Orthodox Stoicism regarded punishment as merely the unflinching application of the penalty decreed by law. Justice must prohibit room for discretion in either direction, for that would be corrupt. Chrysippus, a Stoic (c. 279 BC–c. 206 BC) and founder of propositional logic, believes the judge as "priest of Justice" should be

> dignified, holy, austere, incorruptible, proof against flattery, pitiless and inexorable towards the wicked and guilty, upright, lofty and powerful, terrifying thanks to the force and majesty of equity and truth.[86]

The Stoic sense of forgiveness or pity as a violation of justice and a threat to curbing the "wicked and guilty" (or evil) are important concepts and figure in as well to modern philosophical and psychological arguments against forgiving.

According to Braund, forgiveness as it is generally understood in modern times was not practiced in ancient Greece, and the Roman cultural focus on power, hierarchy, and social status precluded the practice. However, beginning around the mid-first century B.C.E. we find in Roman mythology the emergence of the goddess *Clementia*, an "abstract deity" who received her first public cult in Rome in association with Caesar.[87] The concept of *clementia*, while eventually associated with the interpersonal attitudes of mercy and gentleness, functioned primarily in military contexts, displayed on the battlefield by a Roman general toward a defected foreign enemy, or as a political tool used by royalty in the discretionary administration of justice.

> [T]his term that we might regard as a Roman equivalent of "forgiveness" turns out to be inextricably associated with absolute power: *clementia* implies hierarchy. . . . Only someone in a position of superiority can grant *clementia*; the corollary is that he also has the power to act severely and punitively. This is exactly what Seneca says in his definition of *clementia* at *De Clementia* 2.3.1: "Clemency is restraint of the mind when it is able to take revenge, or the leniency of the more powerful party toward the weaker in the matter of setting penalties."[88]

Under Caesar the concept of *clementia* was applied arbitrarily: in 49 B.C.E Caesar refers to his own mildness and generosity as his new way of successful conquest, yet after the battle with Thapsus in 46, he chose to slaughter roughly ten thousand enemy soldiers.[89] In this way, the Stoics' warning against the corrupting influence of forgiveness proved correct, for as Braund writes, such imperial forgiveness "often bestowed upon and benefitting the all-powerful privileged . . . turns out to be terrifyingly arbitrary and a long way from modern conceptions of 'forgiveness' molded by Christian thought."[90] While seemingly "a long way" from current conceptions of forgiveness, it is important to note that within the heart of forgiveness may lie the "corrupting" seeds of power and hierarchy, an idea to be explored later in the study.

Conclusion

The evidence bears out Hillman's assertion that the gods forgive little and rarely. The beginning conceptions of modern forgiveness are not to be found in ancient Greek and Roman politics, philosophy, or mythology. Forgiveness in the classical political sphere was either seen as a weakness in political power or used as a mere tool to gain political advantage. In early Greek and Roman philosophy, the emphasis on moral perfection and justice deems forgiveness irrelevant—as humankind was not considered "fallen" and hence not in need of spiritual redemption from "sin"—or unjust, insofar as forgiveness interferes with fair consequences or just punishment. And forgiveness in mythology is practically nonexistent; forgiveness from the gods, insofar as it signifies the act of forgetting, is anathema to their existence. The relationship between gods and mortals is instead characterized by sacrifice, rape and abduction, and punishment, in particular toward acts of *hubris*.

Hubris emerges as an important psychological element in the examination of the early history of forgiveness. We may wonder what it is about hubris that both the gods and humankind—or psyche—find so unpardonable and intolerable on the one hand, yet seductive and compelling on the other. If the basis of religious feeling rests upon the experience of absolute dependence (Schleiermacher), the defiant *independence* given by hubris marks its opposite. Hell, as portrayed in Milton's *Paradise Lost*, was founded on the absolute unwillingness to accept the authority of God; as Lucifer says, "Here at least we shall be *free* . . . better to reign in Hell than serve in Heaven."[91] Hubris would mark the fundamental split away from the soul's divine origin that must take place for consciousness to develop, yet if wildly unchecked threatens the foundation of its own existence. When the power and authority of the gods are forgotten or defied, the wax wings melt, the earth is destroyed by the unruly sun, and hell itself comes into being.

Hillman relates the ego's hubris to its need for forgiveness. He observes a modern form of hubris in Sartre's existential humanism: "Man is nothing else but that which he makes of himself. . . . Man is responsible for what he is. Thus, the first effect of existentialism is that it puts every man in possession of himself as he is, and places the entire responsibility for his existence squarely upon his shoulders."[92] In leaving the gods out of the picture, we are left to bear the burden of archetypal guilt alone and are compelled to seek forgiveness. As Hillman describes it:

> Of course we fail, and since there is no power to call upon other than this ego, we beg forgiveness. . . . Our human relations, overcharged with archetypal significance, break down. We cannot carry the Gods because we are human. Were we not alone responsible, but supported by their persons and sharing in their myths, then burdens, blame, *and forgiveness would no longer be so central* . . . As it is now, of course our mothers fail, for they must always be Great, having to be each an archetype,

> having to supplant the dead depersonified world and be the seasons and the earth, the moon and the cows, the trees and the leaves on the trees. All this we expect from persons when we have lost the myths. And who can be a God? Of course our lovers fail, having to be Heroes, to release us from the dragon, to be Eros and flames of fire, to be marvelous wise, or quickening with the divine word.[93]

As Hillman sums up, "All fail and all are guilty and all would be forgiven."[94] Forgiveness in this context becomes merely an ego function, enabling the ego to keep itself in place—as "alone responsible for [its] existence," as first cause, free from the gods, or free to *play* God, as it were.

A person imagined as "alone responsible" for him or herself in effect "kills" the gods, evoking Freud's image of totem sacrifice. The cycle inherent in "All fail and all are guilty and all would be forgiven" parallels Freud's cycle of the murder of the father, guilt, and sacrifice. Here, sacrifice as the final act is also the first insofar as it unconsciously reenacts the original sin of killing and unconsciously engenders guilt, thereby requiring repetition and reinforcing its need to exist. Hillman's forgiveness would likewise register psychologically as a "spiritual" failure in that it validates the ego's archetypal identification and neglect ("killing") of the gods, thereby engendering unconscious guilt, followed by endless repetition (for if the ego was not indeed supremely responsible, there would be nothing to forgive).

Hillman prescribes that we acknowledge the role of the gods and our shared responsibility with them. "Were we not alone responsible . . . then burdens, blame, and forgiveness would no longer be so central"[95] The ego's appropriation of forgiveness that Hillman describes, the ego's resistance to employing forgiveness (foreshadowed by the classical philosophers and politicians), and the very important question of the "unforgivable," or evil as it relates to forgiveness, will be explored in later chapters.

We have seen how forgiveness was not a practice revered in the ancient world, and from this we might assume that psyche had little need of forgiveness, that forgiveness as such was apparently not psychologically required or necessary. Still, though forgiveness was absent in early history, primary elements of forgiveness were nevertheless present and active; the ancient ritual of sacrifice *itself* achieved primary outcomes of forgiveness, including the assuagement of guilt, renewal, and rebirth, and the restoration of positive relations with the deity. As sacrifice became spiritualized, however, "emphasis shifts away from the literal act of the sacrifice to the disposition of the sacrificer" and the sacrificial act was no longer *itself* able to carry the unconsciously projected image of atonement and accomplish its goal. The effectiveness of the sacrificial ritual to literally restore divine relations broke down. As sacrifice became interiorized, the enormous responsibility held externally came home to the psyche, and the crucial and necessary psychological benefits were no longer bestowed through ritual sacrifice. As we shall later see, another phenomenon holding the potential of atonement and renewal—that of *repentance*—begins to emerge in the collective psyche.

Notes

1. While John Paull II's apologies were relatively audacious and sweeping, his pleas for forgiveness for centuries of attacks on Jews, women, and minorities were primarily directed at God. Reflecting a more modern shift, Pope Francis asked forgiveness directly from those who were harmed (e.g., gay individuals who have been offended by the church, the poor, women who have been mistreated, children exploited for labor, and for having blessed so many weapons)—basically, from anyone whom the church could have defended and failed to do. See "Pope Francis Strives to Back up Apologies with Action." *Crux*, August 15, 2016. https://cruxnow.com/vatican/2016/08/15/pope-francis-strives-back-apologies-action/.
   "Pope Francis Says Church Should Apologize to Gays." *The New York Times*, June 26, 2016. http://www.nytimes.com/2016/06/27/world/europe/pope-francis-gays-christians-apologize.html.
2. Pope Francis asked forgiveness for the Roman Catholic Church's "non-Christian and inhumane" treatment in the past of the Waldensians, a tiny Protestant movement the Vatican tried to exterminate in the fifteenth century. "On behalf of the Catholic Church, I ask forgiveness for the un-Christian and even inhumane positions and actions taken against you historically," he said. "In the name of the Lord Jesus Christ, forgive us!"
3. For excellent elaborations on the modern concept of soul in psychology, see Wolfgang Giegerich, *What Is Soul?* (New Orleans, LA: Spring Journal Inc., 2012) and James Hillman, *Re-Visioning Psychology* (New York: Harper & Row, 1975), Introduction.
4. Hillman, *Re-Visioning Psychology*, 187.
5. Michael Kinnucan, "Incest, Cannibalism, and the Gods: The Rise of the House of Atreus," *The Hypocrite Reader* (2011), retrieved on June 12, 2016, from http://www.hypocritereader.com/4/incest-cannibalism-and-the-gods.
6. Page duBois, "Achilles, Psammenitus, and Antigone: Forgiveness in Homer and Beyond," in C.L. Griswold & D. Konstan (Eds.), *Ancient Forgiveness: Classical, Judaic, and Christian* (Cambridge: Cambridge University Press, 2012), 31–47; David Konstan, "Assuaging Rage: Remorse, Repentance, and Forgiveness in the Classical World," in C.L. Griswold & D. Konstan (Eds.), *Ancient Forgiveness: Classical, Judaic, and Christian* (Cambridge: Cambridge University Press, 2012), 17–30.
7. Roberto Calasso, *The Marriage of Cadmus and Harmony* (New York: Knopf, 1993), 403.
8. Kinnucan, "Incest, Cannibalism, and the Gods," section 3.
9. Wolfgang Giegerich, "Killings," in *Soul Violence* (Vol. 3, pp. 189–266) (New Orleans, LA: Spring Journal Books, 2008) (Original work published 1993).
10. Kinnucan, "Incest, Cannibalism, and the Gods," section 4.
11. Ronald Schenk, *The Soul of Beauty: A Psychological Investigation of Appearance* (Lewisburg, PA: Bucknell University Press, 1992), 132.
12. Jeffry Andresen, "The Motif of Sacrifice and the Sacrifice Complex," *Contemporary Psychoanalysis* 20 (1984), 526–559.
13. Herbert Kuhn, *Das Problem Des Urmonotheismus* (Mainz, Germany: Akademie Der Wissenschaften Und Der Literatur, 1950).
14. Andresen, "The Motif of Sacrifice and the Sacrifice Complex," 526–559.
15. Sylvia Perera, *The Scapegoat Complex* (Toronto: Inner City Books, 1986), 17.

16. Salman Akhtar, *Good Stuff: Generosity, Resilience, Humility, Gratitude, Forgiveness, and Sacrifice* (Lanham, MD: Rowman & Littlefield, 2012), 144.
17. Robert Enright & The Human Development Study Group, "The Moral Development of Forgiveness," in W. Kurtines & J. Gewirtz (Eds.), *Handbook of Moral Behavior and Development* (Hillsdale, NJ: Erlbaum, 1991), 123–152.
18. Andresen, "The Motif of Sacrifice and the Sacrifice Complex," 531.
19. *Sublation* describes a dialectical notion where that which is negated, e.g. the offense to be forgiven, is not *merely* canceled out or forgotten but also is preserved in memory, however not as an imminent presence. Sublation occurs as the result of the dialectical process of absolute negation which is discussed at length in Chapter 6.
20. Sigmund Freud, *Totem and Taboo*, trans. by James Strachey (2nd ed.) (London; New York: Routledge, 2001), 176.
21. Kenneth Wapnick, *Forgiveness and Jesus* (Roscoe, NY: Foundation for A Course In Miracles, 1998), 52.
22. In ancient *molk* rituals, firstborn children were killed and offered to the god El, thereby securing divine status for the sacrificed baby.
23. R. Daly, *The Origins of the Christian Doctrine of Sacrifice* (Philadelphia: Fortress Press, 1978).
24. Stephen Finlan, *Problems With Atonement: The Origins Of, and Controversy About, the Atonement Doctrine* (Collegeville, MN: Michael Glazier, 2005).
25. I.U. Dalferth, "Christ Died For Us: Reflections on the Sacrificial Language of Salvation," in S.W. Sykes (Ed.), *Sacrifice and Redemption: Durham Essays in Theology* (Cambridge: Cambridge University Press, 1991), 299–325.
26. Plato, *Laws*, 10.909B (Bury, LCL).
27. Giegerich, "Killings," 174.
28. Giegerich, "Killings," 203.
29. Giegerich, "Killings," 211.
30. Giegerich, "Killings," 215.
31. Giegerich, "Killings," 212.
32. Giegerich, "Killings," 213.
33. Giegerich, "Killings," 212.
34. Giegerich, "Killings," 214.
35. Giegerich, "Killings," 214.
36. Charles Griswold, *Forgiveness: A Philosophical Exploration* (Cambridge: Cambridge University Press, 2007), 128.
37. Wolfgang Giegerich, "Once More the Reality/Irreality Issue: A Reply to Hillman's Reply," (1994) Retrieved from http://www.rubedo.psc.br/reply.htm, para 5.
38. Lucy Allais, "Wiping the Slate Clean: The Heart of Forgiveness," *Philosophy & Public Affairs*, 36, no. 1 (2008): 33–68, doi:10.1111/j.1088-4963.2008.00123.x, 68.
39. Allais, "Wiping the Slate Clean," 57.
40. Wolfgang Giegerich, *Soul Violence (Collected English Papers, Vol. III)* (New Orleans, LA: Spring Journal, Inc., 1998/2008).
41. Kinnucan, "Incest, Cannibalism, and the Gods," section 8.
42. Eva C. Keuls, *The Reign of the Phallus: Sexual Politics in Ancient Athens* (Berkeley: University of California Press, 1993), 49.
43. Susan Brownmiller, *Against Our Will: Men, Women, and Rape* (New York: Ballantine Books, 1993).
44. Eva C. Keuls, *The Reign of the Phallus: Sexual Politics in Ancient Athens* (Berkeley, CA: University of California Press, 1993), 47.
45. Nicholas A. Groth, *Men Who Rape: The Psychology of the Offender* (Cambridge, MA: Da Capo Press, 2001), 12.

46. Erich Neumann, *Great Mother: An Analysis of the Archetype* (1st ed.) (London: Routledge & Kegan Paul PLC, 1955), 14.
47. Hillman, *Re-Visioning Psychology*; Florence L. Wiedemann & Polly Young-Eisendrath, *Female Authority: Empowering Women through Psychotherapy* (New York; London: Guilford Press, 1991); Marion Woodman. *Addiction to Perfection: The Still Unravished Bride: A Psychological Study*. 1st ed. (Toronto: Inner City Books, 1988).
48. Mary R. Lefkowitz, *Women in Greek Myth* (2nd ed.) (Baltimore, MD: The Johns Hopkins University Press, 2007).
49. Lefkowitz, *Women in Greek Myth*, 54.
50. Lefkowitz, *Women in Greek Myth*, 56.
51. Lefkowitz, *Women in Greek Myth*, 56–57.
52. Donald G. Dutton & Susan Painter, "Emotional Attachments in Abusive Relationships: A Test of Traumatic Bonding Theory," *Violence and Victims*, 8, no. 2 (January 1993): 107.
53. Dutton & Painter, "Emotional Attachments in Abusive Relationships".
54. Hillman, *Re-Visioning Psychology*, 187.
55. Paul Tillich, *Systematic Theology* (Chicago: University of Chicago Press, 1975), 50.
56. Tillich, *Systematic Theology*, 50.
57. Publius Ovid Naso, *Metamorphoses*, trans. John Dryden (London: Wordsworth Editions, 1998) Book VI, 32–38.
58. Ovid, Book VI, 43–51.
59. Ovid, Book VI, 194–209.
60. Tillich, *Systematic Theology*, 51.
61. Tillich, *Systematic Theology*, 51.
62. Tillich, *Systematic Theology*, 51.
63. Tillich, *Systematic Theology*, 51.
64. Cecile Gray as cited by Randolf Severson, "Puer's wounded wing: Reflections on the psychology of skin disease," in James Hillman (Ed.), *Puer Papers* (Irving, TX: Spring Publications, 1987), 141.
65. Giegerich, *What Is Soul?*.
66. See Wolfgang Giegerich's *Neurosis: The Logic of a Metaphysical Illness* (New Orleans, LA: Spring Journal, Inc., 2013).
67. Susanna Braund, ed., *Seneca: De Clementia* (Oxford: Oxford University Press, 2009); Susanna Braund, "The Anger of Tyrants and the Forgiveness of Kings," in C.L. Griswold & D. Konstan (Eds.), *Ancient Forgiveness: Classical, Judaic, and Christian* (Cambridge: Cambridge University Press, 2012), 79–96; Konstan, "Assuaging Rage"; Charles Griswold, "Preface," in C.L. Griswold & D. Konstan (Eds.), *Ancient Forgiveness: Classical, Judaic, and Christian* (Cambridge: Cambridge University Press, 2012), xi–xv; Page duBois, "Achilles, Psammenitus, and Antigone: Forgiveness in Homer and Beyond," in C.L. Griswold & D. Konstan (Eds.), *Ancient Forgiveness: Classical, Judaic, and Christian* (Cambridge: Cambridge University Press, 2012), 31–47.
68. Konstan, "Assuaging Rage," 17.
69. Braund, ed., *Seneca: De Clementia*, 81.
70. duBois, "Achilles, Psammenitus, and Antigone".
71. duBois, "Achilles, Psammenitus, and Antigone," 44.
72. duBois, "Achilles, Psammenitus, and Antigone," 35.
73. duBois, "Achilles, Psammenitus, and Antigone," 47.
74. duBois, "Achilles, Psammenitus, and Antigone," 33.
75. U.S. Department of State, "Trafficking in Persons Report (2013)," retrieved from http://www.state.gov/documents/organization/210737.pdf

76. duBois, "Achilles, Psammenitus, and Antigone," 48.
77. Konstan, "Assuaging Rage," 20.
78. Aristotle, *Nicomachean Ethics*, trans. by Terence Irwin (2nd ed.) (Indianapolis, IN: Hackett Publishing Co., 1999), 6.
79. Jonathon Jacobs, "Forgiveness and Perfection: Maimonides, Aquinas, and Medieval Departures from Aristotle," in C.L. Griswold & D. Konstan (Eds.), *Ancient Forgiveness: Classical, Judaic, and Christian* (Cambridge: Cambridge University Press, 2012), 225.
80. Jacobs, "Forgiveness and Perfection," 226.
81. Jacobs, "Forgiveness and Perfection," 217.
82. Moses Maimonides, *The Book of Knowledge: From the Mishneh Torah of Maimonides* (Jersey City, NJ: Ktav Publishers Inc, 1983), 89.
83. Jacobs, "Forgiveness and Perfection," 217–218.
84. Aristotle, *Nicomachean Ethics*, 137.
85. Braund, *Seneca*, 66–67.
86. Braund, *Seneca*, 67.
87. Zsuzsanna Várhelyi, "'To Forgive Is Divine': Gods as Models of Forgiveness in Late Republican and Early Imperial Rome," in C.L. Griswold & D. Konstan (Eds.), *Ancient Forgiveness: Classical, Judaic, and Christian* (Cambridge: Cambridge University Press, 2012), 115–136.
88. Braund, *Seneca*, 89.
89. Várhelyi, "'To Forgive Is Divine".
90. Braund, *Seneca*, 95.
91. John Milton, *Paradise Lost*, Edited by Stephen Orgel & Jonathan Goldberg, Reissue edition (Oxford: Oxford University Press, 2008), 1: 259–226.
92. Jean-Paul Sartre & Stephen Priest, *Jean-Paul Sartre: Basic Writings* (Hove, UK: Psychology Press, 2000), 29.
93. Hillman, *Re-Visioning*, 186, emphasis added.
94. Hillman, *Re-Visioning*, 186.
95. Hillman, *Re-Visioning*, 187.

3 Defining Forgiveness

For many, forgiving would seem to be fairly straightforward and intelligible.[1] At some point in our lives, we have likely experienced forgiveness—either through receiving it (or *not*), granting or denying it, or both/neither. In other words, we know it when we see it—and at times forgiveness appears even more recognizable by its absence. That being said, the "commonsense" definition of forgiveness can vary dramatically when specific contingent factors are considered. For James Hillman, for example, forgiveness "is only a term unless one has been fully humiliated or fully wronged . . . and meaningful only when one can neither forget nor forgive."[2] He continues:

> Anyone can forget a petty matter of insult, a personal affront. But if one has been led step by step into an involvement where the substance was trust itself, bared one's soul, and then been deeply betrayed in the sense of handed over to one's enemies, outer or inner . . . then forgiveness takes on great meaning.[3]

Hillman is distinguishing another "version" of forgiveness altogether: forgiveness is only meaningful when, confronted with forces beyond our conscious control, we are "unable" to grant it. Jacques Derrida makes a similar claim, explored later in the chapter, that the possibility of true forgiveness only arises when one is confronted with that which is unforgivable (i.e., when forgiveness is impossible). This line of thinking takes us to the question of forgiveness in the face of the unforgivable, or what we would call "evil." Before taking on that question in Chapter 4, let us first explore various perspectives on what forgiveness actually *is*.

What Is Forgiveness?

There currently exists no general consensus for a universal definition of forgiveness in psychological literature.[4] Each scholar, thinker, and researcher must therefore borrow, invent, or tailor a definition as a starting point.

In exploring what it means to forgive, important questions emerge, such as *why* forgive (purpose)? *How* does forgiveness actually occur (process)?

When does it occur (context)? From a psychological perspective, we might also be concerned with "*who*" is doing the forgiving (i.e., which inner aspect of the personality), and *to whom* (the perceived, projected, or imagined offender) forgiveness is offered. *From where* does forgiveness issue (the ego/persona, or non-ego/Self/Other)?

Academic discussions of forgiveness often combine, conflate, or assume multiple of the above elements. For example, in a psychoanalytic article examining forgiveness, retaliation, and paranoid reactions we read the following:

> It has been suggested that clinical states ranging from grudgingness and habitual bitterness to delusions of persecution are best resolved by forgiving. The process of forgiving requires that previously unacknowledged impulses, particularly aggressive ones, are accepted in oneself and others. If the therapist is aware of this, he or she can, in the transference, reinforce the patient's good introjects by providing a nonjudgmental, accepting model for the patient and thereby facilitate the adoption of the forgiving attitude.[5]

Forgiveness is defined here as that which accomplishes the resolution of "grudgingness and habitual bitterness to delusions of persecution." Forgiveness as a process is described as acceptance by the forgiver of "previously unacknowledged impulses, particularly aggressive ones" in his or herself and others. The final sentence rests upon the assumption that the *why* or purpose of forgiveness is a given and lays out various ways in which the therapist can facilitate "the adoption of the forgiving attitude." Such an ethical prescription is inherent in many psychological, social, and philosophical discussions of forgiveness; the problem of forgiveness occurs for many as a moral one. A duty to evade the powerful grip of resentment and revenge is assumed. "What a struggle it is to resist the cycle of retaliation!" laments the philosopher Griswold.[6]

> Revenge impulsively surges in response to wrong, and becomes perversely delicious to those possessed by it. . . . Vengefulness, resentment, and moral hatred cloud judgment but seem sweet to the one they possess, transforming a peaceful character into a connoisseur of violence. Personal and national credos proudly anchor themselves in tales of unfairness and the glories of retaliation. Oceans of blood and mountains of bones are their testament. It is an addictive cycle.

Forgiveness, then, would serve as an antidote to the perversely dark shadow of revenge. Griswold offers the following answer as to why we should forgive and why it is a "moral good":

> Utilitarian considerations provide a first answer: without forgiveness, human life is worse off. Egoist considerations provide a second answer: without forgiveness, my life is worse off. But there is a third reason, one that cuts deeper: forgiveness is a virtue, and expresses a commendable

> trait of character. And what makes that characteristic itself valuable? The answer brings us back to the ideals that articulate the moral good, namely those of truth-telling, responsibility-taking, spiritual and moral growth, reconciliation, and love. Given the moral imperfection endemic to the world as we have it, these may seem to be merely ideal, abstract, and irrelevant in practice. But that is not so. We necessarily measure our actions according to some conception of the good. Our success or failure, both in discerning accurately the nature of the good, and in living up to that conception, decisively mold the moral character of our lives. These are practical ideals, and we ignore them at our peril.[7]

Certainly where forgiveness is present, so too is the shadow, our "moral imperfection" manifesting as the violence of the offense, or the vengeful response by the victim. A psychological inquiry into a topic that is overwhelmingly seen as a *moral* question requires care on the part of the researcher to stay within a psychological perspective and resist the temptation to "takes sides," so to speak. What I have outlined above speaks to the unconscious complexes of the many writers and researchers of forgiveness, for as C.G. Jung noted, it is our complexes that lead us into our research. Forgiveness is inextricably tied with guilt; it would follow that guilt colors these complexes, and the lean in toward the assuagement of guilt via greater consciousness and forgiveness would follow.[8] As Hillman observes: "Ego feels guilt; ego lifts the repression and recognizes the faults and sins, ego atones and is redeemed. In all this *agon*, there remains the heroic conviction that moral effort can alter psychological nature."[9]

Yet trying to use moral means to change psychological life "keeps psychology locked in subjectivity, and prevents us from seeing the soul of the world."[10] To behold "the soul of the world," or the *objective* psyche, one would recognize that to see the shadow merely in moral terms—thereby reducing the shadow to an enemy that must be fought and ultimately triumphed over—evokes the even more difficult *psychological* shadow. Hillman (1994) describes the psychological shadow as

> the never-ceasing darkening of the light in every search, a darkening of the light of certainty, the light's own sense that however an "I" searches for soul, that same "I" is inherently biased against the object of its searching and therefore biases the methods it employs for its search. Shadow both keeps us searching and prevents us finding. It is the obstruction that does not want to find what it's looking for. Embedded in the very consciousness that is the instrument of our [search], shadow is the unconsciousness of consciousness itself. Reframing the shadow question from morality to psychology results in different feelings regarding shadow, a different sense of discomfort than the guilt of moral wrong-doing. The basic psychological question at the bottom of all shadow issues is the question which has set the course for the psychoanalytic adventure since its inception—where is the unconscious now;

> how is it affecting consciousness; how can I perceive these effects and alter them (i.e., become conscious of unconsciousness)?[11]

Giegerich also alludes to the psychological shadow when he says that "the psychology of the Self, the soul, the daimon [can be] a huge defense mechanism against the soul, against the self, against the daimon,"[12] which is why psychological discourse "has to *be as* the negation of the ego, and the psychologist has to speak as one who has long died as ego-personality."[13] Hillman's last question, "how can I perceive these effects and alter them (i.e., become conscious of unconsciousness)?" betrays an agenda or an intended outcome and thus involves the subjective ego. According to Giegerich, seeing "the soul of the world" would demand an advance of one's perspective to a point of *indifference* in observing the unconscious. "The art of psychological discourse is to speak as someone already deceased."[14] As such, the question of *why* (or *why not*) forgive will be examined as a function of the ego or psyche, but not taken up intentionally as moral question by this study. I would still acknowledge, however, the already always presence and subterfuge of the psychological shadow—the "unconsciousness of consciousness"—at the ready.

Standard Definitions

To answer the question, "what is forgiveness?" I will begin by noting several standard dictionary definitions, then review several other definitions in the field of psychology, classical studies, and philosophy that are helpful in illuminating various shades of forgiveness relevant to our beginning point.

According to formal dictionary definitions, if one were to "forgive," then one would "give up resentment of or claim to requital" or "cease to feel resentment against (an offender)," "grant free pardon and give up all claim on account of an offense or debt,"[15] "excuse for a fault or offense," "stop feeling anger or resentment against," or "absolve from payment."[16] An expanded notion of "to forgive" denotes the following:

1. To cease to resent OR to pardon, overlook, dismiss from the mind, efface from the memory, pocket the affront, forgive and forget, let pass, palliate, excuse, condone, remit, forget, relent, bear no malice, exonerate, exculpate, let bygones be bygones, laugh it off, let it go, kiss and make up, bury the hatchet, turn the other cheek, charge to experience, make allowance, let up on, write off, charge off; see also FORGET
2. To absolve or to acquit, pardon, release; see absolve, excuse.[17]

Finally, clusters of related words include the following:

> *forgiven* (2002): absolved, taken back, excused; see PARDONED
>
> *forgiveness* (2002): absolution, pardon, acquittal, exoneration, remission, dispensation, reprieve, justification, amnesty, respite

It is significant to note that none of the standard definitions of forgiveness explicitly address the nature of the offense or characterize the offender in any way. Forgiveness as thus defined is focused solely upon the "victim"—or the one in the position to offer forgiveness to the (implicit) offender.

Also relevant to our inquiry is the ambivalent nature of the definition with regard to whether forgiveness is an intentional, conscious process, an involuntary, unconscious phenomenon, or something else altogether. Phrases such as "give up resentment" and "grant free pardon" indicate active intent,[18] while others such as "cease to feel resentment," "stop feeling anger," and even "forgetting" better describe unconscious movements in the psyche. The psychological nature of forgiveness insofar as it occurs as an intentional and ethical choice sourced from the *conscious* mind, in contrast to a spontaneous movement sourced from the *unconscious* depths of the soul, is an essential question of this study. This question parallels that of the nature of love noted by Freud, who considered the commandment to forgive—or love—one's enemies to be inexplicable due to the unconscious nature of love.[19] In a footnote, however, Freud seems to count forgiveness as a conscious act, comparing forgiving "a slight from someone of whom one is fond" to a mathematical operation of subtracting "the feeling with the lesser intensity from that with the greater and to establish the remainder in consciousness."[20] Whether such a simple conscious calculation is possible when the offense to be forgiven is greater than a mere "slight" far from certain.

Because forgiveness is apt to be associated (both positively and negatively) with *forgetting*, particularly in James Hillman's writings on forgiveness, I will also add the following definition:

> *forgotten* (2002): not remembered, not recalled, not recollected, lost, out of one's mind, erased from one's consciousness, beyond recollection, relegated to oblivion, past recall, not recoverable, blanked out, lapsed, see also ABANDONED

As we will see, many researchers and philosophers explicitly exclude the element of "forgetting" from the definition of forgiveness, insisting that the offense be remembered, else forgiveness become nothing more than the neurotic defense of denial.[21] However, the fact remains that forgetting *is* associated with forgiving in most major English language thesauri, as is condoning, pardoning, and excusing—also problematic concerns for researchers and philosophers on moral grounds. Prescriptive and constructed definitions of forgiveness are important to consider, but so too is the way in which forgiveness is held in the psyche at large—including its paradoxes, so-called moral weaknesses, and "neurotic defenses." Allowing the association of forgiving with forgetting to stand, the notion of something "forgotten" as "lost, out of one's mind," or "erased from one's consciousness" evokes a psychic location no longer *inside* of consciousness, possibly "beyond" and "past" an egoic state of awareness into something other.

The verb *forgive* comes from the Old English *forgiefan* meaning to "give, grant, allow; forgive," also "to give up" and "to give in marriage;" from for- "completely" + giefan "give."[22] The Latin compounds composing the word ***īgnōscō***, meaning "I forgive," are derived from *in*, "not", and *(g)nosco*, "know." Remarkably, "to forgive," then, is to "ignore" or "not to know." Latin scholar Charles Knapp (1918) observes,

> If *ignosco*, "to pardon," "to forgive", means fundamentally "not to know", we have in this word a very lofty conception, ethically, of forgiveness, a much loftier conception, for instance, even than one sees in *condonare culpam*, "to forgive a fault."[23]

Indeed, one could argue that by definition, in the forgiven state, the forgiven offense no longer exists in the sense of having influence or relevance in any way. We might even say the past is of no consequence, and knowledge of it would cease to be. Forgiveness as pardoning a "sin" while "not knowing" of it speaks to the paradox of the "disappearance" of the offense effected by forgiveness. "Not known," while at first glance may seem to have much in common with our term *forgotten*, cannot share with it the meaning of something once known which is now no longer known; "not to know" does not imply that one had previously known and then lost the knowledge. "Not to know" is very interesting from the perspective of psyche, as it thrusts one into an even deeper level of the unconscious than does merely forgetting a thing; the subject of our forgetting disappears altogether. It is important to keep in mind the distinction Knapp makes between *ignosco* and *condonare culpam*, for if we are truly "not to know," then we would be fundamentally unaware of a "fault" of which to forgive in the first place. Here we find another important link between forgiveness and the unconscious psyche.

Psychological Definitions of Forgiveness

As noted above, the primary dilemma with empirical forgiveness research in psychology is a lack of consensus on its definition. Definitions of forgiveness range from a slight decrease in negative affect[24] to a complete absence of any negative thoughts, feelings, and behavior[25] to defining forgiving as a loving and compassionate gift,[26] voluntarily offered to release an offender from obligation.[27] From an empirical perspective, researchers must often construct limits or boundaries on the definition of forgiveness to elicit quantifiable and measurable outcomes. Qualitative researchers tend to alter the standard dictionary definition of forgiveness to address various moral, judicial, and practical concerns. Such resulting definitions often explicitly note the unacceptability of the offense, include the caveat that forgiveness does not condone the offense, or assert that the offender still deserves punishment.

Psychoanalytic definitions of forgiveness tend to run closer to the standard dictionary definitions, making no requirement that the relationship be restored (or, for that matter, that the offender apologize or make amends, which as we shall discover is a significant requirement in philosophical definitions). According to Horwitz, the primary requirement of intrapsychic forgiveness is "the ability to let go of obsessive rumination about the injurious behavior of the offending party, as well as the wish for some form of retribution."[28] Mere possession of the "ability to let go" of obsessive rumination about the offense and offender does not necessarily include the act of actually *letting go*, and it is far short of the ability to absolve, "or acquit, pardon, release; to pronounce free from guilt or blame."[29]

While alterations and conditions made by many psychological definitions of forgiveness are common, there is also the proclivity to go in the other direction. A popular mainstream book on forgiveness (with over 120,000 copies sold) titled *Radical Forgiveness* makes the claim: "Radical Forgiveness has no limits whatsoever and is completely unconditional. If Radical Forgiveness cannot forgive Hitler, it can forgive nobody. Like unconditional love, it's all or nothing."[30] Such "unconditional" or "unilateral" forgiveness is often undertaken by the forgiver to avoid or obviate the suffering that often accompanies the wounding, or "to shed the painful and toxic emotion of retributive hatred."[31] As stated by Father William A. Menninger, "It is extremely important from the very beginning to understand that the primary consideration and motivation for [unconditional] forgiveness is ourselves. We forgive others, in the first place, for our own sake."[32]

In the book *The Sunflower*, Harold Kushner, a rabbi and influential author, offers the following description of forgiveness:

> Forgiving is not something we do for another person. . . . Forgiving happens inside us. It represents a letting go of the sense of grievance, and perhaps most importantly a letting go of the role of victim. For a Jew to forgive the Nazis would not mean, God forbid, saying to them "What you did was understandable, I can understand what led you to it and I don't hate you for it." It would mean saying "What you did was thoroughly despicable and puts you outside the category of decent human beings. But I refuse to give you the power to define me as a victim. I refuse to let your blind hatred define the shape and content of my Jewishness. I don't hate you; I reject you." And then the Nazi would remained chained to his past and to his conscience, but the Jew would be free.[33]

Theories of forgiveness focusing upon the well-being of the forgiver tend to treat the offender as "absent" or intentionally split off from the process. Definitions of forgiving termed as "unconditional," "unilateral," or "radical" focus upon the forgiver gaining inner freedom from the profound psychological wounding caused by the offense as opposed to viewing forgiveness as a means of healing relations with the object.

One exception is that of Bishop Desmond Tutu, who in his book titled *No Future Without Forgiveness* describes an attitude of unconditional forgiveness that includes the well-being of all parties. Such a perspective, which he describes as "ubuntu," is one which recognizes that, "my humanity is caught up, is inextricably bound up, in yours" and "what dehumanizes you inexorably dehumanizes me."[34] A person with *ubuntu* knows that "he or she belongs in a greater whole and is diminished when others are humiliated or diminished, when others are tortured or oppressed, or treated as if they were less than who they are."[35] While Bishop Tutu's description of *ubuntu* may reveal a highly ethical and humanitarian consciousness, in philosophical terms it begins to approach what Hegel describes in the preface to the *Phenomenology of Mind* as "true reality"—the process of "reinstating self-identity, of reflecting into its own self in and from its other. . . . It is the process of its own becoming, the circle which presupposes its end as its purpose, and has its end for its beginning; it becomes concrete and actual only by being carried out, and by the end it involves." We shall further explore Hegel's notion of *comprehensive subjectivity* and its crucial relevance to forgiveness in Chapter 6.

Philosophical Perspectives on Forgiveness

In the book of collected essays titled *Ancient Forgiveness* (2012), a number of classical scholars investigating the history of forgiveness work from a theory of forgiveness put forward by epistemologist Adam Morton, who writes, "Forgiveness is above all the transcendence of blame." Morton expands the definition to describe what he calls the "territory of forgiveness" involving a combination of various families of emotions, specifically "resentment-like emotions of the forgiver, abasement-like or repentance-like emotions of the forgiven, and a process of transition joining them, in the course of which reconciliation-like emotions can occur on both sides."[36]

Morton's idea expands the notion of forgiveness by including the "forgiven" party in the process. He describes the "typical" case of forgiveness as having

> an emotional background, involving resentment, blame, or some similar emotion directed by one person at another in connection with some action of the other. Then there is an emotion of overcoming that background. But in the typical case there is also a relationship between the two people that changes at the moment of forgiveness. This is something that does not consist in the emotions of either person. The relationship changes so that, while the offender was unforgiven, now an act of forgiveness has occurred.[37]

In this scenario, both forgiver and offender experience an emotion of "overcoming the background" of resentment or blame—both are changed. The phenomenon of forgiveness is extended to include the offender.

Recall that the primary aim or purpose of unconditional forgiveness is cited as the forgiver's relief from suffering.[38] Morton asserts two different purposes of forgiveness: "The first is to return to a previous cooperative relationship that is of benefit to both parties (or to establish one if none existed). . . . The second is to allow each to imagine the situation of the other."[39]

The first reason makes sense given the obvious benefit of a return to cooperative relations; the purpose of forgiveness is to restore relationship. The second reason, while arguably somewhat arbitrary and prescriptive, is interesting from a psychological perspective because it acknowledges a depth psychological claim on forgiveness; the purpose of forgiveness is to allow imagination.

Another influential and expanded definition of forgiveness cited in classical studies is put forward by philosopher Charles Griswold, who writes,

> Three conditions must be met for [the threshold of forgiveness] to be crossed: the victim must be willing to lower his or her pitch of resentment to the degree appropriate to the injury, and to forswear revenge; the offender must take minimal steps to qualify for forgiveness, namely to take responsibility and apologize; and the injury must be humanly forgivable. Between that threshold, and perfected forgiveness, lies a spectrum of cases.[40]

The requirements that the victim "lower one's pitch of resentment" and "forswear revenge" align with normative definitions. Specifying forgivable injuries as those that are "humanly forgivable," while at first glance seems self-evident, upon further reflection unconceals the presence of the impossible (the "unforgivable") and the divine (or "not human") as elements bound to forgiveness. The fundamental requirement that the offender "take responsibility and apologize" adds a significant new dimension to the standard concept of forgiveness and extends the primarily intrapsychic nature of forgiveness discussed up to this point to the interpersonal domain. Similar to Morton's definition, forgiveness now literally involves a forgiver/offender dyad. Indeed, forgiveness here cannot be accomplished without active participation from both parties; it becomes a function of concrete relationship.

Griswold observes that, "To forgive someone . . . assumes their responsibility for the wrongdoing."[41] Griswold here reveals a shadow element of forgiveness: to forgive another requires seeing them as wrong, at fault, to blame, or worse. Forgiveness *needs* this perspective in order to come into existence. Griswold then makes the following assertion: "Indeed, part of what makes forgiveness so interesting is that it represents a change in the moral relation between wrongdoer and wronged *that accepts the fact that wrong was indeed done*, and done (in some sense) voluntarily."[42] In other words, in Griswold's definition the opportunity for forgiveness at once vindicates the victim and implicates the offending party—an assumption not explicitly included in standard definitions. "At a minimum, the scene must include two people, one of whom has intentionally harmed the other and who is thus responsible and blamable for the wrong (putting aside the problematic case of self-forgiveness for wrongs one has done to oneself)."[43] Again, this is a significant addition to the standard definition of forgiveness, which makes no mention of the "blamable" victim, nor does it explicitly affirm the validity or "intentionality" of the offense.

Care must be taken to discern the *environment* of forgiveness, as there may be at least four distinct perspectives involved: (1) the injured party who willingly seeks to forgive, or the "forgiving victim" (for example, victims of apartheid in South Africa who participated in the Truth and Reconciliation Committee proceedings), (2) the agreeing *object* of the forgiving victim, or the acknowledged perpetrator or "guilty sinner" (such as perpetrators who came forward during the TRC and admitted their crimes), (3) the *disagreeing* object of the forgiving victim, or the "defiant offender" (those who admit no fault or crime), and finally (4), the victim who rejects the request for forgiveness from a "guilty sinner," who could be called the "withholding victim." We might also add (5) the perspective of one who has been clearly injured but denies the injury, and this perspective could be described as the "denying victim."[44]

From this arrangement we can see that Griswold's definition of forgiveness accurately characterizes the relationship between a (1) "forgiving victim" and (2) "guilty sinner" but fails to address the possibility of forgiveness within other permutations of perspectives. For example, forgiveness would not be possible between a (1) "forgiving victim" and (3) "defiant offender," which, as any parent with a teenager knows, is incorrect. Forgiveness *does* occur in the parent/child relationship regularly, and as we shall see, in spiritual terms, the (1:3) relationship is often used to characterize that of "God" and man.

Lucy Allais argues for the possibility of unconditional forgiveness in the sense of "wiping the slate clean" through separating the offense from the offender, such that the person is not defined by or reduced to their act by the forgiver. According to Allais,

> forgiveness constitutively involves the victim making some kind of separation between the wrongdoer and his wrong act in the way she feels about him, such that the wrong act does not play a role in the way the victim affectively sees the wrongdoer.[45]

In noting that the fundamental wish of the person asking for forgiveness as to be seen as redeemed or rehabilitated in the eyes of the victim, Allais's perspective of forgiveness speaks to the longing of the offender, whose psychological experience of forgiveness has until now been largely absent in the discussion. She writes:

> [W]e all do unjustifiable, inexcusable wrong, for which we do not simply want to be understood; we want to move forward in relationships

> in which we are not defined by this wrongdoing; yet we cannot prove that we are worthy of this. In forgiving us, the victim of our wrongdoing gives us a chance to do this. Forgiveness enables us to not fix our attitudes towards each other on the basis of our worst acts. . . . Forgiveness offers something that punishing cannot give: in forgiving, we allow the wrongdoer to make a genuinely fresh start; the slate is wiped clean.[46]

It is as if the offender beseeches the victim thus: *Please do not reduce me to my worst self, my shadow. Allow me to be born again in your eyes.* Hannah Arendt states,

> Without being forgiven, released from the consequences of what we have done, our capacity to act would, as it were, be confined to one single deed from which we could never recover; we would remain the victims of its consequences forever.[47]

Arendt speaks to the liberation from bondage to one's past, sins, and shadow self through forgiveness. "The possible redemption from the predicament of irreversibility—of being unable to undo what one has done . . . —is the faculty of forgiving."[48]

The Paradox of Forgiveness

While according to Morton, forgiveness "above all else is the transcendence of blame," Allais points out the logical challenge of such a statement as it pertains to forgiveness:

> The first difficulty is simply to *make sense* of what is involved in ceasing to hold an action against someone while continuing to regard it as wrong and as attributed to the perpetrator in the way which is necessary for there to be something to forgive. Forgiving seems to mean ceasing to blame, but if blaming means holding the perpetrator responsible, then forgiveness requires *not* ceasing to blame, or else there will be nothing to forgive.[49]

This paradox is one of several that lie at the heart of forgiveness. For in saying, "I forgive my brother for betraying me," I am at once acknowledging the offense of "betrayal" while intending it "wiped clean" through the act of forgiveness. Forgiveness of sin constitutes the reality of sin it forgives. Once forgiveness has occurred and the slate is wiped clean, there is no such notion of abuse nor therefore of forgiveness. *The act of forgiving negates itself.* As Derrida observes, "a pure forgiveness cannot . . . exhibit itself in consciousness without at the same time denying itself. . . . Forgiveness is thus mad. It must plunge, but lucidly, into the night of the unintelligible. Call this the unconscious or the non-conscious if you want."[50] Here Derrida proposes a defining role of "the unconscious or the non-conscious" in forgiveness. Until this point, forgiveness had been considered to originate solely from the conscious will, as if an intention, decision, or choice. He writes:

> In order to approach now the very concept of forgiveness, logic and common sense agree for once with the paradox: it is necessary, it seems to me, to begin from the fact that, yes, there is the unforgivable. Is this not, in truth, the only thing to forgive? The only thing that *calls* for forgiveness? If one is already prepared to forgive what appears to be forgivable . . . then the very idea of forgiveness would disappear. If there is something to forgive, it would be what in religious language is called mortal sin, the worst, the unforgivable crime or harm. From which comes the aporia . . . : forgiveness forgives only the unforgivable. One cannot, or should not, forgive; there is only forgiveness, if there is any, where there is the unforgivable. That is to say that forgiveness must announce itself as impossibility itself. It can only be possible in doing the impossible.[51]

If one is "already prepared to forgive what appears to be forgivable" then one's free will is engaged and forgiveness occurs as a conscious choice—yes or no. Such "forgiveness" appears merely as an exertion of one's moral power gained from the offense, a deliberate decision whether to retain or give up the right to injury imparted by the transgression. While strategic in nature, it is a maneuver performed on the level of common sense and everyday thought and requires no real reflection. However, with the assertion that one "cannot, or should not, forgive; there is only forgiveness, if there is any, where there is the unforgivable," Derrida perverts forgiveness away from the commonsense perspective into the philosophical domain.[52] Forgiveness no longer exists on the horizontal, ego level but is transported into the vertical domain of the *soul's* logic, shedding not only ego concerns but the ego's own logic; the concept of forgiveness is not found on the ordinary, everyday level of discourse, on which level it is logically impossible because, for the ego, "doing the impossible" is out of the question.

Derrida continues: "'Forgiveness died in the death camps.' [Jankélévitch] says. Yes. Unless it only becomes possible from the moment that it appears impossible. Its history would begin, on the contrary, with the unforgivable."[53] We have seen how forgiveness paradoxically insists upon sin and simultaneously (retroactively) posits innocence. Now we find a paradox on another level; the possibility of forgiveness is constituted by its own impossibility—a dialectical relation that can only be grasped at the logical level of thought. Not only is the ego's inaccessibility to forgiveness confirmed,[54] but the birth of forgiveness occurs on the level of the non-ego, or soul.

A modern historical event fraught with unforgivable crimes is World War II, in particular, the Holocaust. If Derrida is correct, and the history of true forgiveness begins with the unforgivable, let us consider the experiences of a young Jewish concentration camp prisoner and his confrontation with an impossible request of forgiveness.

Notes

1. Regarding the recognition of forgiveness, I am referring here to Western and individualistic cultures only. While revenge is considered a "human universal," the types and levels of forgiveness varies across cultures. Rachel E. Lennon, "A Meta-Analysis of Cultural Differences of Revenge and Forgiveness," (UNF Thesis and Dissertations, 2013). http://digitalcommons.unf.edu/etd/476.
2. James Hillman, *Senex and Puer: Uniform Edition of the Writings of James Hillman* (Vol. 3, 1st ed.) (Putnam, CT: Spring Publications, 2005), 209.
3. Hillman, *Senex and Puer*, 209.
4. M.E. McCullough, K.I. Pargament, & C.E. Thoresen, eds., *Forgiveness: Research, Theory, and Practice* (New York: The Guilford Press, 2000); P. Strelan & T. Covic, "A Review of Forgiveness Process Models and a Coping Framework to Guide Future Research," *Journal of Social & Clinical Psychology*, 25, no. 10 (2006): 1059–1085.
5. R.C. Hunter, "Forgiveness, Retaliation and Paranoid Reactions," *The Canadian Psychiatric Association Journal/La Revue De L'association Des Psychiatres Du Canada*, 23, no. 3 (1978): 167.
6. Charles Griswold, *Forgiveness: A Philosophical Exploration* (Cambridge: Cambridge University Press, 2007), xiii.
7. Charles Griswold, "Forgiveness and Apology: What, When, Why?," *Tikkun* (2008, March): 26.
8. James Hillman, *Re-Visioning Psychology* (New York: HarperCollins, 1975); Kenneth Wapnick, *Forgiveness and Jesus* (Roscoe, NY: Foundation for A Course in Miracles, 1998).
9. James Hillman, *Insearch: Psychology and Religion* (2nd ed.) (Putnam, CT: Spring, 1994), 135.
10. Hillman, *Insearch*, 134.
11. Hillman, *Insearch*, 134.
12. Wolfgang Giegerich, *The Soul's Logical Life* (Frankfurt: Peter Lang, GmbH, 2008), 20.
13. Giegerich, *The Soul's Logical Life*, 24.
14. Giegerich, *The Soul's Logical Life*, 24.
15. J.A. Simpson & E.S.C. Weiner, *The Oxford English Dictionary* (Oxford: Clarendon Press, 1989).
16. Forgive, *The American Heritage College Thesaurus* (1st ed.) (Oxford: Oxford University Press, 2004).
17. Forgive, *Roget's II: The New Thesaurus* (Cleveland, OH: Wiley Publishing, 2010).
18. S. Akhtar, "Forgiveness: Origins, Dynamics, Psychopathology, and Technical Relevance," *Psychoanalytic Quarterly*, 71, no. 2 (2002): 175–212.
19. H.F. Smith, "Leaps of Faith: Is Forgiveness a Useful Concept?," *International Journal of Psychoanalysis*, 89, no. 5 (2008): 919–936.
20. Sigmund Freud, *Totem and Taboo: Some Points of Agreement between the Mental Lives of Savages and Neurotics*, trans. by J. Strachey (Florence, KY: Psychology Press, 2001), 73.
21. Smith, "Leaps of Faith".
22. C. Knapp, *The Classical World* (Classical Association of the Atlantic States, 1918), 12.
23. Knapp, *The Classical World*, 12.

24. e.g., C.E. Thoreson, Fred Luskin, & A.H.S. Harris, "Science and Forgiveness Interventions: Reflections and Recommendations," in E.L. Worthington, Jr. (Ed.), *Dimensions of Forgiveness: Psychological Research and Theological Speculations* (Philadelphia: Templeton Foundation Press, 1998), 163–192; K.C. Gordon, D.H. Baucom, & D.K. Snyder, "The Use of Forgiveness in Marital Therapy," in M.E. McCullough, K.I. Pargament, & C.E. Thoresen (Eds.), *Forgiveness: Theory, Research and Practice* (London: Guilford Press, 2000), 203–227.
25. K.C. Gordon & D.H. Baucom, "Understanding Betrayals in Marriage: A Synthesized Model of Forgiveness," *Family Process*, 37 (1998): 425–449; L.Y. Thompson, C.R. Snyder, L. Hoffman, S.T. Michael, H.N. Rasmussen, L.S. Billings, L. Heinze, J.E. Neufeld, H.S. Shorey, J.C. Roberts, & D.E. Roberts, "Dispositional Forgiveness of Self, Others, and Situations," *Journal of Personality*, 73 (2005): 313–359.
26. R.D. Enright & C.T. Coyle, "Researching the Process Model of Forgiveness within Psychological Interventions," in E.L. Worthington (Ed.), *Dimensions of Forgiveness* (Radnor, PA: Templeton Foundation Press, 1998), 139–162.
27. J.J. Exline & R.F. Baumeister, "Expressing Forgiveness and Repentance: Benefits and Barriers," in M.E. McCullough, K.I. Pargament, & C.E. Thoresen (Eds.), *Forgiveness: Theory, Research and Practice* (London: Guilford Press, 2000), 133–155.
28. L. Horwitz, "The Capacity to Forgive: Intrapsychic and Developmental Perspectives," *Journal of the American Psychoanalytic Association*, 53, no. 2 (2005): 487.
29. "Absolve," in *Collins English Dictionary* (New York: HarperCollins Reference, 2007).
30. C. Tipping, *Radical Forgiveness: A Revolutionary Five-Stage Process to Heal Relationships, Let Go of Anger and Blame, Find Peace in Any Situation* (Louisville, CO: Sounds True, 2009), 60.
31. Griswold, "Forgiveness and Apology: What, When, Why?", 23.
32. As cited by Griswold, "Forgiveness and Apology: What, When, Why?", 23.
33. S. Wiesenthal, *The Sunflower: On the Possibilities and Limits of Forgiveness* (New York: Schocken Books, 1969/1998), 186.
34. Desmond Tutu, *No Future without Forgiveness* (London: Random House, 1999), 31.
35. Tutu, *No Future without Forgiveness*, 31.
36. Adam Morton, "What Is forgiveness?," in C.L. Griswold & D. Konstan (Eds.), *Ancient Forgiveness: Classical, Judaic, and Christian* (1st ed., pp. 3–16) (Cambridge: Cambridge University Press, 2012), 7–8.
37. Morton, "What Is Forgiveness?", 7.
38. Tipping, *Radical Forgiveness: A Revolutionary Five-Stage Process to Heal Relationships, Let Go of Anger and Blame, Find Peace in Any Situation*; Griswold, "Forgiveness and Apology: What, When, Why?".
39. Morton, "What Is Forgiveness?", 13.
40. Griswold, "Forgiveness and Apology: What, When, Why?", 24.
41. Charles Griswold, "Plato and Forgiveness," *Ancient Philosophy*, 27, no. 2 (2007): 275.
42. Griswold, "Plato and Forgiveness," emphasis added.
43. C.L. Griswold & D. Konstan, eds. (2012). *Ancient Forgiveness: Classical, Judaic, and Christian* (Cambridge: Cambridge University Press, 2012), xiv–xv.
44. In the case of self-forgiveness, the pairs are internalized and a person might experience a "forgiving victim" paired with a "guilty sinner" (1:2), indicating an ego-syntonic inner relation, whereas a "forgiving victim" and "defiant offender" pair (1:3) may indicate an anti-social perspective. The common "withholding

victim"/"guilty sinner" pair (4:2) would indicate a self-punishing superego. An internal "denying victim"/"guilty sinner" pair (5:2) might characterize the inner experience of an addict suffering through the throes of addiction.

45. Lucy Allais, "Wiping the Slate Clean: The Heart of Forgiveness," *Philosophy & Public Affairs*, 36, no. 1 (2008): 51.
46. Allais, "Wiping the Slate Clean," 67–68.
47. Hannah Arendt, *The Human Condition* (Chicago: University of Chicago Press, 1998), 236.
48. Arendt, *The Human Condition*, 236.
49. Allais, "Wiping the Slate Clean," 32.
50. Jacques Derrida, *On Cosmopolitanism and Forgiveness* (Oxford: Taylor & Francis, 2007), 49.
51. Derrida, *On Cosmopolitanism and Forgiveness*, 33.
52. Foucault's call, "Let us pervert good sense," implies that a good sense must be perverted to enable the philosophical act of critical thinking (as distinct from unreflective thought). The difference in levels between common sense thought or representational appearance and reflective thought or interiority is also found in Giegerich's notion of "the psychological difference."
53. Derrida, *On Cosmopolitanism and Forgiveness*, 37.
54. A common psychological situation is one in which a person "wants" to forgive but finds that he or she cannot; the offense occurs as "unforgivable," forgiveness seems impossible and not a matter of conscious choice, confirming Derrida's observations. The encounter of forgiveness as "impossible" and the important psychological experience of "I want" and "I can't" together will be explored as a crucial element of psychological forgiveness in Chapter 6.

4 Forgiveness in the Face of the Unforgivable

> For as the sun is the blossom of fire, and the heavenly sun is the right eye of the world, so also the copper, when purification makes it to blossom, is an earthly sun, a king upon earth, like the sun in heaven.[1]

The guiding image for this chapter of the study is given by the story in Simon Wiesenthal's book *The Sunflower: On the Possibilities and Limits of Forgiveness*, in which a dying Nazi soldier summons a Jewish prisoner (Wiesenthal himself) to his deathbed to receive his confession of unforgivable crimes. The encounter between these two men portrayed in *The Sunflower* provides a context for examining the psychological relationship between forgiveness and what may be considered as the objectively unforgivable crimes of the Holocaust.

Whereas the first segment of *The Sunflower* documents the extraordinary story of Simon Wiesenthal's life as a concentration camp prisoner, his unforgettable encounter at the deathbed of a Nazi soldier, and his subsequent personal coming to terms with his experience, the second segment of the book consists of numerous essays in which contemporary theologians, philosophers, and well-known authors and thinkers offer their perspective on the fundamental question of forgiveness of the unforgivable.

The Sunflower

In his book, Simon begins by recounting his soul-numbing experience as a prisoner in a Nazi concentration camp. During a forced march one day, he describes how his column came to a halt at a crossroads. He writes:

> I noticed on the left of the street there was a military cemetery. It was enclosed by a low barbed wire fence. The wires were threaded through sparse bushes and low shrubs, but between them you could see the graves aligned in stiff rows.
>
> And on each grave there was planted a sunflower, as straight as a soldier on parade.

> I stared spellbound. The flower heads seemed to absorb the sun's rays like mirrors and draw them down into the darkness of the ground as my gaze wandered from the sunflower to the grave. It seemed to penetrate the earth and suddenly I saw before me a periscope. It was gaily colored and butterflies fluttered from flower to flower. Were they carrying messages from grave to grave? Were they whispering something to each flower to pass on to the soldier below? Yes, this was just what they were doing; the dead were receiving light and messages.
>
> Suddenly I envied the dead soldiers. Each had a sunflower to connect him with the living world, and butterflies to visit his grave. For me there would be no sunflower. I would be buried in a mass grave, where corpses would be piled on top of me. No sunflower would ever light into my darkness, and no butterflies would dance above my dreadful tomb.[2]

Wiesenthal's exquisite capacity to imagine the experience of the (dead) German soldiers is pushed to impossible lengths when he soon thereafter finds himself inexplicably summoned by a hospital nurse to the bedside of a dying young SS soldier named Karl. Over the course of several hours, the soldier, who is gravely injured, blind, and near death, gropes for Simon's hand and begs him to listen as he recounts his unspeakable crimes. Karl confesses in brutal detail the horrific memory that torments him, in which he participates in the merciless slaughter of innocent Jewish civilians and children. Karl ultimately expresses his longing to receive forgiveness from "a Jew." Simon, who maintains his silence throughout the encounter, ultimately responds by leaving the room.

Before proceeding, I wish to include a significant portion's of Karl's admission so that the magnitude of the act for which he seeks forgiveness is understood and a possible glimpse of what Simon might have endured in listening to Karl may be conveyed. What follows is Karl's confession as described by Simon:

> "I know," muttered [Karl], "that at this moment thousands of men are dying. Death is everywhere . . . I am resigned to dying soon, but before that I want to talk about an experience which is torturing me. Otherwise I cannot die in peace . . .
>
> "I must tell you something dreadful . . . Something inhuman. It happened a year ago . . ."[3]
>
> "I must tell you of this horrible deed—tell you because . . . you are a Jew."[4]
>
> "An order was given," he continued, "and we marched toward the huddled mass of Jews. There were a hundred and fifty of them or perhaps two hundred, including many children who stared at us with anxious eyes. A few were quietly crying. There were infants in their mothers' arms, but hardly any young men; mostly women and graybeards.
>
> "As we approached I could see the expression in their eyes—fear, indescribable fear . . . apparently they knew what was awaiting them . . .

"A truck arrived with cans of petrol which we unloaded and took into a house. The strong men among the Jews were ordered to carry the cans to the upper stories. They obeyed—apathetically, without a will of their own, like automatons.

"Then we began to drive the Jews into the house. A sergeant with a whip in his hand helped any of the Jews who were not quick enough. There was a hail of curses and kicks. The house was not very large, it had only three stories. I would not have believed it possible to crowd them all into it. But after a few minutes there was no Jew left on the street."

He was silent and my heart started to beat violently. I could well imagine the scene. It was all too familiar. I might have been among those who were forced into that house with the petrol cans. I could feel how they must have pressed against each other. I could hear their frantic cries as they realized what was to be done to them.

The dying Nazi went on: "Another truck came up full of more Jews and they too were crammed into the house with the others. Then the door was locked and a machine gun was posted opposite."

I knew how the story would end. My own country had been occupied by the Germans for over a year and we had heard of similar happenings in Bialystok, Brody, and Gródek. The method was always the same. He could spare me the rest of his gruesome account.

So I stood up ready to leave but he pleaded with me: "Please stay, I must tell you the rest."

I really do not know what kept me. But there was something in his voice that prevented me from obeying my instinct to end the interview. Perhaps I wanted to hear from his own mouth, in his own words, the full horror of the Nazis' inhumanity.

"When we were told that everything was ready, we went back a few yards, and then received the command to remove safety pins from hand grenades and throw them through the windows of the houses. Detonations followed on after another. . . . My God!"

Now he was silent, and he raised himself slightly from the bed. His whole body was shivering.

But he continued: "We heard screams and saw the flames eat their way from floor to floor. . . . We had our rifles ready to shoot down anyone who tried to escape from that blazing hell. . ..

"The screams from the house were horrible. Dense smoke poured out and choked us. . . ."

His hand felt damp. He was so shattered by his recollection that he broke into a sweat and I loosened my hand from his grip. But at once he groped for it again and held it tight.

"Please, please," he stammered, "don't go away, I have more to say."

I no longer had any doubts as to the ending. I saw that he was summoning his strength for one last effort to tell me the rest of the story to its bitter end.

> "Behind the windows of the second floor, I saw a man with a small child in his arms. His clothes were alight. By his side stood a woman, doubtless the mother of the child. With his free hand the man covered the child's eyes . . . then he jumped into the street. Seconds later the mother followed. Then from the other windows fell burning bodies. . . . We shot. . . . Oh God!"
>
> The dying man held his hand in front of his bandaged eyes as if he wanted to banish the picture from his mind.
>
> "I don't know how many tried to jump out of the windows but that one family I shall never forget—least of all the child. It had black hair and dark eyes."
>
> He fell silent, completely exhausted.[5]

Karl continues his narrative, explaining that weeks later he and his platoon were awaiting orders to attack:

> "[W]e climbed out of the trenches and charged, but suddenly I stopped as though rooted to the ground. Something seized me. My hands, which held my rifle with fixed bayonet, began to tremble. In that moment I saw the burning family, the father with the child and behind them the mother—and they came to meet me. 'No, I cannot shoot at them a second time.' The thought flashed through my mind . . . And then a shell exploded by my side. I lost consciousness."[6]
>
> ". . . I lie here waiting for death. The pains in my body are terrible, but worse still is my conscience. It never ceases to remind me of the burning house and the family that jumped from the window.
>
> ". . . I cannot die . . . without coming clean. This must be my confession."[7]

Karl finally expresses his longing to Simon, saying

> "I know that what I have told you is terrible. In the long nights while I have been waiting for death, time and time again I have longed to talk about it to a Jew and beg forgiveness from him. Only I didn't know whether there were any Jews left. . . .
>
> "I know that what I am asking is almost too much for you, but without your answer I cannot die in peace."[8]

The question of precisely what Karl means by "forgiveness" may be many things, as we have seen. The term *forgiveness* is not explicitly defined by Simon in his book (nor do the respondents do not define it in their responses). However, Simon likens Karl's request to asking for "help" and describes his own response thusly:

> Two men who had never known each other had been brought together for a few hours by Fate. One asks the other for help. But the other was himself helpless and able to do nothing for him.

> I stood up and looked in his direction, at his folded hands. Between them there seemed to rest a sunflower.
>
> At last I made up my mind and without a word I left the room.[9]

After the war, Simon made a trip to visit Karl's mother to confirm what Karl had shared about his childhood, never revealing his identity or the truth about Karl to her. Simon experienced a preoccupation for many years over his encounter with Karl and what may seem like guilt over his silent response. His own anguish over his silence is revealed in the following passage:

> [I kept] silent when a young Nazi, on his deathbed, begged me to be his confessor. And later when I met his mother I again kept silent rather than shatter her illusions about her dead son's inherent goodness. And how many bystanders kept silent as they watched Jewish men, women, and children being led to the slaughterhouses of Europe?[10]

Wiesenthal's response of silence is considered by John Knapp in the following passage of his psychological study of the Holocaust:

> It seems that . . . the silence of Wiesenthal communicated a shade of silence that bears the mark of an unforgivable act. Might Wiesenthal's silence be filled with shock–aghast at the audacity of a dying soldier to seek forgiveness for an unforgivable act? Is such silence a greater form of communication than words might allow? If here, on paper, Wiesenthal's silence upon this man's request for forgiveness were to appear, what would it look like? Is one blank page enough? Could it even be described? Could it even be spoken? How dare this soldier speak! How dare he ask for forgiveness![11]

At this point, Knapp presents five blank pages to the reader, powerfully symbolizing the profound significance of Wiesenthal's silent response to the Nazi soldier. "5 pages of rage—a silence that distances, separates, and hates but does not love, pardon, or forgive." Did Simon's silence, Knapp wonders, contain "the seeds of his violent hatred of this Nazi murderer?"[12]

Indeed, Wiesenthal's self-questioning attitude, his generosity toward Karl demonstrated by his willingness to endure Karl's abhorrent confession, along with the kindness he offered Karl's mother, can occur as somewhat mystifying given the horrors and brutality he had to endure over many years as a concentration camp prisoner. Many members of his family, along with dear friends, were killed during the war, and he nearly died himself on numerous occasions. Mere silence in response to Karl's outrageous request of forgiveness of the unforgivable seems more than kind. Was something else concealed by Wiesenthal's silence? A desire for vengeance? Murderous rage or hatred, as Knapp suggests?

It is impossible to imagine what it might have been like to be in Simon's shoes, to have suffered such profound emotional and physical anguish, so violent a betrayal and loss of soul, to have undergone hell on earth, and then to be confronted by the face of the demon himself in the bandaged visage of Karl, yet astonishingly, that is what Simon asks of the reader.

Wiesenthal addresses various theologians, writers, and influential thinkers in putting forward the following statement:

> Was my silence at the bedside of the dying Nazi right or wrong? This is a profound moral question that challenges the conscience of the reader of this episode, just as much as it once challenged my heart and my mind. There are those who can appreciate my dilemma, and so endorse my attitude, and there are others who will be ready to condemn me for refusing to ease the last moment of a repentant murderer.
>
> The crux of the matter is, of course, the question of forgiveness. Forgetting is something that time alone takes care of, but forgiveness is an act of volition, and only the sufferer is qualified to make the decision.
>
> You, who have just read this sad and tragic episode in my life, can mentally change places with me and ask yourself the crucial question, "What would I have done?"[13]

Wiesenthal's rush to the question of forgiveness leaves a nagging sense of something crucial overlooked. *Was my silence at the bedside of the dying Nazi right or wrong?* Such a question, when posed before the backdrop of the unspeakable monstrosity of the Shoah, begins to resemble less a "profound moral question" than a profoundly *insignificant* one. By asserting the crux of the matter to be, "of course, the question of forgiveness," Wiesenthal seems to elevate the ethical dilemma of offering forgiveness to Karl to the moral category of Karl's unforgivable crimes of the cold-blooded murder of innocents. Are not such crimes are beyond the pale of morality altogether? Like Knapp, some respondents note Karl's utter audacity in assuming that forgiveness of his crimes would even be a *remote* possibility. Yet astonishingly, Simon takes Karl's request for forgiveness *seriously*. Not only that, Simon relates a deeply humanized portrait of Karl to the reader by meticulously recounting the details of the confession that convey Karl's torment and vouching repeatedly for Karl's genuine repentance. And while Wiesenthal does not explicitly offer forgiveness to Karl, he still keeps *alive* the idea of forgiveness by honoring it as *valid option* in the face of the overwhelmingly unforgivable—even writing a book about it! His portrayal of forgiveness thereby fulfills the major conditions set by Derrida of "true" or "pure" forgiveness: that it be extraordinary, exceptional, and present only in the face of the unforgivable. Karl's imminent death also cancels out the "economic" motivation of forgiveness, as there can be no further relationship between the two men, and nothing can be gained from Simon's bestowing forgiveness upon Karl. While the story of *The Sunflower* reflects upon the question of forgiveness's *absence* conveyed by Wiesenthal's silence, it also *presences* forgiveness as a remarkably profound and important moral question (justifiably or not) and depicts an unusually heightened form of forgiveness as reflected in Derrida's "true" forgiveness.

***

Though he confessed, many respondents insist that Karl must not be forgiven. What factors disqualify one who requests forgiveness from receiving it? When does the hope of forgiveness become arrogant or repugnant? Echoing Knapp's expression of fury at the audacity of Karl's confession, numerous respondents in *The Sunflower* contest Karl's "right" to ask Simon for forgiveness. Eugene Fischer writes,

> I believe it is the height of arrogance for Christians to ask Jews to forgive them. . . . [W]e have no right to put Jewish survivors in the impossible moral position of offering forgiveness, implicitly, in the name of the six million. . . . Placing a Jew in this anguished position further victimizes him or her. This . . . was the final sin of the dying Nazi.[14]

At first blush, any request for forgiveness would seem welcome; would it not explicitly convey the offender's genuine remorse and wish to "undo" the sin? However, Fischer identifies the intrusive burden surreptitiously cast by the offender onto the other through the request for forgiveness.

Also noting that the demand for forgiveness may be cut from the same cloth as the initial offense, from Eva Fleischner we read:

> I am not only struck by the agony of the dying man, but his obliviousness to the suffering, the inhuman condition, of Simon and his fellow Jews (he did not even ask Simon his name, although he did give him his possessions upon his death). The mere fact of having Simon summoned to his room exposes the Jew to punishment, if not death. Yet Karl insists on seeing "a Jew"—any Jew—in the hope of being able to die in peace. His own suffering completely blinds him to the suffering of the Jews.[15]

Here the quest for forgiveness is revealed as narcissistic and cruel, again adding further to the offender's crimes. Rebecca Goldstein writes:

> Yes, the SS man came to see, to some extent, his guilt, but not, I think, to the full extent in which that guilt exists and always will. For had he understood the enormity of his crimes, he would never have dared to ask for forgiveness. Never. To have truly seen his guilt would have been to know himself as utterly dispossessed of all chances for forgiveness. It would have been to know himself as having forfeited forever any questionable right to "die in peace." Perhaps then, and only then, in knowing his absolute unforgivability, would it even be conceivable that

> he be granted forgiveness—and then only by those three burning souls, multiplied by millions.[16]

Goldstein is open to the possibility of forgiveness for Karl if and only if he could comprehend his own unforgivability. This hearkens back to Derrida's assertion that forgiveness occurs only in the face of its impossibility.

These writers insist that not only is Karl unforgivable, but that his request for forgiveness is the nail in the coffin, so to speak. "To have truly seen his guilt would have been to know himself as utterly dispossessed of all chances for forgiveness." Karl's expressed yearning for forgiveness before Simon meant that he did not yet "know himself" as unforgivable. He was blind to this psychological truth, and his stated desire for forgiveness gave him away and disqualified him from receiving it. The encounter portrayed in *The Sunflower* illustrates the psychological truth of Derrida's assertion that *the prerequisite of true forgiveness is its own impossibility*.[17] From this we might also observe that Simon's response of silence was consistent with the *truth* of forgiveness. Its prerequisite had not been fulfilled. The question still remains as to *why* the impossibility of forgiveness is necessary for forgiveness.

Let us consider for a moment the problem inherent with the demand of forgiveness in general, amplified so well in the figure of the repentant Nazi soldier in particular. For Karl, the receipt of forgiveness would finally mean relief from the psychological torment caused by the traumatic memories of his horrific crimes. In his fantasy, forgiveness holds the promise of his finally "dying in peace." As the respondents point out, it is obvious here that Karl is still in it only for *himself*: his utter lack of concern for Simon (as noted above, he didn't even bother asking his name) displays the same dehumanizing logic that gave rise to his crimes. For Karl, forgiveness holds the promise of relief from the consequences of his former reality *without his having to abandon that reality of which he himself is a part*. The wish for forgiveness is equivalent to the avoidance of the wholesale rejection of the former logic and the wish to salvage any part of it.

Therein lies the problem: because Karl failed to acknowledge the *impossibility of forgiveness* for himself, he failed to insist upon the absolute unworkability of the former logic. "Please forgive me," conveys a consciousness that *wants to want* absolution but is unwilling to absolve it*self* of the logic *as which* it exists. To beg forgiveness betrays the hidden wish to preserve the self and world that gave rise to the offense; the request for forgiveness serves as a mere *simulation* of the earlier logic's demise in the seductive form of "Forgive me!" Karl's longing for forgiveness indicates an insistence (conscious or not) that the former reality remain intact and in play. Forgiveness holds the promise of acknowledgment, validation, and freedom to be without constriction or consequence. What better tactic to preserve the status quo than to beg forgiveness?

***

The responses in *The Sunflower* demonstrate the purely psychological nature of forgiveness, for nothing *of substance* is at stake in Karl's request (save possibly his "spiritual" salvation, the question of which *is* at stake according to others as discussed below). Karl is on the verge of death, precluding any future interpersonal relationship. Whether or not Simon forgives Karl is of no consequence, *except psychologically*. Here forgiveness lies completely within the purview of the mind. What would it mean, then, psychologically, to grant or gain forgiveness? Why rail so adamantly against one's right to ask, or beg so blindly and desperately for forgiveness? What does forgiveness offer? What does it accomplish? *Why does it matter?* There are a myriad of answers. On a subjective level, the ego, in its constant and feverish attempt to rehabilitate itself in its own eyes, grants and gains forgiveness for its own preservation and salvation (including, for example, the ability for Karl to "die in peace"). In an ego sense, there are tremendous stakes involved with forgiveness. Yet is anything "more" going on (i.e., at the objective level of consciousness)? Does *The Sunflower* help answer the question of whether forgiveness matters *per se*? In *The Sunflower*, because Simon *neither offered forgiveness nor condemned Karl*, the question of forgiveness is allowed to arise as a purely symbolic one, an enigmatic expression of consciousness at large. The encounter between Karl and Simon qualified as a *soul event*, powerful enough to forever alter the life of Simon.

Religious Ethics of Forgiveness and Repentance

The majority of responses to Wiesenthal's questions are dominated by the moral question of forgiveness and fall along theological lines; each is predictable given each author's particular religious affiliation. One author notes this phenomenon at large:

> Over the past twenty years I have frequently used *The Sunflower* as a text in my Holocaust course; it has invariably led to animated discussions. One striking feature has been that, almost without exception, the Christian students come out in favor of forgiveness, while the Jewish students feel that Simon did the right thing by not granting the dying man's wish.[18]

Indeed, Christian writers are compelled to forgive in accordance with scriptural mandates, as noted by Cardinal Franz Konig: "For Christians, the binding answer is in the Gospels. The question of whether there is a limit to forgiveness has been emphatically answered by Christ in the negative".[19]

The respondents who claimed neither to be Jewish nor Christian—for instance, two Buddhists (including the Dalai Lama)—advocated for forgiveness, also citing spiritual prescriptions. ("For a Buddhist, forgiveness is always possible and one should always forgive.")[20]

Likewise, the Jewish essayists cite religious laws governing forgiveness in the Jewish faith that preclude and even prohibit the possibility of Simon's forgiveness of Karl. They unanimously agree with Simon's response of silence toward Karl; "No one can forgive something that has not been done to them directly."[21] Lipstadt states that in Judaism,

> If I sin, I cannot go to someone else who has some remote connection with the person I have harmed and ask that third party for forgiveness. . . . The Jew who had been burned to death by this soldier had not authorized anyone to forgive on their behalf.[22]

It would seem, then, from a Jewish perspective, Simon's question is a moot point—any affirmative response to Karl would have been "wrong" according to Judaic law. In the same way, to withhold forgiveness would be "un-Christian" and erroneous from a Christian perspective.

While there is an absence of support for the possibility of forgiveness for Karl among the Jewish respondents, support for the unlimited possibility of *atonement* does exist in Judaism in a more general context. Rabbi Lopiansky writes: "One of the wonders of the Creation is *teshuvah*—the ability of a sinner to repent and atone for his evil actions and, in effect, clean his slate as if he had never committed the sins."[23] According to Rabbi Eliyahu Touger, "Every person can do *teshuvah*. No matter how low he has descended, there is nothing that can prevent him from reversing his conduct, and establishing a bond with G-d."[24] And the *Jerusalem Talmud*[25] states: "The Holy One, blessed be His name, said to Elijah, 'Behold, the precious gift which I have bestowed on my world: though a man sins again and again, but returns in penitence, I will receive him."[26] While Karl's status as a baptized Catholic guaranteed his salvation and forgiveness of all future sins—short of apostasy—in the eyes of the church (in fact, "every act of confession is a recapitulation of baptism"[27]), he took no obvious comfort in this notion. Indeed, Karl was deeply remorseful and in obvious anguish. Wiesenthal acknowledges that in Karl's confession "there was true repentance . . . the way he spoke and the fact that he spoke to me was a proof of his repentance."[28] In the Judaic tradition, the act of repentance enables reconciliation with others and with God, and according to Lipstadt, "*teshuvah* can result in the sinner returning to a repaired relationship with both God and with his/her fellow human, even as God returns to the sinner."[29] Repentance—a form of *teshuvah* and a precondition for atonement and forgiveness in Jewish teachings—is discussed fifty-three times in Wiesenthal's short book about forgiveness and requires further consideration.

Excursion on Repentance

As we saw in Chapter 2, the beginning conceptions of modern forgiveness are not to be found in ancient Greek and Roman mythology, philosophy, or politics, but rather in the early Judaic tradition as a feature of man's relationship with God.[30]

The modern, less divine, and more interpersonal nature of forgiveness is quite different from the concept of forgiveness found in the Hebrew Bible, midrashic collections, the Mishnah, and the Talmud, where forgiveness is intermingled with a cluster of the related concepts of law, sin, sacrifice, justice, mercy, repentance, atonement, purification, and pardon. Two key elements of forgiveness in rabbinic literature are (a) the primacy of divine-human interaction in which the primary offender/victim pair is the human against God (as opposed to another person), and (b) the emphasis of action focused upon the perpetrator—that is, the responsibility for reparation by the sinner. *This focus on the perpetrator as opposed to the victim highlights a corresponding emphasis upon repentance.* Morgan notes that ancient Jewish texts focus on the requirement to repent as an important, perhaps a necessary condition of forgiveness. Moreover, "the forgiveness of interest is God's forgiveness and not the forgiveness of any human victim of wrongdoing, if there is one."[31] While repentance is a necessary condition of reconciliation in all cases, for serious transgressions, differing ritual practices of atonement must also be performed, such as fasting, cessation of work, sacrifices, and purgation to enable the sinner's purification and atonement as described in the Torah (see Leviticus 16; Exodus 30:10, Leviticus 23:27–31; 25:9; Numbers 29:7–11). Morgan notes that such practices are in themselves

> an expression of God's purification and his confirmation of the reconciliation with the sinner; in a sense, they manifest God's acceptance of the repentance and hence His mercy, the cancellation of the punishment.[32]

Similar to the way in which acts of ritual sacrifice contain within themselves their own meaning,[33] such rituals of atonement (including sacrifice) literally "manifest" God's acceptance and forgiveness.

When the offense against God involves an offense against another person—for example the violation of biblical codes prohibiting stealing, lying, swearing falsely, ignoring the poor, and so on—interpersonal forgiveness still remains a secondary issue; the human victim of the wrongdoing is an "incidental factor" in the sinner's efforts to reconcile with God. Not only that, once compensated for their loss, "the victim should receive the compensation and *issue his own forgiveness without reluctance*, in order to facilitate God's ultimate act of pardon."[34] Forgiveness here lacks emotional tone or change of heart; it is merely a directive to be followed, a law to be obeyed.

Turning back to Karl, it was noted earlier that while he may have been genuinely repentant, the second precondition for atonement was impossible for him to accomplish, as his victims were deceased and unable to receive restitution.[35] In *The Sunflower* essays, much is made of the inability of God to forgive misdeeds among people; only the victim has the right to forgive the perpetrator, no one else.[36] "According to Jewish tradition, even God Himself can only forgive sins committed against Himself, not against man."[37] The insistence that performing *teshuvah* only absolves one from sins committed against God, while sins against another person are absolved only when restitution has been made and the pardon of the offended party has been obtained, is a difficult paradox. It is hard to imagine that Karl's actions against his fellow man were *not also* sins against God. According to Morgan's reading of early Judaic teachings, any sin committed against man is also a sin against God. God's forgiveness of the sinner would be granted only upon the successful act of forgiveness by the victim. In this sense, God would be "waiting" for the victim to forgive, implying that divine forgiveness is inextricably linked to interpersonal forgiveness; in order to forgive us, God needs us to forgive one another.

Morgan notes an interesting distinction in ancient Jewish texts between repenting out of *fear* of God's punishment for the transgression and repenting out of *love* for God and a feeling of devotion. In the first case, while the sinner may properly repent, even performing all the necessary rituals of atonement, he "is still the same person; his openness to sin is checked by knowledge of the penalties, but the sinfulness is not removed."[38] Repentance performed out of fear of God's punishment allows one to avoid the consequences for sinful actions, but one's character is not changed by the "sin"; the semantics or contents of one's heart are the focus, rather than the syntax or foundation of the heart itself. In repenting out of love and devotion, however, the sinner undergoes a profound *metanoia*:

> Repentance from fear involves a kind of separation from the particular sin in question; it requires a public confession and elicits from God a pardon or act of mercy. Repentance from love involves a more radical separation from sinfulness itself; it requires inward repentance and elicits from God forgiveness, for the penitent has left behind one self, the sinful self, and engaged in an act of self-creation in which he has become a new person.[39]

In a move of deep interiority and self-creation, the penitent is numinously reborn. Indeed, in the Talmud we read that in a place where people who have done *teshuvah* stand, the purest *zadik* (righteous person) cannot stand.[40]

Returning to *The Sunflower*, the question emerges as to whether Karl's repentance was out of fear or out of love, and whether through the extent of his repentance he accomplished *teshuvah*, or "connectedness with God."[41] It would seem that in the moment in which Karl caught sight of the little child about to be burned to death, love fell upon him. He was finally and suddenly gripped by love, a traumatically enlightening soul event that pierced open his blackened heart and began the process of his redemption. Yet while the "unforgettable" image of the doomed child "with dark hair and dark eyes" initiated the process of redemption, Karl's subsequent objectification of Simon was proof he had not yet fully "left behind his former self." Part of the process of Karl's atonement seemed to require the act of confession, of which Simon unwittingly found himself a part.

Confession

"I cannot die . . . without coming clean. This must be my confession."[42] *The Sunflower* powerfully depicts the confession of Karl's unspeakable sins, and in a broader sense the book itself serves as Simon's own very public and courageous confession of a profound and deeply personal moral decision.

Confession can be defined as "the act of stating one's sin to another person who is sanctioned to 'hear' and to supply the reassurance of pardon and forgiveness."[43] The act of confession is inherent to forgiveness as the revelation of that which seeks to be forgiven. In Judaism, confession (*vidui)* is a crucial element of repentance (*teshuvah*) allowing for atonement with God.[44] In Catholicism, confession is designated as one of the sacred sacraments, symbolizing an outer reflection of inner "grace" given by baptism.

Jung describes "the extraordinary significance of genuine, straightforward confession"[45] as the prototype of "all analytic treatment of the soul,"[46] citing a proverb of the Greek mysteries: *Give up what thou has, and thou wilt receive*. That which is given up and revealed in confession, according to Jung, is the shadow element of the psyche. He explains:

> How can I be substantial without casting a shadow? I must have a dark side too if I am to be whole; and by becoming conscious of my shadow I remember once more that I am a human being like any other. . . . [I]f this rediscovery of my own wholeness remains private it will only restore the earlier condition . . . [and] prolong my isolation. . . . But through confession I throw myself into the arms of humanity again, freed at last from the burden of moral exile.[47]

In "giving up" the unconscious shadow, one may receive and be received into community. Confession is seen as an archetypal act reflecting the need to be forgiven and reconciled. With confession,

> The penitent is relieved of strain and tension. He is reconciled and welcomed back into the arms of humanity. Jung valued confession as an aid to psychological health. The chief value of confession lies in the aspect of relief of strain and the resultant reconciliation.[48]

Rabbi Aaron Lopiansky emphasizes the *defiant* element of sin, signaling an attitude of "independence" from God that in effect severs one's connection to the Other.[49] The way to rectify this distancing autonomy must be through an act of submission before God, or *hisbatlus*, described as a kind of self-cancellation or negation by Lopiansky. The role of confession here is that the act of sharing one's sin is seen as a literal expression the Holy Spirit or *ruach*—the part of man's soul that connects one indestructibly and eternally to God. Thus, *vidui*, by virtue of activating the *ruach* through speech, negates the independent sinful self, thus reestablishing one's eternal dependence and the reality of the unbroken divine bond.

The idea that confession obviates an intense experience of alienation from one's community is paramount according to Jung. He writes,

> The tremendous feeling of relief which usually follows a confession can be ascribed to the readmission of the lost sheep into the human community. His moral isolation and seclusion, which were so difficult to bear, cease. Herein lies the chief psychological value of confession.[50]

Jung's characterization of confession as allowing for such a reunion evokes an image of the penitent cut off and cast out in agonizing isolation outside the gates of humanity, then gloriously received back into its arms upon the "giving up" of the shameful shadow element. Similar to the Prodigal Son coming home to publicly acknowledge his misdeeds and ask for forgiveness, confession makes possible a shift in one's social location, so to speak, from outside the fold to inside. If we return to our story, we might agree that a motivation for Karl's confession is his wish to avoid a continued experience of "moral isolation and seclusion." We hear a longing for the presence of the other in Karl's desperate pleadings "Please stay, I must tell you the rest,"[51] "'Please, please,' he stammered, 'Don't go away, I have more to say'"[52] and from his repeated groping for Simon's hand. "Without your answer," begs Karl, "I cannot die in peace."

Evil and Forgiveness

The ancient confrontation between good and evil in *The Sunflower* seems apparent; Simon, representing the slaughtered Jewish people, and Karl, representing the Nazi murderers, together function as a microcosm of the Holocaust at large, evidenced by the way respondents invoke the general question of the Holocaust when considering Karl's sins. For instance, one author asks, "Is it morally possible to say, 'I am sorry for the Holocaust?' Or to apologize for individual acts of murder whose great aggregate yielded the murder of millions of Jews?"[53] Another writes, "The Holocaust involved . . . murder and the defamation of the Jewish people . . . No matter how much atonement is expressed for these crimes, no restitution is possible, and no forgiveness can follow."[54] Karl's sins are thus conflated with all Nazis' crimes against humanity and situated inside the dimension of archetypal evil; as Friedlander observes, "[T]he extermination of the Jews of Europe is perceived by many as the ultimate standard of evil, against which all degrees of evil may be measured."[55]

Here we are faced with probably the most pressing concern in the study of forgiveness, which is the question of forgiveness in the face of willful malevolence, or "evil." Of course the most obvious "problem" with forgiveness in this context is that such forgiveness might blunt or dilute the significance of the problem of evil; forgiveness would seem to regard as acceptable that which is unacceptable, thus consciously making a place for that which there *is no allowable place* in consciousness.

While the expression of evil made manifest in the Holocaust is so extreme as to be rendered incomprehensible and unspeakable, Bartlett argues against the notion that it is unique, unintelligible, or even an aberration of human nature.

> We unfortunately find the same forces of hatred, violence, cruelty, atrocity, and mass murder in other genocides. Among them, the Holocaust stands as the most horrifying obscene eruption of human evil in man's history. . . . But the same fundamental pathology is involved, the same human evil.[56]

Before Bartlett, Jung referred to "barbarities and blood baths perpetrated . . . throughout European history,"[57] all of which "show us a picture of the common human shadow that could hardly be painted in blacker colors. The evil that comes to light in man and that undoubtedly dwells within him is of gigantic proportions."[58] He continues:

> Man has done these things; I am a man, who has his share of human nature; therefore I am guilty with the rest and bear unaltered and indelibly within me the capacity and the inclination to do them again at any time. Even if, juristically speaking, we were not accessories to the crime, we are always, thanks to our human nature, potential criminals. In reality we merely lacked a suitable opportunity to be drawn into the infernal melee. None of us stands outside humanity's black collective shadow. [59]

Arendt's well-known observation of "the banality of evil" points to the fact that so-called normal people can be led to perpetrate unthinkable evil. While Arendt speaks of the normal in pathological, Jung and Bartlett are speaking also of *the pathological in normality*. Bartlett analyzes the psychological factors present in the behaviors of the perpetrators of the Holocaust and argues that such factors are present in so-called normal people. These characteristics include

> projective thinking, dehumanization, doubling, splitting, use of abusive/euphemistic language, psychic numbing, and the gratifications that come from finding an emotional home in the struggle for a cause, from conformity with one's group, and from enjoyment of violence.[60]

Bartlett cites the following additional inherent psychological traits, which, together with those noted above, *virtually guarantee the persistence of pathological behavior in humanity*:

> Human aversion to unpleasant self-knowledge; denial; individual and group narcissism and species-wide homocentrism; . . . the adrenalin rush

> of killing; the sense of personal empowerment of focused hatred; a steadfast and self-chosen blindness to humanity's reproductive proliferation; its self-centered avarice for land and natural resources; humanity's selfishness in its careless destruction of the world's biodiversity; the insistence of . . . the superiority of their . . . nations and their political and religious ideologies; . . . mankind's single-minded appetite only for the hopeful and the consoling; the universality of patterns of thought . . . that are self-defeating, self-undermining, and meaningless; a pronounced rigid commitment to all of these affective and cognitive habits, [and] antagonism toward attempts to question them and to break free from the old constraints.[61]

Our combined "aversion to self-knowledge; denial;" and "single-minded appetite only for the hopeful and the consoling" lead Bartlett to draw a compelling though disturbing conclusion with regard to forgiveness. He writes:

> Forgiveness serves to erase and to deny that which we must remember if we are to learn from our past. Like hope, forgiveness is a second-order pathology, which contributes to the perpetuation of human evil rather than to its abatement.[62]

Bartlett argues that the presence of forgiveness in the face of evil is itself pathological, a denial of reality. He cites Charny and Rapaport (1982):

> There can be no forgiveness; there can be no dampening of our outrage and protest against the killing of men. My desire is to understand how these terrible events come to be and what we might do to stop them, not to forgive.

The ubiquitous nature of evil within the human psyche leads Bartlett to conclude that human evil is a pathology, a disease; any psychologically "healthy" person may succumb to evil if the conditions are right. As such, it should be approached and treated in the same way as one might a disease. Forgiveness, he argues, is not a valid response to evil, for we do not "forgive" those afflicted with disease. "Should we 'forgive' our species for its destructive, cruel, and vicious pathology?" he asks. "Should we instead 'blame' it? Or neither?"[63] Bartlett claims that forgiveness is problematic because it does not motivate us to undertake the task of taking seriously

> the need to curtail very significantly the proliferation of the pathogen, and to undertake, by whatever measures are effective and socially and politically expedient, to change the basic psychological and cognitive constitution of the race.[64]

Anger, however, says Bartlett, can be a helpful response to the extent that it is expressed as the exclamation, *No more!* According to Bartlett, outrage is the only appropriate way to meet and overcome evil.

Bartlett points to the way forgiveness can be used by the ego to neglect and reject the unacceptable and intolerable parts of itself via the psychological defense mechanism of denial. "The only thing that must happen for evil to triumph is for human beings to be convinced they are good."[65] Forgiveness, insofar as it shields us from the intolerable darkness of our own shadow, serves to further the pathological pattern of human evil. Does true forgiveness actively *deny* the existence of evil, as Bartlett contends, and thereby itself constitute a form of pathology? Let us consider further the personal ego's defensive structure and its relation to evil and forgiveness.

The Ego's Relation to Forgiveness

The ego has as its primary aim its own survival.[66] Giegerich observes:

> I am ego as long as I am defined as an existing being and consequently have as my prime interest my self-preservation—not only literal physical self-preservation, not only emotional self-preservation, but also *logical* self-preservation, i.e., the preservation of the very definition of me as existing entity or being.[67]

From the ego's perspective, everything would be evaluated and utilized (or rejected) in the interest of self-preservation, including forgiveness. James Hillman observes the ego's predictable use of forgiveness for its own ends. He notes forgiveness's hidden, circular function of propping up the ego by blaming it—seen in our seemingly endless attempts to forgive and gain forgiveness. Such forgiveness Hillman characterizes "as [the] ego's cry for relief from carrying the whole world on its shoulders."[68] From this perspective, forgiveness is seen as a shutting down, a forgetting of the very symptoms, pathos, and complexes that connect us to soul. He says: "Forgiveness of the confusions in which I am submerged, the wounds that give me eyes to see with, the errant and renegade in my behavior, blots out the Gods' main route of access."[69]

From an archetypal perspective, appealing to the ego for forgiveness of the ego's own failings is an endless and fruitless cycle, for the ego devoid of soul is utterly incapable of meeting the archetypal demands of the soul and must always fail when it ignores the myths and denies the gods. "Of course we fail," Hillman says, "and since there is no power to call upon other than this ego, we beg forgiveness."[70]

Freud reminds us that punishment must be exacted.[71] Rarely is forgiveness viewed as an acceptable exception to the rule of justice; rather, forgiveness is often held hostage by the ego's seeming commitment to justice and revenge. Forgiveness may require giving up getting to be "right" about one's experience of another, threatening the ego's solidity, pride, and sense of personal dignity. Forgiving may seem to diminish the self, as if in giving something away one is left with less, for one is giving away the upper hand, the right to retribution, and the right to the pain caused by injustice. Indeed, "true" forgiveness is "aneconomic,"[72] delivering no "benefit" to the forgiver. Yet the ego has a difficult time "forgiving" without getting *something* in return—compensation, or an apology from the offender,[73] for example.

Ego defenses are important to consider in the study of forgiveness because of the manner in which forgiveness is actively withheld on their behalf.[74] Horwitz articulates the following set of secondary ego defense mechanisms that prevent the victim from giving up anger and desire for vengeance, making forgiveness virtually impossible:[75]

> *Fear of retraumatization.* People who have been traumatized and hurt have a fear of letting down the barriers of distrust lest they once again experience the same kind of psychic injury from others.
>
> *Wish for retaliation.* The person who has suffered at the hands of another wishes to even the score by making the offending party suffer in equal measure.
>
> *Sadistic pleasure.* By holding on to one's anger, one finds gratification not only in retaliating but in the exercise of power and control, a defense against hopelessness and feelings of deadness.[76]
>
> *Holding on to the relationship.* Ongoing hostility involves not letting go of a significant but ambivalent relationship. This is frequently based on a difficulty in mourning or unresolved dependency.[77]
>
> *Avoidance of shame.* When victims feel guilty or ashamed of their contribution to the narcissistic injury, they often externalize their shameful feelings by clinging to a blaming attitude.[78]
>
> *Superego pathology.* A harsh superego may lead to the repression of hostility lest one face the possibility of abandonment or other negative consequences. In addition, the expectation of perfection in oneself (an inability to forgive oneself) and in others may lead to an intolerance of any behavior by another that falls short of one's impossibly high expectations.[79]
>
> *Envy.* The destructive wish to deprive envied others of the abilities they possess is accompanied by the fantasy of attaining superiority over them.[80]
>
> *Overcoming powerlessness.* By adopting an unrelenting angry stance toward an individual who has treated one badly, one can, at least in fantasy, gain a sense of power to replace the sense of powerlessness created by the narcissistic injury.
>
> *Free will and personal agency.* Both forgiveness and self-forgiveness are mediated by the sense that the offending person had freedom of choice in a given behavior. The greater the choice, the more difficult it is to forgive or self-forgive.[81]

Despite the egoic objections to forgiving as noted above, we commonly see the active utilization of forgiveness by the ego for its own defense and protection. For example, Smith views forgiveness as a compromise formation, and as such, the attempt to forgive

> will always include a defensive effort to ward off the unbearable affect associated with intense aggressive and erotic wishes and the self-punishments that accompany them. . . . Frequently, what we call forgiveness is a form of denial or disavowal of a traumatic reality (internal or external), as if to say, "It never happened" or "It doesn't matter". . . .[82]

Smith argues against the explicit use or goal of forgiveness in psychoanalytic work; forgiveness is rather to be understood as "the complex result of the everyday work of analysis."[83] The resulting forgiveness is not seen as a defensive measure but as a psychological consequence of making conscious one's unconscious defenses. Likewise, Lansky presents a compelling psychoanalytic formulation in which forgiveness ultimately involves the resolution and "working through" of the primitive defense mechanism of splitting, where it first manifests as an unforgiving attitude, or "vehement retributive states of mind such as resentment, vengefulness, grudge, envy, bitterness, blame, and spite."[84]

In its apparent form, forgiveness is based upon an acknowledgment of wrongdoing, or attack, and thus can mask somewhat dubious intentions, as noted by Kenneth Wapnick:

> Psychologically speaking, we are not able to forgive while we believe something has been done to hurt us (or those loved ones with whom we identify). . . . Forgiveness that follows from a perception of attack cannot truly forgive, for it seeks to pardon where it has seen wrongdoing or sin. It itself, then, becomes a subtle form of attack in the guise of a "holier-than-thou" attitude, taking this form: "You are a terrible person because of what you have done to hurt me, an innocent victim of your unjustified attack. But, in the goodness of my heart, I will forgive you anyway, praying that God have mercy on your sinful soul." There is obviously no love in such a statement . . . This is one more example of the ego's deceptiveness, having us focus on the sins outside, so that we do not deal with the sins we believe are inside.[85]

In "offering" forgiveness in this way, the offender is doubly guilty; once for the initial sin against the forgiver and twice for the undeserved gift of the forgiver's beneficence. Such "forgiveness," as described by Aladjem, "forgets the sin, so to speak, on the condition that it *could* remember, so that the sinner will remember himself, and he and others will revere it in perpetual gratitude."[86] Such forgiveness would conceal the ego's covert wish to see the offender as sinful[87] and does not fulfill the condition of true forgiveness described by Derrida, which is "unconditional, gracious, infinite, aneconomic forgiveness granted to the *guilty as guilty*, without counterpart, even to those who do not repent or ask forgiveness."[88]

The question inevitably emerges regarding the compatibility of the ego and forgiveness. We have seen how forgiveness is either avoided altogether or actively utilized by the ego to satisfy its system of defenses. "Every instance of what we call forgiveness can be seen to serve a different defensive function," claims Smith.[89] Yet "true" forgiveness "is based on defenseless*ness*," observes Wapnick,[90] implicating true forgiveness as a non-ego or soul function. According to Giegerich, "It is the very job of the ego to be blind to the soul."[91] Because of such blindness, is true forgiveness, in the way Derrida describes, even possible for the ego to accomplish? Hillman (2005) poignantly offers an answer:

> We must be quite clear that forgiveness is no easy matter. If the ego has been wronged, the ego cannot forgive just because it "should," notwithstanding the wider context of love and destiny. The ego is kept vital by its *amour-propre*, its pride and honor. Even where one wants to forgive, one finds one simply can't, because forgiveness doesn't come from the ego.[92]

As noted above, the ego has as its primary goal its own survival, but this would seem to make it merely an unwitting accomplice to evil, rather than its source. Indeed, the question of evil also extends beyond the subjective shadow to what Hillman describes as the "psychological shadow" and what Giegerich terms the "sick soul," both referring to the aspect of objective consciousness that *insists upon its own untruth*. Recall Hillman's description of the psychological shadow as

> the never-ceasing darkening of the light in every search, a darkening of the light of certainty, the light's own sense that however an "I" searches for soul, that same "I" is inherently biased against the object of its searching . . . Shadow both keeps us searching and prevents us finding. It is the obstruction that does not want to find what it's looking for. Embedded in the very consciousness that is the instrument of our [search], shadow is the unconsciousness of consciousness itself.[93]

The unconsciousness of consciousness, the psychological shadow, and the sick soul—while all having the identical intent of relentlessly undermining and preventing the unfolding of truth—do not speak to the substantive existence of "evil."[94] Whereas Jung asserts a definite reality to evil and rails against the notion of evil as *privatio boni*, or the absence of Good, Giegerich asserts that evil as a *privatio boni*

> makes perfect sense within the logic of Love. For this logic, evil is not a substance, not for example, the body, particular desires, drives, or passions. It is not anything ontic, a natural "entity" like "the shadow." Nature is neither good nor evil. No, evil is something logical and, as such, negative (a *privatio*): namely one's NOT negating one's natural

> impulses and naturalistic imaginal perspectives, one's NOT placing oneself under supersensory ethical laws, one's NOT humbling oneself all the way and NOT (logically) bowing under the evil and evils in the world. It is the omission or rather refusal, to overcome, time and again, one's "original sin" by rising to the sphere of logos and the concept.[95]

Giegerich makes clear the ego's role in "evil" as its relentless "refusal" to submit to or place itself/bow under something other than itself (which would ironically result in its "rise" into the vast sphere of interiority and inner infinity, or the realm of soul). The ego's refusal to "give up" the primacy of substantiality, the semantic domain over which it presides, reflects the notion of "original sin" as that of the hubris-laden refusal to humble oneself to God. The ego has no access to true forgiveness because it has no access to the realm of soul, by its own refusal to enter. Thus if one identifies solely with the ego, the experience of true forgiveness is impossible.

Projection of the Shadow

Recall Jung's lament, "The evil that comes to light in man and that undoubtedly dwells within him is of gigantic proportions."[96] Humankind's most significant challenge, however, lies in its defiant unawareness of this inherent evil. Echoed by Bartlett's assertion that, "The only thing that must happen for evil to triumph is for human beings to be convinced they are good,"[97] Jung's frustration with humanity's seemingly obstinate ignorance is apparent:

> Since it is universally believed that man *is* merely what his consciousness knows of itself, he regards himself as harmless and so adds stupidity to iniquity. He does not deny that terrible things have happened and still go on happening, but it is always "the others" who do them. And when such deeds belong to the recent or remote past, they quickly and conveniently sink into the sea of forgetfulness, and that state of chronic woolly-mindedness returns which we describe as "normality." In shocking contrast to this is the fact that nothing has finally disappeared and nothing has been made good. The evil, the guilt, the profound unease of conscience, the obscure misgiving are there before our eyes, if only we would see.[98]

Humankind's unwillingness "to see" constellates the primary difficulty in dealing with evil, as we have no capacity to address that of which we are unaware. "In fact," Jung states

> this negligence is the best means of making [man] an instrument of evil. Harmlessness and naïveté are as little helpful as it would be for a cholera patient and those in his vicinity to remain unconscious of the contagiousness of the disease. On the contrary, they lead to projection of the unrecognized evil into the "other."[99]

Here Jung introduces a crucial outcome of the unawareness of evil: the psychological projection of the shadow.

Jung developed his theory of psychological evil in terms of a metaphor he described as the *shadow*, defined as "the 'negative' part of the personality, namely the sum of the hidden, disadvantageous qualities, inadequately developed functions, and contents of the personal unconscious."[100] The shadow's unwanted and intolerable nature leads to its near total suppression. Jung also proposed a *collective* shadow reflecting instincts and forms of perception that are inherited. The collective shadow comprises the "unrecognized, deficient, unattractive, and repellant side of a group, nation or race"[101] and is similarly denied or suppressed. In general, the personal and collective shadows tend to constellate that which is considered "evil" in a society.[102]

Giegerich rightly reminds us that the term *shadow* is merely a personified concept in Jungian psychology, an interpretation, not a name for an actual thing or fact.[103] When using the word "shadow" there is a tendency to reduce and compartmentalize unconscious aspects of the personality (e.g., the "bad" or "unwanted" parts), forgetting that Jung also referred to the shadow as an expression of the entirety of the unconscious, in the form of a presentation or appearance in which the soul presents itself (to itself) in a particular moment. Giegerich explains:

> The shadow is that guise or self-interpretation of the soul that the soul wants or needs to take when it happens to have defined itself as ego . . . and now wants to present itself to itself, i.e., to the ego-form of itself, as its own other. But because that on which it wants to impress itself as its own other is itself-*in-the-guise-of* "the ego," and because it is the very nature of "the ego" not to have any sense of soul, this other cannot really show itself as what it actually is (the soul's own other), but only as *the* Other, the wholly Other—absolutely incompatible and thus dark and threatening (namely to the ego-personality)[104]

Projection, the psychological defense that serves to rid the self of this "absolutely incompatible and thus dark and threatening" shadow, is essentially related to the fundamental denial of one's inner psychic reality,[105] wherein the intolerable and threatening parts of the personality are denied/rejected. The defense of projection then makes the ingenious added move of attributing the unwanted/incompatible parts to the Other (or others), in the hopes of destroying the evidence, so to speak. Projection would thus modify and extend Bartlett's assertion in the following way: "The only thing that must happen for evil to triumph is for human beings to be convinced they are good *and others are bad*."

It was Freud who first introduced the term *projection* to describe a somewhat covert psychological strategy that assigns any unpleasant or intolerable emotions to another person.[106] Freud originally imagined projection to be a response to the profound human longing for an original state of undifferentiated union as experienced in the mother-infant dyad.[107] To the extent that a person's ego boundaries are underdeveloped and simulate the original state of unity, internal psychic events and experiences are mistakenly attributed to objects outside the self to others and the world. Freud eventually altered the definition of projection to refer more specifically to an emotional defense used to avoid the awareness of intolerable feelings in oneself. "In this second sense," he writes, "a projection results when one attributes to others one's own rejected propensities."[108]

In his analysis of evil and the Holocaust, Bartlett notes that prejudice and persecution are essentially projective. He writes:

> The negative feelings and images that people project into their conceptions of others are frequently not based in reality, but are expressions of bigotry. The persecution of others who are perceived in this way is built upon projection. This point of view has led to the observation: "It may very well be that unless and until we have tools for containing projection processes, most of the heroic efforts we make toward world justice and peace will be to little avail".[109]

And because projection is wholly *unconscious*—wherein lies its power as a defense mechanism—it cannot be readily recognized and addressed by the conscious mind. Bartlett observes this problem in groups: "[B]y definition, [projection is] relatively impervious to a group's self-awareness. Sources of projective hatred will always be located in the hated group, and not in the prejudiced and persecuting group."[110]

As a psychological defense mechanism, projection is doubly effective; it serves to block overt expression of unacceptable thoughts or feelings and at the same time gain relief by expressing in disguised form that which is unacceptable. When aggressive feelings are projected onto another person, for example, the one using the defense blocks ownership of those feelings but is still able to experience the aggression as coming from the other and covertly gratify aggressive wishes.[111] Here the ego is having its cake and eating it too, making projection a very (unconsciously) attractive means of relating with others.

The following paragraph is a helpful summation of Jung's perspective on projection as it affects human relations in general:

> Just as we tend to assume that the world is as we see it, we naively suppose that people are as we imagine them to be. In this latter case, unfortunately, there is no scientific test that would prove the discrepancy between perception and reality. Although the possibility for gross deception is infinitely greater here than in our perception of the physical world, we still go on naively projecting our own psychology into our fellow human beings. In this way everyone creates for himself a series of more or less imaginary relationships based essentially on projection. . . . A person whom I perceive

> mainly through my projections is an *imago* or, alternately, a carrier of *imagos* or symbols. All the contents of our unconscious are constantly being projected into our surroundings, and it is only by recognizing certain properties of the objects as projections or *imagos* that we are able to distinguish them from the real properties of the objects. But if we are not aware that a property of the object is a projection, we cannot do anything else but be naively convinced that it really does belong to the object. All human relationships swarm with these projections. . . . [W]e always see our own un-avowed mistakes in our opponent. Excellent examples of this are to be found in all personal quarrels. Unless we are possessed of an unusual degree of self-awareness we shall never see through our projections but must always succumb to them, because the mind in its natural state presupposes the existence of such projections. . . . Thus every normal person of our time, who is not reflective beyond the average, is bound to his environment by a whole system of projections.[112]

Projection, insofar as it serves to displace the shadow onto the other, plays a very important role in the phenomenon of forgiveness. If the source of malevolent intent is denied and relocated from the self to the other through projection, it becomes "the evil which one does not see in one's own bosom but always in somebody else's."[113] The *other* is now perceived as guilty and reviled, while we ourselves stand blameless:

> [With projection,] the mind's guilt has now been perceived outside in the world, leaving us with the self-concept of the *face of innocence*.[114] It is our suffering at the hands of another, in whatever form, that establishes our sinlessness for all to see. Following the ego's reigning dictum of hate—*one or the other, kill or be killed* [115]—another's guilt proves we are innocent of all sin, and this person deserves the punishment that we secretly [unconsciously] believe is our just desert.[116]

The more one "suffers" at the hands of another, the more "innocence" and relief from guilt is experienced by the projecting mind. Projection would condemn the other as evil and guilty, and only the condemned are in need of forgiveness. Yet evil, insofar as it exists as an (unconsciously projected) characteristic or behavior exhibited in the other, does not in actuality *warrant* forgiveness of the other. For what is to be forgiven—one's own projection? Forgiveness of the other in response to projected evil validates and cements both the primitive ego defenses of denial (i.e., "*I* am not bad") and projection ("*You* are bad"), with the added bonus of gratifying the ego with an explicit experience of innocence ("I am *good* because I am merciful/kind"). Forgiveness in response to unconscious projections thus functions as a powerful "triple-strength" ego defense. Bartlett's wholesale rejection of forgiveness as a "second-order pathology" contributing to the perpetuation of human evil is valid when evil is seen through the veil of denial and projection.

Personal vs. Archetypal Shadow

Both Jung and Hillman make distinctions between the personal and collective shadow. Theoretically, projections emanating from the personal unconscious, if identified as such, are able to be withdrawn and successfully integrated back into the personality, albeit with significant effort, for as Jacobi notes, "Nobody likes to admit his own darkness, for which reason most people put up—even in analytical work—the greatest resistance to the realization of their shadow."[117] For Jung, the suitable response to the problem of evil is the identification and withdrawal of projected shadow elements of the personality, a process foundational to analytical work. Jung writes,

> If you imagine someone who is brave enough to withdraw these projections, then you get an individual conscious of a pretty thick shadow. . . . Such a man knows that whatever is wrong with the world is in himself, and if he only learns to deal with his own shadow then he has done something real for the world.[118]

For both Jung and Bartlett, the crucial weapon in effectively dealing with the problem of evil must include the identification and withdrawal of projections. As noted earlier, forgiveness of the other's "sins" without examining the possibility those sins are projected reduces forgiving to a mere tool in the ego's arsenal to prop itself up as blameless and morally superior to the other. For as long as one is unaware of a projection, the projected characteristic really does belong to the other[119] and can therefore never truly be forgiven—only repeatedly denied, ignored, repressed, and resisted. And when another opportunity for projection presents itself, the sensation of offense and pain will reoccur and the work of "false" forgiveness would need to begin again. The psychological endeavor of withdrawing and subsequently integrating projections and its relation to forgiveness will be examined further in Chapter 5.

When collective shadow contents are projected—in the form of powerful nationalistic movements, societal racism/apartheid, or genocide, for example—individuals may find themselves in the grip of external "archetypal" forces not amenable to integration. For Hillman, archetypal evil is not a pathology lying dormant in the human personality, as Bartlett argues, treatable as any other biological disease might be. Rather, absolute evil is imagined as mythic, transcendent, and impersonal, becoming actualized when joined with the human ego to do its bidding. For Hillman,

> When evil takes on godly form (Loki, Lucifer, Hermes-Mercury, the Trickster), it has a double nature and, like the spirit, it can blow for ill or good. It reaches its enormity only when it is half-human. When it is joined with the human ego, the will and reason and desire with which a man can choose a course of action and pursue an end, then does the merely devilish become truly evil.[120]

Because of its transcendent archetypal nature, such evil is unstoppable and thereby inevitable in human experience. This is the reality of evil; it can "neither be cured nor integrated nor humanized. It can only be held at bay."[121] Hillman, then, approaches evil from the perspective of discernment—one is to distinguish or separate "the strands of the shadow which can be lived and integrated from those which irredeemably belong in Hell."[122]

Psychological Perspectives

Let us return to our story in *The Sunflower*. As noted earlier, many respondents claim Karl's request as invalid—it was *wrong* of him to ask Simon for forgiveness. But as Native American Jose Hobday notes, "That is beside the point, because he *does* ask."[123] If we are to look at the encounter from a psychological perspective, the focus is not on ethics, that is, whether his request is right or wrong, but rather on "the soul, the psychological situation, the soul level. What does the soul, the objective psyche, want? What is the soul content of this . . . phenomenon? What is the thought or feeling inherent in the phenomenon?"[124] The question of whether or not Karl should have asked for forgiveness or Simon should or should not have offered it is a secondary issue, psychologically speaking. Rather, the psychological perspective offers acceptance of the phenomenon *as it is given* and interacts with it as such, with a focus on the soul content. For example, when analyzing a dream, we do not typically "argue" with the dream in the sense of disagreeing with what happened. Rather, we accept the dream as a valid psychic artifact of consciousness.[125] What is the psyche 'saying' about itself via the dream?

Seen with a psychological eye, then, what elements emerge in the scene of the hospital room described by Wiesenthal? Here we might examine what the figures of Karl and Simon represent symbolically, and what occurs psychologically between them. What alchemical and archetypal dynamics are at play? What might we imagine is happening in that room from the perspective of the soul, and what might the soul, the objective psyche, "want" to happen?

Before these questions are considered, it is important to note that the situation between Karl and Simon contains a significant disparity that was observed by some of the respondents; Karl wishes forgiveness from a person he did not harm directly. As many mentioned, according to Judaic law, only the party who is directly wronged has the authority to forgive. Because Simon is not the literally offended party, in the exchange Simon becomes a *symbol*—he is "a Jew"—and hence represents a member of the harmed party. In this sense, Simon is a stand-in for "the Jewish people" at large, because the choice of Simon was arbitrary; all that mattered was that he was "a Jew" and anyone out of the entire Jewish population would have sufficed. Thus Simon symbolizes the Jewish people. This creates a problem because Karl, as an empirical person, is appealing to a *symbol* for forgiveness ("the Jewish People") rather than another empirical person. He is thus attempting to relate as a man to a (non-empirical) symbol as if both are realities on the same level. Giegerich alludes to a similar problem when the ego and the soul are presented as realities on the same level, which obscures their "fundamentally different dimensions."[126] To correct this problem, Giegerich assigns a different status to each: the quality of *horizontality* for the ego and *verticality* for the soul, such that "the sphere of soul is . . . at right angles to the world of the ego."[127] Giegerich describes the associated "impossibility of a connection"[128] between the two levels (while they do at times intersect and cause what Giegerich calls a "soul event" and Badiou a "truth event,"[129] their intersection forms a discontinuity or rupture, not a connection).

Seen in this manner, we could interpret Simon's silence as a failure on Karl's part to make a connection with him. Had Karl related to Simon as an empirical *actual person*, if he had relayed even the slightest care or concern for Simon as a human being, there may have been a more human and "felt" connection between them. But Karl was not speaking to "Simon," the man, but to "a Jew," the symbol. As such, Simon was not in "the position," so to speak, to help Karl. Their related psychological positions were mutually exclusive and hence unrelatable. Had Karl *expanded* his request for forgiveness not merely for himself but on behalf of "the Nazis" or "the German People," thereby logically elevating his status also to a symbol, would Simon have been in a better position to offer an answer? Yes—because the request would have gained a logical coherence and seen for the impossible request that it was—but his answer would have obviously been "No!" Even had Karl asked for some measure of forgiveness on behalf of the Nazis, for example, his personal repentance and purification process could not conceivably metabolize and "negate" the sins of such magnitude and number, much less the sins of an entire people! But as it happened, we are left with an untenable situation in which Karl's appeal for forgiveness is psychologically incoherent, thus preventing a response from Simon and making the connection he so longed for impossible.

Conversely, we must also consider the possibility that it was Simon who was unable to make the connection with Karl, which surprisingly may make sense if Karl does in fact accomplish *teshuvah*. Remember, in the Talmud we read: "In a place where people who have done *teshuvah* stand, the purest *zadik* (righteous person) cannot stand." To his friends afterward, Simon has difficulty communicating the depth of his feeling from the encounter, its numinosity and power. Given Karl's near-death condition, his poverty of spirit, his brokenhearted defenselessness, desperation, and humility, dare we consider the possibility that Karl was psychologically "nearer to God" in the moment of their meeting? While it would appear not, as *teshuvah* is "characterized by joy," notes Rabbi Schneerson, in truth, we do not know and are left with the question. Let us attempt to gain insight into Karl's process of atonement from an alchemical perspective.

Alchemical Perspectives on Confession and Repentance

Jung observed in the medieval art of alchemy profound psychological relevance; the various stages of alchemy bore a remarkable similarity to the stages of development of human consciousness, concretized via alchemical imagery and the alchemist's attempt to realize, from the mere ordinary matter of the *prima materia*, the purest gold, the elixir of eternal life, or the fabled Philosopher's Stone.[130] The major alchemical stages of progression in achieving the *opus* include the *nigredo* (the blackening of matter), *albedo* (the whitening), and *rubedo* (the reddening). Within these three major stages, alchemists identified numerous associated processes; the *nigredo* stage has associated with it the processes of *mortificatio* (dying) and *putrefactio* (rotting), for example, and *albedo* is accomplished through processes of "burning" to white ash (*calcinatio*) or "cleansing" (washing or *solutio*, distillation or *separatio*, or purification or *mundificatio*). All of these alchemical processes Jung correlates to psychological processes occurring in individuation, or the full maturation of consciousness.

Jung provides an overview of the alchemical journey or *mystical peregrination* in the following passage:

> Right at the beginning you meet the "dragon," the chthonic spirit, the "devil" or, as the alchemists called it, the "blackness," the *nigredo*, and this encounter produces suffering. . . . In the language of the alchemists, matter suffers until the *nigredo* disappears, when the "dawn" (*aurora*) will be announced by the "peacock's tail" (*cauda pavonis*) and a new day will break.[131]

Such a complete transformation of matter for the alchemist, the achievement of which symbolized nothing less than redemption of humankind and the universe itself, [132] was astonishingly difficult and rife with suffering. "The writings of the alchemists recorded the descent to Hell and the rebirth that can result from the ordeal."[133] So too does the path of human psychological maturation and personal "redemption," in having to traverse the various stages, including "meeting the dragon" and facing the "devil" in oneself, result in profound personal anguish. As Edinger notes, "this fact helps to account for the reluctance sensitive people have to committing themselves to the individuation process. They sense in advance the suffering they are letting themselves in for."[134]

Rosarium Philosophorum

In "The Psychology of the Transference," Jung provides an account of the transference phenomena based on illustrations to the "*Rosarium Philosophorum*,"[135] a series of alchemical woodcuts representing the various stages leading to the achievement of the philosopher's stone or *lapis*. Of the imagery depicted in this series of woodcuts, Jung exclaims, "Everything that the doctor discovers and experiences when analyzing the unconscious of his patient coincides in the most remarkable way with the content of these pictures."[136] Seen as raw expressions of projected unconscious material, the pictures correspond to the psychological stages crucial to achieving the *psychological* opus, individuation, or the realization of the Self (the soul or objective psyche). What follows is a brief examination of five images examined by Jung and their correspondence to Karl's psychological process as reported by Wiesenthal in *The Sunflower*.

The series as presented by Jung contains the following ten images, each representing an alchemical moment contributing to the realization of the alchemical gold.

1. The Mercurial Fountain
2. King and Queen
3. The Naked Truth
4. Immersion in the Bath (*Sublimatio*)
5. The Conjunction (*Coniunctio*)
6. Death (*Putrefactio*)
7. The Ascent of the Soul

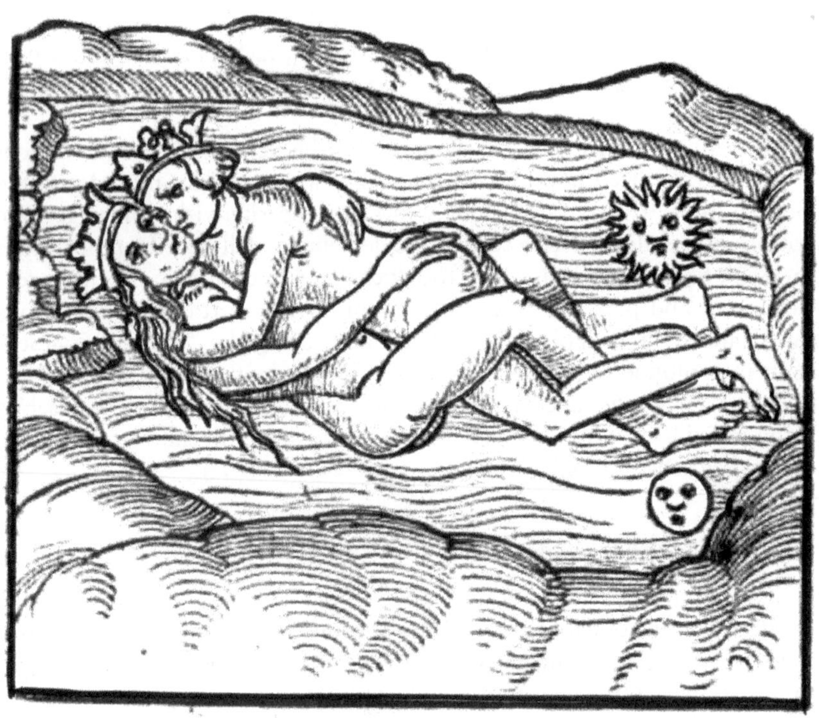

Figure 4.1 "The sea has closed over the king and queen, and they have gone back to the chaotic beginnings, the *massa confusa*."[137]

8. Falling Dew (*Mundificatio*)
9. The Return of the Soul
10. The New Birth

Images five through nine in the *Rosarium Philosophorum* find important parallels to elements in the story of *The Sunflower*. In particular, Jung directly relates the act of confession to Stage 8, "Falling Dew," purification or *mundificatio*. While the assumption that consciousness follows a linear or temporal order of stages, or even progresses toward a goal, is a valid question, the stages immediately preceding Stage 8—*Coniunctio* (5), *Putrefactio* or "Death" (6), and "The Ascent of the Soul" (7), as well as the following stage, "The Return of the Soul" (9)—have remarkable temporal parallels to our story as well and warrant exploration.

Stage 5: Conjunction (Coniunctio) and Identification with the Archetype

The *coniunctio*, as depicted in the *Rosarium* by the sexual coupling of the King and Queen in a bath of water, represents the "union of the opposites"—or psychologically speaking, the meeting of the conscious and unconscious psyche—and is the foundational element of alchemical psychology. To the extent that the *coniunctio* signifies the entirety of consciousness, it is the culmination of the *opus*[138] and symbolizes the Self as "the unity of the unity and the opposition of the opposites."[139]

> [The *Coniunctio*] is produced by a final union of the purified opposites, and because it combines the opposites, it mitigates and rectifies all one-sidedness. Thus the Philosophers' Stone is described as "a stone having power to give life to all mortal, to purify all corrupt. . . ." Again, the Stone (personified as the *Sapientia Dei*) says of itself, "I am the mediatrix of the elements, making one to agree with another; . . . I am the end and my beloved is the beginning."[140]

The *coniunctio* can result in complete psychological transformation, resulting in the emergence of a reconciling symbol, as Jung claims of the *transcendent function*, which occurs when one fully endures the tension of opposites within. Invocation of the transcendent function compels one into a completely transformed state of awareness in which the Self is experienced.

This particular image in the *Rosarium*, however, is *not* the ultimate alchemical stage or "final union of the purified opposites" but rather represents what is referred to as the much more common "lesser *coniunctio*." As such, this image symbolizes instead

> a union in unconscious identity, which could be compared with the primitive, initial state of chaos, the *massa confusa*, or rather with the

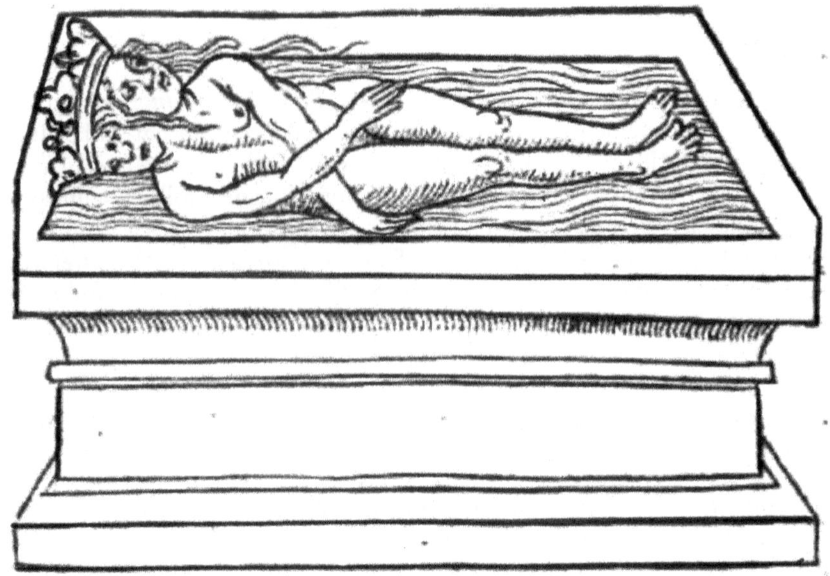

Figure 4.2 "Here King and Queen are lying dead/ In great distress the soul is sped."[141]

> state of *participation mystique* where heterogeneous factors merge in an unconscious relationship.[142]

This lesser *coniunctio* occurs when the ego identifies with the contents emerging from the unconscious, such as the shadow, the *anima* or *animus*, or the Self (the objective psyche).[143] Speaking to its aberrant nature, Jung writes, "The *coniunctio* was incestuous and therefore sinful, leaving pollution behind it."[144]

Such an unholy *coniunctio* is symbolized in *The Sunflower* by Karl's complete identification with his role as an SS soldier, in which the Führer had taken God's place.[145] The *coniunctio* marks Karl's entering into full union with unconscious archetypal evil. In this unholy psychic union, Karl perpetrates unspeakable acts of violence, torture and murder.

Stage 6: Death (Putrefactio)

The alchemical stage of *putrefactio* is marked by "death, darkness, and sin"[146] as the soul parts from the body "in great distress," resulting in a blackened and soulless state. Jung describes the soul's distress as a consequence of punishment for the previous alchemical stage of *coniunctio*. *Putrefactio* is marked by blackness, "the *immunditia* (uncleanliness), as is proved by the *ablutio* that subsequently becomes necessary"[147] in the later alchemical stage of purification. Still reeling from "so catastrophic a consummation"[148] with archetypal darkness, Karl appears to wander in the soulless "Death" stage for some time, up to the point where he is confronted with orders to kill again, which he this time refuses. When the order came to attack, describes Karl,

> we climbed out of the trenches and charged, but suddenly I stopped as though rooted to the ground. Something seized me. My hands, which held my rifle with fixed bayonet, began to tremble.
>
> In that moment I saw the burning family, the father with the child and behind them the mother—and they came to meet me. "No, I cannot shoot at them a second time."[149]

Figure 4.3 Here is the division of the four elements/As from the lifeless corpse the soul ascends.[150]

The enormous psychological shift in Karl is apparent in the moment he confronts again in his mind the death of the family. Advancement toward and into darkness, something that is often vigorously avoided by the conscious ego, is required for psychological transformation. Hillman considers "all movement towards this realm of death, whether they be fantasies of decay, images of sickness . . . repetitive compulsions, or suicidal impulses, as movements towards a more psychological perspective."[151] Ultimately, according to Hillman, "'death' is the most radical way of expressing a shift in consciousness,"[152] as reflected in this alchemical stage.

Stage 7: "The Ascent of the Soul" and Repentance

This alchemical stage depicts a corpse in a coffin, the merged hermaphroditic body of the King and Queen, and is a stage of "deadly darkness" and continued soullessness.[153] In our story, Karl lies broken and bandaged, his body dying and in decay on his "deathbed" in a "death chamber."[154]

An important feature of this stage closely mirroring that of repentance is the experience of the "dark night of the soul." Wiesenthal conveys Karl's inner torment by sharing his words:

> All the time I have been lying here I have never stopped thinking of the horrible deed at Dnepropetrovsk. If only I had not survived that shell-but I can't die yet, although I have often longed to die. . . . The pains in my body are terrible, but worse still is my conscience. It never ceases to remind me of the burning house and the family that jumped from the window.[155]

Jung refers to the writing of St. John of the Cross, who conceived of the "dark night" as supremely valuable, calling it instead the "spiritual night of the soul," in which "the invisible—and therefore dark—radiance of God comes to pierce and purify the soul."[156]

This stage "carries the *putrefactio* a stage further. Out of the decay the soul mounts up to heaven."[157] The flight or "return" of the soul to heaven has parallels with the origin of the term *repentance*, as described in Judaic literature.[158] The "division of the four elements" in this stage refers to the experience of dismemberment, a theme also present in true repentance, from which occurs a "radical separation from sinfulness itself."[159] This alchemical stage, notes Jung,

> corresponds psychologically to a dark state of disorientation. The decomposition of the elements indicates dissociation and the collapse of the existing ego-consciousness. . . . [T]his is the moment when . . . [one] becomes aware of the collective unconscious and the psychic non-ego.[160]

Karl's emotional collapse of ego-consciousness manifests initially as his unwillingness to murder the family a second time. He is no longer the man he knows himself to be, and accordingly "represents the man who is no more, who is destined to decay."[161] Yet this decay and rot makes possible the birth of new life, "the archetype which is inwardly experienced at this stage, namely the birth of the 'divine child' or—in the language of the mystics—the inner man."[162] The spiritual evolution and transformation resulting from *teshuvah* is remarkably similar to this psychological change Jung describes. The repentant sinner is no longer the same person; "the penitent has left behind one self, the sinful self, and engaged in an act of self-creation in which he has become a new person."[163]

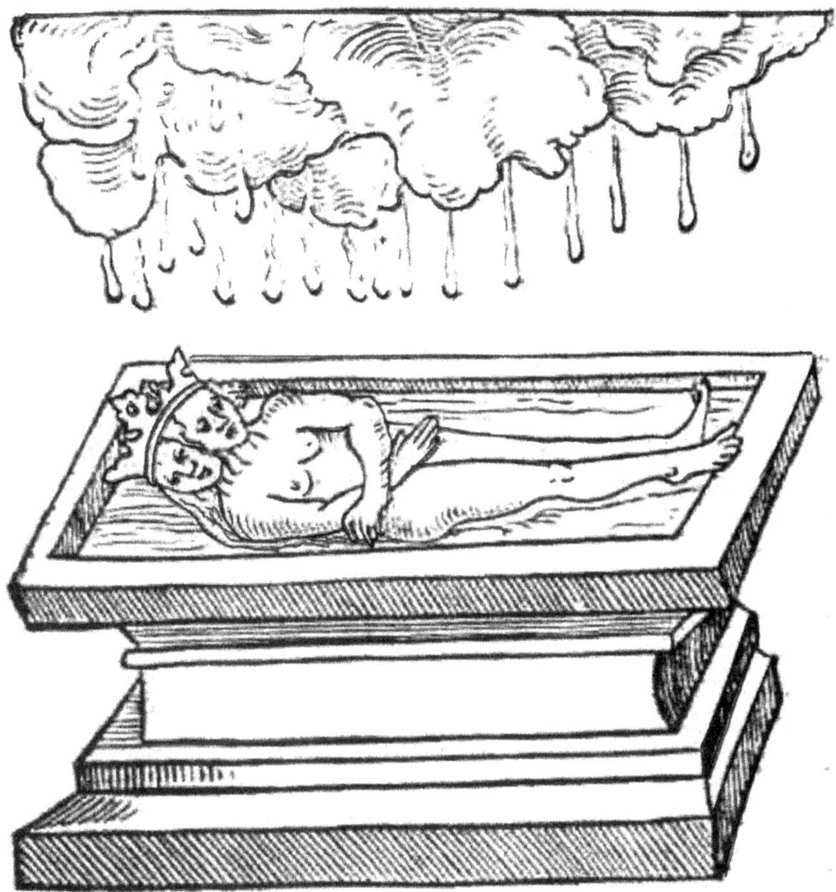

Figure 4.4 Here falls the heavenly dew, to lave/ The soiled black body in the grave.[164]

Stage 8: "Purification" (Mundificatio) and Confession

Karl says to Simon, "I cannot die . . . without coming clean."[165] The notion of having to "come clean" before dying implies that what is intolerable to Karl is not only moral isolation,[166] but his current experience of being "unclean"—a state he must remedy through the act of confession.

In addition to serving as a unifying and integrative act, Jung describes confession as a psychologically *purifying* act, aligning it with the alchemical process of *mundificatio* (purification of the body). *Mundificatio* is depicted in the eighth woodcut of the *Rosarium Philosophorum* series in which heavenly droplets of water rain upon the corpse of the hermaphroditic conjoined couple of the King and Queen lying in a coffin: "Here falls the heavenly dew, to lave/ The soiled black body in the grave."[167]

Psychologically speaking, confession is the process of differentiating the ego-personality from the unconscious; we "confess" that which we have determined does not belong to the self. Jung explains:

> In alchemy the purification is the result of numerous distillations; in psychology too it comes from an equally thorough separation of the ordinary ego-personality from all inflationary admixtures. This task entails the most painstaking self-examination. . . . The process of psychological differentiation is no light work.[168]

Indeed, the ego can be "completely fascinated and overpowered"[169] by projected archetypal elements from the unconscious. Such factors "draw us in like a magnet and at the same time frighten us. . . . The absorptive power of the archetype explains . . . the passionate intensity with which it seizes upon the individual."[170] Jung describes as "contaminated" the psychological state resulting from "the more or less complete identification of the ego with unconscious factors."[171] The confession is an attempt to sort out the unconscious factors in which the person has been caught:

> The rational man, in order to live in this world, has to make a distinction between "himself" and . . . "eternal" truths [that] become dangerously disturbing factors when they suppress the unique ego of the individual and live at his expense.[172]

From this perspective, that which is being "given up" through confession is both "the sin of the unconscious"[173] and the acknowledgment of having surrendered to those dangerously disturbing factors, granting them life at one's own expense.

In Karl's case, his participation as an SS soldier performing unspeakable acts of violence resulted from his ego's identicalness with unconscious archetypal forces, resulting psychologically in "a state resembling death,"[174] as we saw in stages 6 and 7. Confession here becomes the purifying process *differentiating the individual from the unconscious*; of saying, "I am NOT that [archetypal evil] any longer," and to separate "the strands of the shadow which can be lived and integrated from those which irredeemably belong in Hell."[175] Karl in effect says as much in uttering: "No, I cannot shoot at them a second time,"[176] and "I would be ready to suffer worse and longer pains if by that means I could bring back the dead."[177] This process is also reflected in the process of individuation, in which the empirical person undergoes his *de-identification* or distinction from the archetype or unconscious archetypal roles. In this way, "All the mythical garments in which man had hitherto been cloaked can ultimately be taken off. This is what individuation means *practically*; I am just myself, the empirical person that I am, no more, no less, no better, no worse."[178]

Mundificatio is also associated with the cleansing alchemical process of *separatio*[179] in which subject and object are separated and the opposites are brought into awareness—a fundamental feature of emerging consciousness. For, to the extent that the opposites remain unconscious and unseparated,

> one lives in a state of *participation mystique*, which means that one identifies with one side of a pair of opposites and projects its contrary as an enemy. Space for consciousness to exist appears between the opposites, which means that one becomes conscious as one is able to contain and endure the opposites within.[180]

Karl's complete identification with the SS easily allowed him to "live in a state of *participation mystique*," in which he blindly projected his "inner contrary" onto innocent fellow human beings, thereby making them "enemy." The disintegrating effects brought on by an extended *putrefactio* (stages 6 and 7 in the Rosarium) broke down Karl's unconscious identification with the SS, resulting in a collapse of ego-consciousness altogether. Awareness of the "other," or that which he is *not*, arose in Karl's mind as an awareness of the opposites, allowing for psychological awareness to dawn on Karl in the form of repentance. Karl's subsequent confession to Simon enacts the stage of purification, or explicit discernment between the conscious and the unconscious.

Such a "purification" of the psyche involving confessional catharsis requires what Jung describes as a "radical understanding" of the kind which is "impossible without a human partner."[181] For this reason, Jung says, "confessions made to one's secret self generally have little or no effect, whereas confessions made to another are much more promising"[182]—another psychological reason behind Karl's desperate pleading for Simon's presence.

Mundificatio denotes an explicit stage of purification, a final whitening process, or one that results in a stage of "silvering" or *albedo*—the state of purification between the tribulation of the *nigredo* and the final reddening, the achievement of the opus. The "white" thus achieved is distinct from an original, "innocent" white. The alchemical work, as Hillman observes,

> begins on the original white conditions, blackening them by scorching, hurting, cursing, rotting the innocence of soul and corrupting and depressing it into the *nigredo*, which we recognize by its stench, its blind

> impulse and the despair of a mind thrashing about in matter. . . . *Our* white, the second white or *albedo*, emerges from that black, a white earth from scorched earth as the silver from a forest fire. There is a recovery of innocence, though not in its pristine form. . . . [183]

The possibility of a "recovered innocence" emerging through the ordeal of the *nigredo* may help us understand forgiveness as an appropriate response to repentance and confession. According to Jung, "The phase called whitening in alchemy refers to the emergence of psychological consciousness, the ability to hear psychologically, and to perceive *fantasy* creating reality."[184]

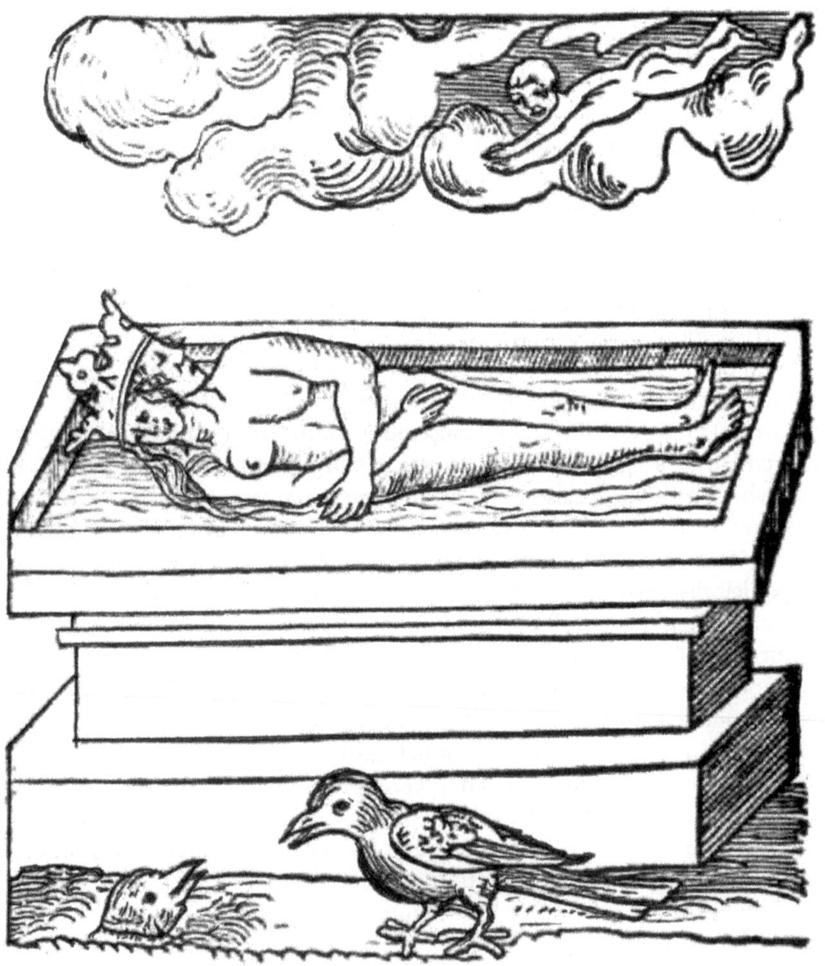

Figure 4.5 Here is the soul descending from on high/To quick the corpse we strove to purify.[185]

Here forgiveness would indeed serve to create and bear witness to a new reality, one devoid of sin.

Stage 9: "The Return of the Soul" and Reconciliation

With repentance and confession we find similar themes to those emerging from earlier sacrificial rituals, namely remaking the past, self-creation or rebirth, and restoration of divine relations (in that true repentance "elicits God's forgiveness"). Indeed, the Rosarium Philosophorum depicts "Purification" as the necessary alchemical stage in preparation for the penultimate stage, Stage 9: "The Return of the Soul." Of this stage, Jung writes: "Here the reconciler, the soul, dives down from heaven to breathe life into the dead body."[186] His description of the soul as "reconciler" suggests that the purifying act of confession makes way for reconciliation, the ultimate outcome of forgiveness. Jung states that here, "the 'soul' which is reunited with the body is the One born of the two, the vinculum common to both. It is therefore the very essence of relationship."[187]

Morgan extends the Judaic concept of "repentance from love" and its ability to elicit God's forgiveness to forgiveness between people by suggesting that interpersonal forgiveness is "both a response to [the sinner's] commitment to being a new person and itself an expression of giving up that hostility that ties the other person to the act that has harmed [one]."[188] Similar to Allais's notion of separating the offense from the offender, Morgan's forgiveness is also motivated as a human response to the offender's genuine wish to become "a new person." Forgiveness would thus seem to acknowledge the *accomplishment* of psychological conversion in another—the achievement of a new life, a new person, the realization of a completed stage (*mundificatio*), the readiness for the rebirth of the soul. Turning back to *The Sunflower*, it would seem as though Simon's withholding of forgiveness signals a refusal to honor Karl's "commitment" to being a new person, thereby "unconsciously acknowledg[ing] the indissoluble bond fusing the criminal to his crime."[189] Simon does, however, acknowledge Karl's sincere repentance. And while the process of purification (*mundificatio*) allows for the "return of the soul," the outcome is not guaranteed—clearly, mutual reconciliation did not occur directly between Simon and Karl. In a psychological sense, however, it does appear that Karl became a part of Simon and never left him.

The Transcendent Function

Within the mythic conflict of good pitted against evil depicted in *The Sunflower*, we see additional pairs of opposites at play. Karl and Simon are in the literal opposing roles of "perpetrator" and "victim." And within Karl's mind, the struggle of differentiation between himself as murdering "sinner" and his passionately declared penitent reformed self signifies another pair of opposites. Simon also displays an internal ambivalence; he stays and hears Karl's confession despite himself. His experience signals a struggle between opposing conscious and unconscious internal forces.

Where pairs of opposites are brought together and remain in tension, such as described here, a psychological phenomenon Jung describes as the *transcendent function* can arise. The transcendent function denotes the psychological process by which internal conflict between incongruent forces or opposing poles is resolved, resulting in a transformative shift in consciousness; "the essence of the transcendent function is to allow something new to emerge from things that are in seemingly irreconcilable conflict."[190] For Jung, the transcendent function "is called 'transcendent' because it makes the transition from one attitude to another organically possible."[191] He proposed the transcendent function to be a natural healing mechanism of the soul as it attempts to integrate disparate parts of itself.

The transcendent function plays a crucial role in "undoing" the ego defenses of projection and denial of the shadow.[192] Miller notes, "The transcendent function is the mechanism through which the shadow will be brought into conversation with the ego and the opposites in each brought together."[193] Hillman concurs that self-realization requires the "embracing of one's untransformed psychopathology," a beholding of the inhuman side of one's humanity. Such a lingering and candid gaze at the darkness within exposes it to the conscious ego, invoking the transcendent function.[194]

The idea of a transformational agent that is activated through the paradoxical coming together and toleration of opposites or disparate parts is similar to the concept of transitional phenomena that are so central to other theoretical perspectives. We find it in the me-yet-not-me paradox of Winnicott's transitional object, which is "to be accepted and tolerated and respected, and . . . not to be resolved."[195] The liminal space that Winnicott describes between reality and fantasy that inspires play, creativity, and individuation is akin to the third, mediatory and containing space of the transcendent function in which opposites are suspended or united through symbol and fantasy. The central developmental movement from Klein's *paranoid-schizoid position* to the *depressive position* shares the core integrative element of the transcendent function;[196] just as opposites are united by the transcendent function, the antitheses of 'good' and 'bad' in the paranoid-schizoid position are brought together in the depressive position. Such a transition involves a key psychological integration, and the depressive position mediates a fundamental either/or quandary, moving it to a space where both coexist.[197]

Other transitional phenomena can be seen in the self-object of self-psychology, which mediates ontological opposites of reality and illusion and inner and outer to allow a transition to a third thing, the newly gained part of the self structure.[198] Like the transcendent function, the self-object allows the paradox of a neither/nor solution to an either/or problem; it creates an intermediate experience where an exchange between "me" and "other" can take place with the result being a new thing, resulting in progress toward the developing self.[199] The self-object is a symbolic (Jungian), me-yet-not-me (Winnicottian) experience that brings fantasy and reality, inner and outer, together for the developing self.

While these examples share varying degrees of commonality with the transcendent function, the concurrent characteristics of teleology, numinosity, and ubiquitousness are unique to the transcendent function. For example, Winnicott's transitional phenomena are limited to certain pairs of opposites (inner/outer, reality/fantasy, and subject/object). The transitional and integrative component of the movement into the depressive position is limited mostly to developmental stages, and many of the transitional concepts are described in phenomenological terms. But as Jung states: "The transcendent function does not proceed without aim or purpose, but leads to the revelation of the essential man. . . . The meaning and purpose of the process is . . . the production and unfolding of the original potential wholeness."[200] Jung's idea of the transcendent function is a more expansive and comprehensive model of how psychological transformation occurs within the context of the evolution of consciousness.

Jung goes so far as to require the transcendent function for individuation of the personality, likening it to the alchemical process of forging the *opus*. He states,

> The secret of alchemy was in fact the transcendent function, the transformation of personality through the blending and fusion of the noble with the base components, of the differentiated with the inferior functions, of the conscious with the unconscious.[201]

The transcendent function describes both the process *by which* the alchemical action occurs and the containing field or vessel *in which* it occurs. The new third element that emerges is actually the "alchemical fourth"; the two opposing psychic states and the third mediating process or container yield the fourth element. This state is "the experience of the Third as it now links to a state of Oneness of existence."[202] When the alchemical fourth emerges, in the form of a reconciling symbol, the result is nothing short of a "totally new consciousness."[203]

While Karl's confession to Simon sets the scene for the transcendent function, it would appear as though a reconciling symbol fails to emerge; Simon leaves the room without a word. This "failure" to achieve the transcendent "alchemical fourth" may have contributed to Simon's deeply ambivalent feelings about his response to Karl; Simon may have felt the unease of guilt, for he "was able to do nothing" for Karl and failed to achieve something significant on a psychological level. Was the offered—and rejected—knapsack of belongings the attempted "reconciling symbol"? Simon's failure to respond could indicate the psychological need for continued tension; the conditions were not yet right; Karl had not yet achieved the depth of repentance or conversion required to truly oppose the "sin" and bring about the transcendent fourth state of reconciliation and oneness.

Yet while the sought-out integration (forgiveness) apparently fails to happen, is it possible that a transcendent state actually *does* occur? Derrida describes a "holy" space that emerges from the act of one truly bearing witness to another, in which a sacred oath to the other implicitly forms.

> There is no bearing witness without some involvement of an oath and without some sworn word. What distinguishes an act of bearing witness from the simple transmission of knowledge, from simple information, from the simple statement or mere demonstration of a proven theoretical truth, is that in it someone *engages* himself with regard to someone else, by an oath that is at least implicit. The witness *promises* to say or to manifest something to another, his addressee: a truth, a sense that was or is in some way present to him as a unique and irreplaceable witness. This irreplaceable singularity links the question of bearing witness to that of the secret but also, indissociably, to that of a death that no one can anticipate or see coming, neither give nor receive in the place of the other. With this attestation, there is no other choice but to *believe* it or *not believe* it. . . . The experience of bearing witness as such thus presupposes the oath. It takes place in the space of this *sacramentum*. . . . This oath is sacred: it marks acceptance of the sacred, acquiescence to entering into a holy or sacred space in the relationship to the other.[204]

In *The Sunflower*, Simon not only hears Karl's confession by staying present at his bedside, but he explicitly bears witness to Karl through painstakingly and publicly detailing his horrific admission, faithfully depicting not only the brutality of his sins but a moving scene of soulful repentance. In so doing, Simon fulfills his "sacred oath" to Karl and honors the *sacramentum* of his confession. The "reconciling symbol" in this case would not be forgiveness per se, but possibly the numinous emergence of that "sacred space in the relationship to the other," reflected in Karl's gift of belongings to Simon, Simon's visit to Karl's mother, and Simon's book *The Sunflower*; though Simon felt he was "able to do nothing" for Karl, in asking what the reader might do in his place, he keeps alive the psychological possibility that others *could* do something.

Archetypal Psychology and Forgiveness

In his groundbreaking concept of Archetypal Psychology, James Hillman proposes a decisive shift in emphasis. For Hillman, the primary metaphor of psychology must be soul, for psychology's job as "the study of soul" is to "provide soul with an adequate account of itself."[205] Hillman acknowledges the elusive nature of this accounting and the difficulty inherent in psychology's attempt to speak of "the soul" in metaphorical terms without substantiating it. Hillman writes, "The soul can be an object of study only when it is also recognized as the subject studying itself by means of the fictions and metaphors of objectivity."[206] Hillman states that to relate psychologically to the world, its literalisms and positivisms must be "seen through" or "psychologized" such that their underlying psychic expressions may appear through symbols. Hillman describes it thus:

> *Psychologizing goes on whenever reflection takes place in terms other than those presented.* It suspects an interior, not evident intention; it searches for . . . something more than meets the eye; or it sees with another eye. It goes on whenever we move to a deeper level.[207]

The reflective perspective—which *is* soul—"mediates events and makes difference between ourselves and everything that happens. Between us and events, between the doer and the deed, there is a reflective moment—and soul-making means differentiating this middle ground."[208] Miller explains, "Just as the transcendent function leads to a transformation of psychological state or attitude, soul leads to a transformation of experience from a physical one to a psychological one."[209] This shift in perspective from literal to metaphorical, from concrete to poetic, introduces a psychological fissure in the hard certainty of reality, opening up the miraculous possibility of *another way* of seeing. Psychologizing also applies to one's own person, causing a severe dislodging and shift of the ego's assumption of itself as cause to that of effect; the "I" who dreams and projects the world is de-literalized and becomes metaphor, a dream and projection of soul itself.

Archetypal psychology proposes a radically different—and challenging—perspective of human relations. An offensive act for which we quickly condemn another would be de-literalized and understood metaphorically, a mere part in a larger unfolding cosmic play; a malevolent crime committed is "seen through" and explored as a meaningful expression of the unconscious at large. According to Hillman, through such psychological reflection one may

> dissolve the literal belief in persons by re-personifying them into metaphors. Then personality may be imagined in a new way: that I am an impersonal person, a metaphor enacting multiple personifications, mimetic to images in the heart that are my fate, and that this soul which projects me has archetypal depths that are alien, inhuman, and impersonal. My so-called personality is a persona through which soul speaks. It is subject to depersonalization and is not mine, but depends altogether upon the gift of belief in myself, a faith given through anima in my worth as carrier of soul. Not I personify, but the anima personifies me, or soul-makes herself through me, giving my life her sense—her intense daydream is my "me-ness"; and "I," a psychic vessel whose existence is a psychic metaphor, an "as-if being," in which every single belief is a

> literalism except the belief of soul whose faith posits me and makes me possible as a personification of psyche.[210]

Where forgiveness is concerned, when the personality is de-personalized, who then is the "I" that has been offended? Or committed a sin? To "whom" is forgiveness offered? If "I" am no longer my own but rather a personification of psyche, then so too is the other a persona through which soul speaks. For Hillman, there but for the grace of the gods, go we—nay, *are* we—and any *personal* claim on justice loses coherence.

How might we consider the story of Karl and Simon from an archetypal perspective? We would take care to refrain from accepting the scene in the hospital room as a concrete reality—the encounter would not be reduced to two literal bodies, one having committed unforgivable crimes against actual persons, confessing and asking forgiveness, with the other hearing the confession and leaving the room. From an archetypal perspective, what might we see instead? What ancient myth might be newly unfolding? What might the soul be "saying" to itself through the actors in this scene? These questions are challenging because they dignify evil with the possibility of meaning. And as we have seen, the ego exhibits profound resistance to the fact of the presence of evil in the psyche; to acknowledge meaning or purpose in evil would be anathema, a threat to the value of meaning itself. Yet from an archetypal perspective, existence in psyche presupposes meaning in psyche.

> The assumption is always that *everything belongs somewhere*: all forms of psychopathology have their mythical substrate and belong or have their home in myths. Moreover, psychopathology is itself a means of reverting to a myth, a means of being affected by myth and entering into myth. Or, as Jung said: "The gods have become diseases" (Jung, 1957/1983, 37 [*CW* 13, para. 54]) so that today it is to our pathologies we must look for finding the Gods.[211]

Seeing metaphorically would allow for symbolic meaning in *all* aspects of human experience, including evil.

Equally challenging to the ego as allowing evil its place in psyche, however, is the idea of de-literalizing and personifying itself and its own perspective. This is because, as Hillman puts it, the "I" as an expression of the ego must take itself *literally*. In the mythical drama of psyche, the ego's necessary perspective is to take itself as literally real. "An ego's specific characteristic, and its specific function, is to represent the literal view: it takes itself and its view for real. Literalism is an ego viewpoint."[212] Insistence upon a metaphorical perspective fundamentally threatens the ego's concrete and literal perspective—that which it knows to be true and takes as real.

With regard to personal relations, the ego's tendency to literalize, in conjunction with its proneness to project, cause many difficulties that appear to lie with other people. Hillman writes: "The obsessive literalism of our belief in other people holds us tighter than any personified totem or fetish. How quick others are to become angels or demons, nymphs or heroes: how we expect—how they disappoint!"[213] In the context of archetypal psychology, "forgiveness" of the other who invariably must fail to embody the ego's literal projection of a divine figure is clearly misdirected.

Returning to the scene in *The Sunflower*, to de-literalize would threaten the ego's version of the truth, since reality from an ego perspective is the literal version—an actual Nazi soldier named Karl murdered innocent people. Yet as Hillman reminds us, *"Through psychologizing I change the idea of any literal action at all—political, scientific, personal—into a metaphorical enactment."*[214] This "metaphorical enactment" transforms our literal scene into one in which "Karl," "murder," and "innocent people" all become symbols representing expressions of psyche or soul. From an ego perspective, Karl committed unforgivable crimes. From the perspective of psyche, Karl's "unforgivable sin" depicts a part of soul destroying (or negating) another part of itself. Karl's "repentance" now becomes the soul's self-display of its *changing its mind* about *itself*. In Simon's willingness to hear Karl's "confession," the soul appears to be bearing witness to its own transformation. And Karl's "request for forgiveness" may symbolize an attempted *coniunctio* within the soul, following the cleansing alchemical stage of *mundificatio*, brought on by Karl's repentance. In the subsequent stage, the soul reenters the purified body. Simon's "withholding of forgiveness" could represent a lack of readiness to enter into this stage; the dismembering work of repentance and purification is not yet complete. Such imaginings are attempts are the "job of psychology" as Hillman says, "to provide soul with an adequate account of itself."

Of the Holocaust, Giegerich continues along this line of thought, suggesting what to the ego, as mentioned above, is unthinkable: the possibility of a psychological *telos* within archetypal evil. Giegerich grants significance to the Holocaust as a meaningful metaphorical enactment that depicts Western consciousness attempting to forever rid itself of its insistence upon the fatal illusion of its own innocence. He writes:

> What was it that the Western soul inflicted upon itself with this event [Auschwitz, the Holocaust]? It was the killing of the innocent belief in the moral Good and in the primary goodness of man. It was a demonstration of the impotence of conscience and morality. Since Plato, and later, with the Christianization of Europe, the idea of the Good—*to agathon, summum bonum*—has been what held the world together metaphysically and ensured the innocence of consciousness. In this century, however, it has been the factual labor of the soul to destroy ruthlessly its own belief in the Good as something sacred, so that the *very innocence* of consciousness, which it had *actually* already lost with the beginning of the Christian West, has now also obviously and undeniably been taken away from it.[215]

For Giegerich, the Holocaust could be seen as that event "in which the soul attacked and ruined for good its own innocent belief in 'the Good,'" for the purpose of "overcoming itself and achieving a higher logical status of itself."[216] The realization of the complete loss of innocence of consciousness represents the accomplished integration of the shadow.

In an interview conducted in 2010, Giegerich put forth a second, "complementary" idea in the form of a *koan*: "The Holocaust is the soul's initiation into Love."[217] When asked for elaboration on this idea, Giegerich declined, saying

> There are times and topics where the ego has to become silent. And whoever would like to understand what could possibly be meant by that dictum will never find out if he or she turns to others for an explanation, for example to me. No, for an understanding one has to turn to nothing else but the bewildering notion itself, here the notion of Love (with a capital L) in connection with the Holocaust, and turn to it in the quiet and loneliness of thought, the thought of the heart, with the patience of being able to wait.[218]

The psychological act of "turning toward *nothing else* but the notion itself" for understanding is quite different than the approach advocated in archetypal psychology, which would "see through" or reflect upon the phenomenon in metaphorical terms *other* than itself. Giegerich also intimates the necessity of a devotedly painstaking and thoughtful attitude to gain insight and enter fully and deeply into the subject matter at hand. Psychology here is defined as *the discipline of interiority* and entails a dialectical approach resulting in the *absolute-negative interiorization* of the subject matter—a process by which psychology pursues its own inner truth.

Psychology as the Discipline of Interiority

Psychology, at its heart, is concerned with interiority and truth. Psychology begins "where any phenomenon (whether physical or mental, 'real' or fantasy image) is absolute-negatively interiorized into itself and I find myself in its internal infinity," writes Giegerich. "This is what it takes, psychology cannot be had for less."[219]

The method of encountering the "internal infinity" of the soul requires a series of Hegelian "negations" of the external positivistic world:

> Transcendence, interiority, or "the soul" do not exist as a positive reality. They are not a special part or region of the empirical world. They come about only *through a logical act*, through the *negation* of externality, of space as such, which negation in turn is possible only through the negation or self-contradiction of a passionately attempted forward movement.[220]

Giegerich describes the negation of externality as a *logical* act. This is important because it introduces a crucial distinction between levels of reality and the differences in their corresponding logic, as can be found in the logical difference between *literal, positivistic* reality and *symbolic* meaning, for example (on a literal or semantic level, letters of the alphabet are memorized and learned, and on the level of symbol or syntax, words are formed and the "meanings" of each literal letter disappear or are sublated into the meaning of the formed word, which itself then "disappears" or is sublated into the meaning of the sentence of which it is a part, etc.). For Giegerich, the soul operates at the level of *absolute negativity* and has a mutually exclusive or orthogonal logic to the empirical world—though it is in and through the empirical world the soul "leaves its tracks," so to speak. A truly psychological perspective follows the soul's logic, attempting to comprehend it on its own terms and from within its own logic, as opposed to imposing on it the world's positivistic logic from the outside. Whereas archetypal psychology 'negates' the literal aspect of a phenomenon by seeing through to its metaphorical meaning, psychology as the discipline of interiority negates the literal aspect *absolutely* so as to reach beyond the symbol to that which the symbol signifies (i.e., to soul or consciousness itself).

With Giegerich's characterization of psychological evolution as dialectical in nature, we are presented with a different dynamic of the development of consciousness from Jung's transcendent function. Instead of a conflict of two fundamental opposites held in tension, we encounter a dynamic based upon commitment to a single initial idea or position. Giegerich writes:

> The dialectical process does not begin with Two, but with One, with a Position. There is, at first, no opposition to this position, no alternatives. . . . Rather, by committedly sticking to this one position that it holds, the mind discovers, or is forced to admit, that this position proves untenable. It does not hold up.

An example from our story might be Karl's initial commitment to the SS as his first position. There really is no alternative in play—that is, until he catches sight of the eyes of the innocent child. In this moment, Karl's "mind discovers, or is forced to admit, that his position has proven untenable. It does not hold up." When Karl is ordered to fire again on innocent people, he no longer can. Giegerich continues,

> This experience amounts to a *Negation* of the initial position. If before the position was A, the negation of the position results in non-A, a contradiction to the original position. The negation, if tested again, proves to be untenable and is accordingly negated.

Though Karl rejected his SS-belief system, resulting in the negation of his original position, this too proved untenable. A simple negation of himself as an SS soldier was not enough; he was unable to "die in peace" and needed to publicly repent and negate himself *absolutely*, including the underlying logic giving rise to his former identity as a Nazi soldier. In this case,

> we get the *Negation of the Negation* (not-[non-A]). But the negation of the negation as such is *Absolute Negation* and as such the reinstitution of the original *Position* (=A). However it is now the Position on a fundamentally new level, because it is no longer the "naïve" (immediate) position of the beginning, as a simple given, but mediated and tremendously enriched by the history of all the negations and as their net *result.* It has been greatly differentiated, is much more subtle, refined. Nothing has been lost or discarded through the negations. The superseded stages are all still there, however now only as sublated moments within the new Position. On this new level the dialectical process can then begin once more with the differentiated result as its starting point, i.e., as the new Position.[221]

In *The Sunflower*, the negation of the negation, or Absolute Negation, comes in the form of Karl's repentance and confession of his unspeakable crimes of murder against innocent Jewish families. With absolute negation we would expect transformation, a new identity. Did the syntax of Karl's consciousness transform, or was it merely semantic? As noted earlier, when a person repents truly, "he is no longer the same person. . . . [F]or the penitent has left behind one self, the sinful self, and engaged in an act of self-creation in which he has become a new person."[222] Did he truly achieve "absolute negation," a syntactic change in consciousness, or did his repentance merely signal a shift in behavior, at the semantic level, and fail to achieve "a logical transformation, a transformation in one's self-definition"?[223] Had Karl achieved the absolute negation of his identity as an SS soldier, he would have returned to himself, but "on a fundamentally new level"—mediated and forever changed by the reality of his crimes.

An important implication to emerge out of the dialectical process is the level of consciousness achieved in absolute negation, which rivals the psychological state accomplished with *teshuvah*, the alchemical state of *albedo*, and the union of opposites achieved by the transcendent function. In all of these conditions, change or advancement occurs at what Giegerich describes as the *syntactic* or structural level of consciousness. Mogenson explains further:

> In his writings, Giegerich frequently distinguishes between the "semantic" or content level of consciousness and the "syntactic" level of its overall structure or form. Change at the semantic level merely involves a shifting around of the contents of consciousness in the light of their having been contradicted in some way. This shifting around, however, as extensive as it may be in many cases, poses no challenge to the form

> of consciousness. None of its contents, that is to say, has yet become the straw that breaks the camel's back. In the negation of the negation, by contrast, the camel's back is broken, the structure of consciousness torn asunder.[224]

Referring back to our earlier discussion of repentance, when one repents out of fear, what changes is merely the *contents* of consciousness (what Giegerich refers to as the *semantic* level), whereas when one repents out of love, the actual *structure* or syntax of consciousness changes: one is no longer the same person.

Dialectics shares the deconstructive elements of alchemy in that it "is a work of 'decomposition,' 'fermenting corruption,' not of constructive synthesis; it is a process of stepping backwards and going under, rather than a utopian waiting for a resolution."[225] The quality of the resulting absolute negation as the reinstitution of the original position yet lacking its naïveté is strikingly similar to the alchemical "second white" achieved in the stage of *albedo*; both states reflect an original wholeness and purity yet are immeasurably enriched through the process of negation or *nigredo*.

Giegerich alerts us to the danger of imagining psychological transformation as occurring in the context of a clash of opposites; such a characterization lends itself to a positivistic and unpsychological perspective in which the opposites are seen as externalized concrete entities. He writes, "A thinking in terms of conflict positions itself in *external* reflection, in the position of an external observer. It does not look from within. A conflict implies the external collision, clash, of two opposite entities."[226] The dialectical process, as noted earlier, does not begin with opposites, nor does it

> *look for* a *creative* solution of . . . conflict. Rather, the process of deepening thought discovers and reveals that the opposites had been united all along in a common Ground. There is no need for a solution here, but rather the *insight* and *realization* that the experience of the opposites was due to a superficial and preliminary view. So the dialectical movement, instead of seeking a future solution, is a going under; it makes explicit the presuppositions that had unwittingly been behind and inherent in one's initial assumptions; it goes back and down to the deeper Ground that had been there all the time and had merely not been seen. As we might put it in psychology, consciousness had been too unconscious, superficial, too undifferentiated, too prejudiced. The *union* of opposites (or the resolution of the contradiction) is precisely the prior reality, and a *reality* from the outset, not something to be created. What has been there from the beginning is allowed to catch up with consciousness, to come home to consciousness.[227]

Karl's repentant confession acknowledges the poverty of consciousness of his former sinful self. Through the ever-deepening dialectical process of absolute negation, Karl gained an awareness that "the opposites had been united all along in a common Ground"—to the extent that he seemed to grieve for the families he killed as if they were his own family.

Where the transcendent function reveals the soul as mediating reflection "between ourselves and everything that happens" and "[b]etween us and events, between the doer and the deed,"[228] the dialectical process explicitly reveals soul as the process of reflection into *itself*, thus continually revealing itself as the infinite "bottomlessness of its own ever-negated base, absolute negativity, 'the soul'"[229] leading down to "the deeper Ground that had been there all the time and had merely not been seen." The dialectical process is thus not one of creation, but of the *self-revelation and self-recognition* of consciousness.

The dialectical process, through its repeated negating of positivity, in effect distills consciousness, absolving it from semantic contents, and exposing an underlying consciousness devoid of positivity, revealing "spirit" in its pure form. The significance of maintaining this division between logical domains shows itself as an ethical concern, for example, in the following statement by Kierkegaard:

> The truth in the Carpocratian view of attaining perfection through sin . . . has its truth in the moment of decision when the immediate spirit posits itself as spirit by spirit; contrariwise, it is blasphemy to hold that this view is to be realized in *concreto*.[230]

Similarly, the Gnostic *Gospel of Mary* characterizes the union of spirit and matter as "adulterous."[231] Consciousness as absolute negativity finds its truth in its ability and willingness to stay in relation to itself, *as* itself. The dialectical process, as a self-revealing and self-recognizing psychological movement, ultimately discloses a consciousness that has transcended the state in which it was gripped by the compulsion to "illicitly" conjoin spirit and matter by literalizing or acting out in *concreto*. Instead, the mind now has access to the "moment of decision" and is no longer compelled to blaspheme or "sin."

The dialectical process may be seen at work in Giegerich's depiction of the process of *symbolization*:

> The invisible soul or logic expresses itself first in symbolic garb, for example, in a sexual phenomenon. Secondly, the phenomenal aspect of the symbol negates itself as follows: "*I (the way I look)* am *not* what I am about—I am not really about sexuality at all". Thirdly, the phenomenal aspect of the symbol points to some other hidden invisible as to that which it is actually about. Fourthly, the symbol says: "But only through me (this my garb) can you get an access to this other". Fifthly, "Because my meaning is absolutely negative, I really mean *nothing*, but not nothing in the sense of total emptiness". The symbol is this internal

drama occurring simultaneously which is a logical drama, the logic of the symbol as a circular, uroboric logic.[232]

Turning back to *The Sunflower*, let us imagine this dialectical process at work by taking Simon's response of *silence* to Karl's confession as an arbitrary example, our *prima materia*. While we do not know the actual meaning behind Simon's silence, it has been suggested that the silence symbolizes rage or hatred, shock or ambivalence—in general, the blunt absence of forgiveness. However, if we follow the dialectical process of symbolization, we come up with a very different possibility. The dialectical process is the following:

(1) The invisible soul or logic expresses itself first in symbolic garb, for example, *Simon's silence* or *denial of forgiveness*.
(2) Secondly, the phenomenal aspect of the symbol negates itself as follows: "I [my silent response] am not what I am about—I am not really about [denying forgiveness]" at all.
(3) Thirdly, the phenomenal aspect of the symbol points to some *other* hidden invisible as to that which it is *actually* about [its negation, which is forgiveness].
(4) Fourthly, the symbol says: "But only through me (this my garb) [my silence] can you get an access to this other [forgiveness]."
(5) Fifthly, "Because my meaning is absolutely negative, I [my silence] really means *nothing* but not nothing in the sense of total emptiness."

When we consider this pivotal scene in the book, the explicit act of forgiveness is not present. Yet Karl leaves his belongings to Simon *as if* he had received forgiveness. Not only that, *he dies that night*, or we might say, he was finally *able* to die following his confession to Simon, implying that he indeed received what he needed from Simon. The proposition of true forgiveness then emerges in Simon's book as a serious question he poses to the reader, and again more explicitly in several of the responses encouraging forgiveness. The possibility of forgiveness, beginning first in Karl's mind, next surfacing in his confession to Simon, then carrying over into Simon's book as the question he poses to readers, can be imagined also as something Simon was unable to authentically or explicitly offer to Karl, yet which possibility he was unwilling or unable to snuff out completely. In this way, the idea of "forgiving the unforgivable" continued its propagation within psyche; maybe Karl would receive some measure of forgiveness, if not by Simon, by someone who read his story.

***

The underlying theme of *The Sunflower* is the endeavor of *psychological healing*. A man who had sacrificed his soul asks for help from another in the form of forgiveness. Yet the other, himself lost by his own admission, was "able to do nothing for him." Both men were suffering greatly and in need of help.

The notion of healing implies a wound or illness. From a psychological perspective, a wound or "psychic illness means that the soul's logical life has become stuck at some point, and healing . . . means nothing else but its becoming fluid again."[233] This "stuckness" can be readily seen in Karl's agony—he is even prevented from dying because of it. "I cannot die . . . without coming clean." We could also interpret Simon's fixation or preoccupation—even obsession—with the "haunting episode"[234] in the hospital room as a kind of psychic "stuckness." The traumatic encounter was *wounding* for Simon as well and left a part of him psychologically trapped in the experience. "Had I anything to reproach myself for?"[235] he continues to ask himself, many years later. His visit to Karl's mother—whose name and address he remarkably remembers years later from a momentary glance at the bundle of Karl's possessions—is inspired not from curiosity, but rather "a vague sense of duty . . . and perhaps the hope of exorcising forever one of the most unpleasant experiences of my life."[236] The sense of duty supports the role of Simon as bearing witness to Karl, as mentioned earlier. Yet the admission of their encounter as one of the most unpleasant experiences of Simon's life is almost shocking given years spent in concentration camps and the many unspeakable horrors he surely faced. The several hours spent with Karl left an indelible image and is evidence of a traumatic and unyielding psychic experience. After his visit with Karl's mother he writes, "the solution of my problem was not a single step nearer."[237] Simon too is in need of healing.

The connection of healing with the notion of the soul's logical life becoming "unstuck," released, or free to continue on its path is also associated with alchemical imagery depicting the emancipation of spirit from matter, or "the liberation of the spirit Mercurius from his imprisonment in the opaqueness of the matter."[238] Karl says, "I can't die yet, although I have often longed to die";[239] "I cannot die . . . without coming clean";[240] "I want to die in peace and so I need. . . . without your answer I cannot die in peace."[241] Here dying, as the literal departure of the soul from the body (death) and the symbolic liberation of the spirit Mercurius from his imprisonment in the opaqueness of the matter (healing), would appear to depend upon forgiveness. It is not difficult to imagine *The Sunflower* itself, following years of inward soul-searching, as a kind of personal confession and implicit prayer for forgiveness (asked in the form "Is what I did right or wrong?") on behalf of Simon's own healing. This may hint to us the soul's use of forgiveness as a kind of alchemical solvent emancipating the spirit and permitting once again the unhindered flow of the soul's logical life.

Conclusion

With the insight gained from our contemplation contained and guided by *The Sunflower*, an image of true forgiveness begins to emerge. From a psychological perspective, forgiveness appears related to that soul aspect that bears witness to a fundamental syntactical advance in its own consciousness via beholding and signaling the rebirth of the other. Such radical conversion attempts to arise in numerous ways as we have seen: true repentance and confession or *teshuvah*, suffering the *nigredo* given by the alchemical stages of *mortificatio* and *mundificatio*, the unification of the opposites via the transcendent function, *psychologizing* and seeing through, and absolute-negative interiorization—all of which result in the relativization of the ego and a profound expansion of context and awareness.

An important insight emerges with respect to the relation between forgiveness and the ego, in that the ego both employs and avoids the practice of forgiveness in the interest and defense of its self-preservation (both literally and psychologically), thus excluding the ego's access to true "undefended" forgiveness.

Bartlett and others claim that forgiveness is pathological in that it denies the reality of evil altogether. Indeed, the practice of "forgiving" projected evil reinforces the misplacement and denial of evil. Forgiveness of the other in response to projected evil assumes the reality of evil in the other, always in the bosom of "somebody else," confirming a psychic denial of reality. Forgiveness as a response to evil is an unpsychological response that validates the unconscious defense mechanism of projection. Jung identifies the psychological response to the problem of evil as the identification and withdrawal of unconsciously projected shadow elements of the personality. Thus a function of forgiveness as a response to evil involves the integration of the shadow.

In archetypal psychology, forgiveness comes into play as an accomplice to the soul-making act of psychologizing and seeing through. An offensive deed for which we quickly condemn another would be de-literalized and viewed metaphorically, a positivistic fact to be seen through and explored as a symbolic expression of the unconscious psyche. When the personality is de-personalized, the question of forgiveness confronts itself; no longer does one claim identicalness with the role of innocent victim or guilty sinner but instead recognizes the inexorable reality and necessity of both aspects in a larger unfolding cosmic play.

Finally, if, as Giegerich writes, "the process of deepening thought discovers and reveals that the opposites had been united all along in a common Ground" revealing "no need for a solution," then through the dialectical process we are also left with the realization that the initial "problem" to solve was merely a lack of "*insight* and *realization* that the experience of the opposites [the conflict] was due to a superficial and preliminary view."[242] In essence, the dialectical process reveals that in reality there was no "sin" to forgive in the ordinary sense in the first place. It is important to emphasize that "nothing to forgive" does not mean that "nothing happened." Rather, it means that "what happened" was merely a function of consciousness having been "too unconscious, superficial, too undifferentiated, too prejudiced" to recognize the "resolution of the contradiction" as "precisely the prior reality, and a *reality* from the outset, not something to be created. What has been there from the beginning is allowed to catch up with consciousness, to come home to consciousness."[243] "Sin" in this context *is a function of unconsciousness*. This idea is explored further in the following chapter, which will be guided by the image of Jesus on the cross crying out, "Father, forgive them, for they know not what they do." Here, *not knowing what one is doing*, as a form of unconsciousness, constitutes the sin warranting forgiveness.

The study of forgiveness in *The Sunflower* is a study of the failure to forgive. In the following chapter, our subject matter turns to the notion of forgiveness in its original and accomplished form.

Notes

1. Berthelot, *Alch. grecs, III, xlii, 1* as cited in C.G. Jung, *Mysterium Coniunctionis* in R.F.C. Hull (Trans.), *The Collected Works of C.G. Jung* (Vol. 14, 2nd ed.) (Princeton, NJ: Princeton University Press, 1970) (Original work published 1963), 262 [CW 14, para. 353]).
2. Simon Wiesenthal, *The Sunflower: On the Possibilities and Limits of Forgiveness* (New York: Schocken Books, Inc., 1969/1998), 14–15.
3. Wiesenthal, *The Sunflower*, 29.
4. Wiesenthal, *The Sunflower*, 30.
5. Wiesenthal, *The Sunflower*, 40–42.
6. Wiesenthal, *The Sunflower*, 51.
7. Wiesenthal, *The Sunflower*, 51–53.
8. Wiesenthal, *The Sunflower*, 54.
9. Wiesenthal, *The Sunflower*, 55.
10. Wiesenthal, *The Sunflower*, 97.
11. John C. Knapp, *Was Psyche Present at Auschwitz?: The Holocaust in Psychology* (Carpinteria, CA: Pacifica Graduate Institute, 2013), 146.
12. Knapp, *Was Psyche Present at Auschwitz?*, 147.
13. Wiesenthal, *The Sunflower*, 97–98.
14. See Fisher's response in Wiesenthal's, *The Sunflower*, 132.
15. See Fleischner's response in Wiesenthal's, *The Sunflower*, 143.
16. See Goldstein's response in Wiesenthal's, *The Sunflower*, 151–152.
17. Jacques Derrida, *On Cosmopolitanism and Forgiveness* (Oxford: Taylor & Francis, 2007).
18. See Fleischner's response in Wiesenthal's, *The Sunflower*, 139.
19. See Cardinal Koenig's response in Wiesenthal's, *The Sunflower*, 182.
20. See Ricard's response in Wiesenthal's, *The Sunflower*, 235.
21. See Loewy's response in Wiesenthal's, *The Sunflower*, 205.
22. See Lipstadt's response in Wiesenthal's, *The Sunflower*, 194–195.
23. Rabbi Aaron Lopiansky, "The Role of Confession in Atonement," in *A Yom Kippur Reader*, retrieved from http://www.yeshiva.edu.
24. Eliyahu Touger, "Keeping in Touch—Volume 1: The Ten Days of Teshuvah," retrieved on August 19, 2016 from http://www.sichos-in-english.org/books/keeping-in-touch-1/ten-days-of-teshuvah.htm.
25. Heinrich Walter, *Guggenheimer: The Jerusalem Talmud: Fourth Order: Neziqin. Tractates Sanhedrin, Makkot, and Horaiot* (Berlin: Walter De Gruyter, 2010).

26. Sanhedrin 28b.
27. Christopher Jones, "Loosing and Binding: The Liturgical Mediation of Forgiveness," in Alistair McFadyen & Sarot Marcel (Eds.), *Forgiveness and Truth* (Bloomsbury Publishing, 2002), 44.
28. Wiesenthal, *The Sunflower*, 53.
29. See Lipstadt's response in Wiesenthal's, *The Sunflower*, 193.
30. Michael Morgan, "Mercy, Repentance, and Forgiveness in Ancient Judaism," in Charles L. Griswold & David Konstan (Eds.), *Ancient Forgiveness: Classical, Judaic, and Christian* (Cambridge: Cambridge University Press, 2011), 137–159.
31. Morgan, "Mercy, Repentance, and Forgiveness in Ancient Judaism," 138.
32. Morgan, "Mercy, Repentance, and Forgiveness in Ancient Judaism," 148.
33. Wolfgang Giegerich, *Soul Violence (Collected English Papers, Vol. III)* (New Orleans, LA: Spring Journal, Inc., 2008).
34. Morgan, "Mercy, Repentance, and Forgiveness in Ancient Judaism," 149, emphasis added.
35. See Heschel's response in Wiesenthal's, *The Sunflower*, 170.
36. See the responses of Heschel, Prager, and Todorov in Wiesenthal's, *The Sunflower.*
37. See Heschel's response in Wiesenthal's, *The Sunflower*, 171.
38. Morgan, "Mercy, Repentance, and Forgiveness in Ancient Judaism," 155.
39. Morgan, "Mercy, Repentance, and Forgiveness in Ancient Judaism," 156.
40. Isadore Twersky, *Introduction to the Code of Maimonides: Mishneh Torah* (New Haven: Yale University Press, 1980).
41. Touger, "Keeping in Touch," para. 5.
42. Wiesenthal, *The Sunflower*, 53.
43. Emily Todd, "The Value and Confession and Forgiveness According to Jung," *Journal of Religion and Health*, 24, no. 1 (1985): 39–48.
44. Morgan, "Mercy, Repentance, and Forgiveness in Ancient Judaism".
45. C.G. Jung, "Problems of Modern Psychotherapy," in R.F.C. Hull (Trans.), *The Collected Works of C.G. Jung* (Vol. 16) (Princeton, NJ: Princeton University Press, 1982) (Original work published 1931), 59 [*CW* 16, para. 133].
46. Jung, "Problems of Modern Psychotherapy," 55 [*CW* 16, para. 123].
47. Jung, "Problems of Modern Psychotherapy," 59 [*CW* 16, para. 134].
48. Todd, "The Value and Confession," 41–42.
49. Rabbi Aaron Lopiansky, "The Role of Confession in Atonement."
50. C.G. Jung, "The Theory of Psychoanalysis," In R.F.C. Hull (Trans.), *The Collected Works of C.G. Jung* (Vol. 4) (Princeton, NJ: Princeton University Press, 1989) (Original work published 1955), 192 [*CW* 4, para. 432].
51. Wiesenthal, *The Sunflower*, 41.
52. Wiesenthal, *The Sunflower*, 42.
53. See Berger's response in Wiesenthal's, *The Sunflower*, 119.
54. See Heschel's response in Wiesenthal's, *The Sunflower*, 172.
55. Saul Friedlander, *Nazi Germany and the Jews: Volume 1: The Years of Persecution 1933–1939* (New York: Harper Perennial, 1998), 1.
56. Steven J. Bartlett, *The Pathology of Man: A Study of Human Evil* (1st ed.) (Springfield, IL: Charles C. Thomas Pub Ltd, 2005), 165.
57. C.G. Jung, "The Undiscovered Self," in R.F.C. Hull (Trans.), *The Collected Works of C.G. Jung* (Vol. 10) (Princeton, NJ: Princeton University Press, 1970) (Original work published 1957), 296 [*CW* 10, para. 571].
58. Jung, "The Undiscovered Self," 296 [*CW* 10, para. 571].
59. Jung, "The Undiscovered Self," 296 [*CW* 10, para. 572].
60. Bartlett, *The Pathology of Man*, 202–203.
61. Bartlett, *The Pathology of Man*, 203.
62. Bartlett, *The Pathology of Man*, 320.
63. Bartlett, *The Pathology of Man*, 320.

64. Bartlett, *The Pathology of Man*, 320.
65. Bartlett, *The Pathology of Man*, 319.
66. Sigmund Freud, "The Ego and the Id," in J. Strachey (Ed. and Trans.), *The Standard Edition of the Complete Psychological Works of Sigmund Freud* (Vol. 19, pp. 3–66) (London: Hogarth Press, 1961) (Original work published 1923).
67. Wolfgang Giegerich, "Jung's Thought of the Self in the Light of Its Underlying Experiences," in *The Neurosis of Psychology* (Vol. 1, pp. 184–185) (New Orleans, LA: Spring Journal Books, 2005) (Original work published 2001).
68. James Hillman, *Re-Visioning Psychology* (New York: Harper & Row, 1975), 186.
69. Hillman, *Re-Visioning Psychology*, 186.
70. Hillman, *Re-Visioning Psychology*, 187.
71. Sigmund Freud, *Civilization and Its Discontents*, trans. by J. Riviere (Mansfield Centre, CT: Martino Publishing, 2010) (Original work published 1930).
72. Derrida, *On Cosmopolitanism and Forgiveness*.
73. Ryan Fehr & Michele J. Gelfand, "When Apologies Work: How Matching Apology Components to Victims' Self-Construals Facilitates Forgiveness," *Organizational Behavior and Human Decision Processes*, 113, no. 1 (September 1, 2010): 37–50.
74. Bartlett, *The Pathology of Man*; Kenneth Wapnick, *Forgiveness and Jesus* (Roscoe, NY: Foundation for A Course In Miracles, 1998).
75. Leonard Horwitz, "The Capacity To Forgive: Intrapsychic and Developmental Perspectives." *Journal of the American Psychoanalytic Association* 53, no. 2 (June 1, 2005): 493–494. doi:10.1177/00030651050530021401.
76. H.F. Searles, "The Psychodynamics of Vengefulness. *Psychiatry* 19 (1956): 31–39.
77. G.O. Gabbard, "Hatred and its Rewards." *Psychoanalytic Inquiry* 20 (2000): 409–420.
78. Melvin R. Lansky, "The Impossibility of Forgiveness: Shame Fantasies as Instigators of Vengefulness in Euripides' *Medea*," *Journal of the American Psychoanalytic Association*, 53, no. 2 (June 1, 2005): 437–464. doi:10.1177/00030651050530021701.
79. Horwitz, "The Capacity to Forgive," 486–511; T.M. Grant, "Forgiveness in Psychoanalysis," (Unpublished paper, 1987).
80. E.B. Spillius, "Varieties of Envious Experiences." in R. Schafer (Ed.), *The Contemporary Kleinians of London* (Madison, CT: International Universities Press, 1997), 141–171.
81. M. Cavell, "Freedom and Forgiveness." *International Journal of Psychoanalysis* 35 (2003): 515–531.
82. Henry F. Smith, "Leaps of Faith: Is Forgiveness a Useful Concept?" *International Journal of Psychoanalysis*, 89, no. 5 (October 2008): 919–936.
83. Smith, "Leaps of Faith," 919.
84. Melvin Lansky, "Forgiveness as the Working Through of Splitting." *Psychoanalytic Inquiry* 29, no. 5 (2009): 374.
85. Wapnick, *Forgiveness and Jesus*, 65–65.
86. Terry K. Aladjem, *The Culture of Vengeance and the Fate of American Justice* (1st ed.) (Cambridge: Cambridge University Press, 2008), 171.
87. Wapnick, *Forgiveness and Jesus*.
88. Derrida, *On Cosmopolitanism and Forgiveness*, 34.
89. Smith, "Leaps of Faith," 919.
90. Wapnick, *Forgiveness and Jesus*, 64, emphasis added.
91. Wolfgang Giegerich, *What Is Soul?* (New Orleans, LA: Spring Journal, Inc., 2012), 130.

92. James Hillman, *Senex and Puer: Uniform Edition of the Writings of James Hillman* (Vol. 3, 1st ed.) (Putnam, CT: Spring Publications, 2005), 209.
93. James Hillman, *Insearch: Psychology and Religion* (2nd ed.) (Putnam, CT: Spring Publications, Inc., 1994) (Original work published 1967), 134.
94. Evil here exists not as substantive entity on the semantic level but as a logic on the level of syntax, the logic of the soul's refusing its own truth.
95. Wolfgang Giegerich, "God Must Not Die!," *Spring Journal*, 84 (2010), 66.
96. C.G. Jung, "The Undiscovered Self," in R.F.C. Hull (Trans.), *The Collected Works of C.G. Jung* (Vol. 8, 2nd ed., pp. 245–305) (Princeton, NJ: Princeton University Press, 1970) (Original work published 1957), 296 [*CW* 10, para. 571].
97. Bartlett, *The Pathology of Man*, 319.
98. Jung, "The Undiscovered Self," 296 [*CW* 10, para. 572].
99. Jung, "The Undiscovered Self," 297.
100. C.G. Jung, "Two Essays on Analytical Psychology," in R.F.C. Hull (Trans.), *The Collected Works of C.G. Jung* (Vol. 7, 2nd ed.) (Princeton, NJ: Princeton University Press, 1966) (Original work published 1917), 66 [*CW* 7, para. 103n].
101. Bartlett, *The Pathology of Man*, 94.
102. Liliane Frey-Rohn, "Evil From the Psychological Point of View," in The Curatorium of the C.G. Jung Institute (Ed.); Ralph Manheim and Hildegard Nagel (Trans.), *Evil: Essays by Carl Kerényi, Geo Widengren, Victor Maag, Marie-Louise von Franz, Martin Schlappner, Liliane Frey-Rohn, Karl Löwith, Karl Schmid* (Evanston, IL: Northwestern University Press, 1967), 170.
103. Giegerich, *What Is Soul?*
104. Wolfgang Giegerich, "Love the Questions Themselves," in R.W. Henderson & J. Henderson (Eds.), *Living with Jung: Interviews with Jungian Analysts* (Vol. 3, pp. 262–302) (Spring Journal, Inc., 2010), 273–274.
105. Rosenfeld, 1983.
106. Sigmund Freud, "The Neuro-Psychosis of Defense," in J. Strachey (Ed. and Trans.), *The Standard Edition of the Complete Psychological Works of Sigmund Freud* (Vol. 3, pp. 43–69) (London: Hogarth Press, 1953–74) (Original work published 1894); Sigmund Freud, "Further Remarks on the Neuro-Psychosis of Defense," in J. Strachey (Ed. and Trans.), *The Standard Edition of the Complete Psychological works of Sigmund Freud* (Vol. 3, pp. 159–188) (London: Hogarth Press, 1953–74) (Original work published 1896).
107. Freud, *Civilization and Its Discontents*, 786.
108. Bartlett, *The Pathology of Man*, 77.
109. Bartlett, *The Pathology of Man*, 168.
110. Bartlett, *The Pathology of Man*, 168.
111. J.H. Porcerelli and S. Hibbard, "Defense Mechanisms and Psychopathology" in S. Haynes, E. Helby, and M. Herson (Eds.), *Comprehensive handbook of psychological assessment* (Hoboken, NJ: Wiley Inc, 2004), 467.
112. C.G. Jung, "General Aspects of Dream Psychology," in R.F.C. Hull (Trans.), *The Collected Works of C.G. Jung* (Vol. 8, 2nd ed., pp. 237–280) (Princeton, NJ: Princeton University Press, 1981) (Original work published 1948), 264–265 [*CW* 8, para. 507].
113. C.G. Jung, "The Undiscovered Self," in R.F.C. Hull (Trans.), *The Collected Works of C.G. Jung* (Vol. 10, pp. 245–306) (Princeton, NJ: Princeton University Press, 1970) (Original work published 1957), 299 [*CW* 10, para. 575].
114. T-31.V.2:6.
115. M-17.7:11.
116. Kenneth Wapnick, "Amor Fati: The Birth of Gratitude," *The Lighthouse*, 23, no. 3 (2010): 2.

117. Jolande Jacobi, *The Way of Individuation* (New York: Harcourt, Brace & World, 1967), 39.
118. C.G. Jung, "Psychology and Religion," in R.F.C. Hull (Trans.), *The Collected Works of C.G. Jung* (Vol. 11, pp. 1–106) (Princeton, NJ: Princeton University Press, 1977) (Original work published 1938), 83 [CW 11, para. 140].
119. C.G. Jung, "On the Nature of the Psyche," in R.F.C. Hull (Trans.), *The Collected Works of C.G. Jung* (Vol. 8, 2nd ed., pp. 159–236) (Princeton, NJ: Princeton University Press, 1981).
120. Hillman, *Insearch*, 90.
121. Hillman, *Insearch*, 90.
122. Hillman, *Insearch*, 94.
123. See Hobday's response in Wiesenthal's, *The Sunflower*, 174.
124. Giegerich as cited by Ann Casement, "The interiorizing movement of logical life: reflections on Wolfgang Giegerich," *The Journal of Analytical Psychology*, 56 (2011): 532–549.
125. While the dream occurs in the unconscious mind, the awareness or memory of the dream is conscious.
126. Giegerich, *What Is Soul?*, 132.
127. Giegerich, *What Is Soul?*, 132.
128. Giegerich, *What Is Soul?*, 130.
129. http://www.lacan.com/zizek-badiou.htm.
130. "Jung's resurrection and psychological interpretation of alchemy is perhaps his central achievement" according to Cheetham. (See Tom Cheetham, *Green Man, Earth Angel: The Prophetic Tradition and the Battle for the Soul of the World* (Albany, NY: State University of New York Press, 2004), 34.
131. C.G. Jung, *Jung Speaking*, ed. by W. McGuire & R.F.C. Hull (Princeton, NJ: Princeton University Press, 1977), 228f.
132. Jung observes, "Alchemy represents the projection of a drama both cosmic and spiritual in laboratory terms. The *opus magnum* had two aims: the rescue of the human soul and the salvation of the cosmos." (Jung, 1977, 228).
133. Cheetham, *Green Man, Earth Angel*, 34.
134. Edward Edinger, *Anatomy of the Psyche* (Chicago: Open Court, 1985), 154.
135. The images displayed here are reproductions of the woodcuts from the Rosarium Philosophorum (Frankfurt, 1550) available in the public domain.
136. C.G. Jung, "The Psychology of the Transference," in R.F.C. Hull (Trans.), *The Collected Works of C.G. Jung* (Vol. 16, pp. 163–326) (Princeton, NJ: Princeton University Press, 1982) (Original work published 1946), 200 [CW 16, para. 410].
137. Caption: C.G. Jung, *The Practice of Psychotherapy (The Collected Works of C.G. Jung, Vol. 16)*, trans. by Gerhard Adler & R.F.C. Hull (2nd ed.) (Princeton, NJ: Princeton University Press, 1966), 247 [CW 16, para. 457]. Woodcut reproduced from *De Alchimia. Opuscula complura veterum philosophorum* (Frankfurt, 1550).
138. Edinger, *Anatomy of the Psyche*, 211.
139. Wolfgang Giegerich, "Jung's Thought of the Self in the Light of Its Underlying Experiences," in *The Neurosis of Psychology* (Vol. 1) (New Orleans, LA: Spring Journal Books, 2005) (Original work published 2001), 183.
140. Edinger, *Anatomy of the Psyche*, 215.
141. Woodcut and caption reproduced from the *Rosarium philosophorum, secunda pars alchimiae de lapide philosophico* (Frankfurt, 1550).
142. Jung, "The Psychology of the Transference," 252 [CW 16, para. 462].
143. Edinger, *Anatomy of the Psyche*, 215.
144. Nathan Schwartz-Salant, *The Mystery of Human Relationship* (London: Routledge, 1998), 70.

145. Wiesenthal, *The Sunflower.*
146. Jung, "The Psychology of the Transference," 260 [*CW* 16, para. 468].
147. Jung, "The Psychology of the Transference," 260 [*CW* 16, para. 468].
148. Jung, "The Psychology of the Transference," 260 [*CW* 16, para. 469].
149. Wiesenthal, *The Sunflower*, 51.
150. Woodcut and caption reproduced from the *Rosarium philosophorum, secunda pars alchimiae de lapide philosophico* (Frankfurt, 1550).
151. James Hillman, *The Dream and the Underworld* (New York: Harper & Row, 1979), 47.
152. Stanton Marlan & David H. Rosen, *The Black Sun: The Alchemy and Art of Darkness* (College Station, TX: Texas A&M University Press, 2005), 78.
153. Jung, "The Psychology of the Transference," 268 [*CW* 16, para. 476].
154. Wiesenthal, *The Sunflower*, 28.
155. Wiesenthal, *The Sunflower*, 52–53.
156. Jung, "The Psychology of the Transference," 271 [*CW* 16, para. 479].
157. Jung, "The Psychology of the Transference," 267 [CW 16, para. 475].
158. See Lipstadt's response in Wiesenthal's, *The Sunflower*, p. 193.
159. Morgan, "Mercy, Repentance, and Forgiveness in Ancient Judaism," 155.
160. Jung, "The Psychology of the Transference," 267 [*CW* 16, para. 476].
161. Jung, "The Psychology of the Transference," 268 [*CW* 16, para. 478].
162. Jung, "The Psychology of the Transference," 272 [*CW* 16, para. 482].
163. Morgan, "Mercy, Repentance, and Forgiveness in Ancient Judaism," 156.
164. Woodcut and caption reproduced from the *Rosarium philosophorum, secunda pars alchimiae de lapide philosophico* (Frankfurt, 1550).
165. Wiesenthal, *The Sunflower*, 53.
166. Jung, "The Psychology of the Transference," [*CW* 16]; Jung, "The Theory of Psychoanalysis," [*CW* 4].
167. Jung, "The Psychology of the Transference," 273 [*CW* 16, para. 483].
168. Jung, "The Psychology of the Transference," 294 [*CW* 16, para. 503].
169. Jung, "The Psychology of the Transference," 293 [*CW* 16, para. 502].
170. Jung, "The Psychology of the Transference," 292 [*CW* 16, para. 501].
171. Jung, "The Psychology of the Transference," 292 [*CW* 16, para. 501].
172. Jung, "The Psychology of the Transference," 293 [*CW* 16, para. 502].
173. C.G. Jung, "The Significance of the Father in the Destiny of the Individual," in R.F.C. Hull (Trans.), *The Collected Works of C.G. Jung* (Vol. 4, pp. 301–323) (Princeton, NJ: Princeton University Press, 1989) (Original work published 1909), 317 [*CW* 4, para. 730]; C.G. Jung, "The Phenomenology of the Spirit in Fairytales," in R.F.C. Hull (Trans.), *The Collected Works of C.G. Jung* (Vol. 9i, 2nd ed., pp. 207–254) (Princeton, NJ: Princeton University Press, 1979) (Original work published 1948), 253 [*CW* 9i, para. 455]; C.G. Jung, "Aion," in R.F.C. Hull (Trans.), *The Collected Works of C.G. Jung* (Vol. 9ii, 2nd ed.) (Princeton, NJ: Princeton University Press, 1979) (Original work published 1951), 192 [*CW* 9ii, para. 299].
174. Jung, "The Psychology of the Transference," 292 [*CW* 16, para. 501].
175. Hillman, *Insearch*, 94.
176. Wiesenthal, *The Sunflower*, 51.
177. Wiesenthal, *The Sunflower*, 53.
178. Giegerich, "Jung's Thought of the Self," 187–188.
179. Edinger, *Anatomy of the Psyche.*
180. Edinger, *Anatomy of the Psyche*, 187.
181. Jung, "The Psychology of the Transference," 294 [*CW* 16, para. 503].
182. Jung, "The Psychology of the Transference," 294 [*CW* 16, para. 503].
183. James Hillman, *Alchemical Psychology: The Uniform Edition of the Writings of James Hillman* (Vol. 1) (Putnam, CT: Spring Publications, 2010), 155.

184. C.G. Jung, "Psychological Types," in R.F.C. Hull (Trans.), *The Collected Works of C.G. Jung* (Vol. 6) (Princeton, NJ: Princeton University Press, 1979) (Original work published 1921), 52 [CW 6, para. 78].
185. Woodcut and caption reproduced from the *Rosarium philosophorum, secunda pars alchimiae de lapide philosophico* (Frankfurt, 1550).
186. Jung, "The Psychology of the Transference," 283 [CW 16, para. 494].
187. Jung, "The Psychology of the Transference," 295 [CW 16, para. 504].
188. Morgan, "Mercy, Repentance, and Forgiveness in Ancient Judaism," 157.
189. See Langer's, response in Wiesenthal's, *The Sunflower*, 187.
190. Jeffrey C. Miller, *The Transcendent Function: Jung's Model of Psychological Growth through Dialogue with the Unconscious* (Albany, NY: State University of New York Press, 2004), 8.
191. C.G. Jung, "The Transcendent Function," in R.F.C. Hull (Trans.), *The Collected Works of C.G. Jung* (Vol. 6) (Princeton, NJ: Princeton University Press, 1979) (Original work published 1916), 73 [CW 8, para. 145].
192. A striking image of the accomplished transcendent function is beautifully reflected in the famous series of conversations documented in Pumla Gobodo-Madikizela's book, *A Human Being Died That Night*, between Madikizela, a psychologist who grew up in a black South African township, and Eugene de Kock, nicknamed "Prime Evil," the commanding officer of state-sanctioned death squads under apartheid. Mirroring the alchemical process of what Jung described as "the blending and fusion of the noble with the base components, of the differentiated with the inferior functions, of the conscious with the unconscious," Madikizela and de Kock spent forty-six hours together in conversation over a period of six months. Their challenging, soulful, and patient dialogue left Madikizela's heart filled with empathy and restored to one "without hate," and inspired in de Kock an extraordinary awakening of conscience and humanity. Both were profoundly transformed (Pumla Gobodo-Madikizela, *A Human Being Died That Night: A South African Woman Confronts the Legacy of Apartheid* (New York: Mariner Books, 2004)).
193. Miller, *The Transcendent Function*, 74.
194. Hillman, *Re-Visioning Psychology*, 188.
195. D.W. Winnicott, *Playing and Reality* (2nd ed.) (Routledge, 2005), xvi.
196. Hanna Segal, *Introduction to the Work of Melanie Klein* (Enlarged ed.) (London: Karnac Books, 1988).
197. Miller, *The Transcendent Function.*
198. Heinz Kohut, *The Analysis of the Self: A Systematic Approach to the Psychoanalytic Treatment of Narcissistic Personality Disorders* (Chicago: University of Chicago Press, 2009).
199. Miller, *The Transcendent Function.*
200. C.G. Jung, "Two Essays on Analytical Psychology," in R.F.C. Hull (Trans.), *The Collected Works of C.G. Jung* (Vol. 7, 2nd ed.) (Princeton, NJ: Princeton University Press, 1966) (Original work published 1917), 110 [CW 7, para. 186].
201. C.G. Jung, "Two Essays on Analytical Psychology," 219 [CW 7, para. 360].
202. Schwartz-Salant, *The Mystery of Human Relationship*, 65.
203. Miller, *The Transcendent Function*, 128.
204. Jacques Derrida, *Sovereignties in Question: The Poetics of Paul Celan*, ed. by T. Dutoit & O. Pasanen (3rd ed.) (Bronx, NY: Fordham University Press, 2005) (Original work published 2004), 83–84.
205. Hillman, *Insearch*, 28.
206. Hillman, *Insearch*, 30.
207. Hillman, *Re-Visioning Psychology*, 135.
208. Hillman, *Re-Visioning Psychology*, xvi.
209. Miller, *The Transcendent Function*, 96.

210. Hillman, *Re-Visioning Psychology*, 51.
211. Hillman, *Re-Visioning Psychology*, 50.
212. Hillman, *Re-Visioning Psychology*, 48.
213. Hillman, *Re-Visioning Psychology*, 46–47.
214. Hillman, *Re-Visioning Psychology*, 127.
215. Wolfgang Giegerich, "Killings," in *Soul Violence* (Vol. 3, pp. 189–266) (New Orleans, LA: Spring Journal Books, 2008) (Original work published 1993), 265.
216. Giegerich, "Killings," 270.
217. Giegerich, "Love the Questions Themselves," 271.
218. Giegerich, "Love the Questions Themselves," 271.
219. Wolfgang Giegerich, "Is the Soul Deep?," in *The Soul Always Thinks* (Vol. 4, pp. 131–163) (New Orleans, LA: Spring Journal, Inc., 2010) (Original work published 1998), 161–162.
220. Wolfgang Giegerich, David L. Miller, & Greg Mogenson, *Dialectics & Analytical Psychology: The El Capitan Canyon Seminar* (New Orleans, LA: Spring Journal, Inc., 2005), 16.
221. Giegerich et al., *Dialectics & Analytical Psychology*, 5–6.
222. Morgan, "Mercy, Repentance, and Forgiveness in Ancient Judaism," 156.
223. Giegerich, "Jung's Thought of the Self," 185.
224. Giegerich et al., *Dialectics & Analytical Psychology*, 93.
225. Giegerich et al., *Dialectics & Analytical Psychology*, 6–7.
226. Giegerich et al., *Dialectics & Analytical Psychology*, 2.
227. Giegerich et al., *Dialectics & Analytical Psychology*, 5.
228. Hillman, *Re-Visioning Psychology*, xvi.
229. Giegerich et al., *Dialectics & Analytical Psychology*, 103.
230. Soren Kierkegaard, *The Concept of Anxiety: A Simple Psychologically Orienting Deliberation on the Dogmatic Issue of Hereditary Sin (Kierkegaard's Writings, VIII)*. ed. by Reidar Thomte (Princeton University Press, 1981), 104.
231. (7.15–16).
232. As cited by Ann Casement, "The Interiorizing Movement of Logical Life: Reflections on Wolfgang Giegerich," *The Journal of Analytical Psychology*, 56 (2011): 536.
233. Giegerich, "Love the Questions Themselves," 299.
234. Wiesenthal, *The Sunflower*, 84.
235. Wiesenthal, *The Sunflower*, 84.
236. Wiesenthal, *The Sunflower*, 85.
237. Wiesenthal, *The Sunflower*, 94.
238. Giegerich, "Love the Questions Themselves," 299.
239. Wiesenthal, *The Sunflower*, 52.
240. Wiesenthal, *The Sunflower*, 53.
241. Wiesenthal, *The Sunflower*, 54.
242. Giegerich et al., *Dialectics & Analytical Psychology*, 5.
243. Giegerich et al., *Dialectics & Analytical Psychology*, 5.

5 Forgiveness and the Self

> And when they came to the place which is called The Skull, there they crucified him, and the criminals, one on the right and one on the left. And Jesus said, "Father, forgive them; for they know not what they do."
>
> (Luke 23:32–34)

From a historical perspective, Jesus's prayer ushers in a starkly different viewpoint of forgiveness than that of the traditional scriptural laws. Jesus validates forgiveness as a response to his own murder, overriding the previous requirement for *teshuvah*—no atonement is asked for, no reparation, no apology, no repentance, no conversion. Jesus proposes a radical new idea of forgiveness not based on justice, condition, or economy. The primary issue is not the sin *per se*—no purification or cleansing or negation of the sin (or sinner) is required. Rather, the problem seems to be the state of mind that gives rise to the sin—those committing the sin *do not know* what they are doing. They are blind to the impact or meaning of their actions. The sin is committed in the absence of consciousness. Recall that forgiveness stems from the Latin root *ignosco*, meaning fundamentally "not to know,"[1] which in his final prayer Jesus aligns with "not knowing" what one is doing. Forgiveness would seem here to dispatch the mind of the forgiver into the fog of unawareness as well, along with the sinner's. One might then translate Jesus as pleading, *Father, do not know them in their unconsciousness*. Stay unaware of them in their sin, as they too are unaware.

One might also infer that if they *were* conscious of what they were doing, they would not be doing it. Knowing, awareness, consciousness is the point, and presumably would prevent the sin, would prevent the expression of evil. In parallel with the notion of evil as the absence of good (*privatio boni*), which Jung rejected, here evil seems to rest on *the absence of consciousness*, awareness, or understanding. In this case, Jesus's murderers were in error due to a lack of understanding, and their unforgivable sin is perceived instead as a mistake, an error in judgment. What is initially inexplicable—the brutal torture and murder of an innocent man—is seen as a tragic mistake to be forgiven rather than as a sin to be punished.

On the other hand, one may also infer that if they *had known* what they were doing, forgiveness would not be offered, implying the very opposite—consciousness and evil coexist. Consciousness carries with it the responsibility for committing evil, and the two are intrinsically related, as asserted by Hegel, who defines consciousness as a "stepping away" or "stepping forth" from an implicit state of pure being, goodness, or oneness with the divine. The resulting rupture or cleavage that *is* consciousness is symbolized in the individual as the distinction between judgment (or thought, discernment) and action (for example, animals do not possess a cleavage between action and judging, they are not inwardly divided, they do not "know" what they "do"). For Hegel,

> Knowledge of good and evil is itself evil. Cognition entails a judging or dividing—a self-distinguishing within oneself. This cleavage is the contradiction—that which is evil. But in the same way that this cleavage is the *source* of evil, it is also the standpoint of the conversion that consciousness contains within itself whereby the division in consciousness is overcome.[2]

Overcoming the division entails the full consciousness and acknowledgment of the sin or evil to be forgiven:

> Evil must be recognized as what it is before it can be sublated. The "judgment" of the judging consciousness is a necessary moment; without it there can be no reconciliation. . . . True forgiveness has to be preceded by full recognition of the act which is to be sublated. [3]

It would seem certain that Jesus himself—*and only he*—had "full recognition of the act . . . to be sublated." He thus could function as mediator or reconciler between man and God. In a sense one might imagine his prayer to be, *Father, I have full awareness of this sin, that I carry while in the absence of theirs, upon which achievement it will be "overcome" or sublated.*

The Conditional Forgiveness of Jesus

Before examining further psychological implications given by the image of Jesus's prayer for forgiveness, I wish to consider a very different perspective on Luke 23:34, one in which Jesus's plea for forgiveness is not unconditional at all but serves instead to cloak persecutory hatred and vengeance and amplify blame toward Jews. Biblical scholar Jennifer Knust surveys numerous scriptural revisions noted by scholars that suppress Jesus's call for unconditional forgiveness in an effort to eradicate mercy for the Jewish community, noting the likely possibility that other New Testament authors may have suppressed the passage (which is found only in Luke) in response to the destruction of Jerusalem, linking it with the death of Jesus and the apostles.[4] Knust cites Streeter (1925): "Twice within seventy years Jerusalem had been destroyed and hundreds of thousands of Jews massacred and enslaved. It followed that, if Christ had prayed that prayer, God had declined to grant it."[5] Second-century theologian Irenaeus of Lyons referred often to Luke 23:34 when instructing followers to exhibit long-suffering patience and compassion, and to pray for those who persecute them. However, Knust points out that in reality Iranaeus cited Christ's prayer

> not so that [a person] can lovingly welcome and forgive those who have injured him, but so that he can demonstrate how wrong and objectionable they actually are. "For when an account is demanded for their blood and they obtain glory," [Irenaeus] argues, "then all who dishonor their martyrdom will be put to shame by Christ." . . . In other words, the love and forgiveness extended by Christ and the martyrs at the moment of death only postpones the violence and death God actually intends for the persecutors. Their forgiveness serves as a warrant for God's violence, their love as an excuse for the eternal death that necessarily awaits them.[6]

Knust acknowledges that in its initial appearance in Luke, the passage illustrates that "Jesus' exemplary forgiveness also affirms his divinity."[7] However when taken in the larger context of Luke and Acts, the biblical author(s) rework material and add contextual details such that

> the forgiveness Jesus extends to . . . his murderers at the moment of death is gradually revoked, so that by the end of Luke's two-volume work, the Gospel and the Acts of the Apostles, the blame for killing Christ and the Christians has been shifted to Jewish critics of the Jesus movement, who are promised eternal punishment.[8]

The introduction of forgiveness with no conditions was novel and as such met with severe resistance. Despite Jesus's prayer, the primary focus in Luke-Acts is still on "*repentance* as a necessary requirement for forgiveness, not on the unconditional love shown by God toward all people irrespective of their sins."[9] In her conclusion, Knust opines that "appeals to unconditional forgiveness appear to . . . be a poor strategy"[10] to attain the "worthy goal" of reparation. "All too often, such appeals work to preserve a sense of superiority on the part of the forgiver, divine or human, not to enable the kind of truth telling that might make reconciliation possible."[11]

Knust's analysis demonstrates the ego's penchant for annexing moments of the Self for its own ends.[12] Jesus's brand of unconditional forgiveness is inaccessible to the ego (as we have seen earlier), and must thus be altered and adapted, reworked, and even suppressed altogether, ultimately taking on its *negated* meaning—Jesus's forgiveness "serves as a warrant for God's violence," his love a mere cover "for the eternal death that necessarily awaits [the sinner]."

Forgiveness as Release from Projection

Jesus's prayer on the cross refers to unconsciousness in the form of "not knowing what one is doing." As noted by Jung, that of which we are unconscious reveals itself to us first in the outer world as projections. As Edinger observes, Jesus illuminates humankind's proclivity toward psychological projection two thousand years prior to depth psychology when he asks,

> Why do you look at the speck of sawdust in your brother's eye and pay no attention to the plank in your own eye? How can you say to your brother, "Brother, let me take the speck out of your eye," when you yourself fail to see the plank in your own eye?
>
> (Luke 6:41–42)[13]

The passage is situated within the context of judgment, condemnation, and forgiveness, occurring soon after Jesus's statements: "Do not condemn and you will not be condemned. Forgive and you will be forgiven" (Luke 37–38). Jesus seems to associate condemnation with the "looking at the speck" in the brother's eye and forgiveness as a superior response to perceived sin. If we go directly to the Greek text of the New Testament, the term "forgive" in Luke 6:37 is taken from the word "ἀπολύετε" (transliteration = apolyete), which literally means to "release" or "set free."[14] Psychologically speaking, as a projection is recognized and seen through, one who had before been the carrier of the projection is "set free" or released from the bonds of judgment and condemnation; one's brother is liberated from the humiliating torment of their sin, the disfiguring "speck."

Arendt asserts that the very faculty of forgiveness lies in its ability to liberate and deliver one from one's past, offering "redemption from the predicament of irreversibility—of being unable to undo what one has done . . ."[15] Allais also speaks of forgiving as releasing another from the past. "Forgiveness enables us to not fix our attitudes towards each other on the basis of our worst acts. . . . [I]n forgiving, we allow the wrongdoer to make a genuinely fresh start; the slate is wiped clean."[16] Arendt equates forgiveness with the release from the consequences of our transgression, without which "our capacity to act would, as it were, be confined to one single deed from which we could never recover; we would remain the victims of its consequences forever."[17]

The idea of *forgiveness as release* is also similar to that explored in the previous chapter, in which the soul function of forgiveness is imagined metaphorically as an alchemical solvent that liberates the Mercurial spirit to allow once again the unhindered flow of the soul's logical life. Forgiveness in this case also evokes an image of freeing oneself from the identification of unconscious elements, thereby shedding "the mythical garments in which [one] had hitherto been cloaked. . . . This is what individuation means *practically*; I am just myself, the empirical person that I am, no more, no less, no better, no worse."[18] Such deliverance from the bondage of identity with the archetypes occurs authentically through the ordeal of shadow integration, which we have seen in various forms as *teshuvah* (repentance), unification of the opposites (via the transcendent function), and absolute negation, or absolute-negative interiorization, which Giegerich defines explicitly as that reality which is "*released* into its truth" amounting to "the freeing of the Mercurius imprisoned in the physicalness of the matter."[19]

Turning back to projection, according to Jung, "If we are not aware that a property of the object is a projection, we cannot do anything else but be naively convinced that it really does belong to the object,"[20] that is, one feels *certain* of the reality of the speck in a brother's eye. If one suspects but is not sure, dispassionate, or equally open to the possibility that there is no speck, it is unlikely to be a projection, for it is the *subjective factor* that reveals projections. "Exaggeration indicates, in most cases, an interpretation on the subjective level"[21] and "the more subjective and emotional [an] impression is, the more likely it is that the property will be a projection."[22] With regard to forgiveness, certain subjective factors such as negative judgment, condemnation, self-righteousness, vengefulness, etc., come into play. Forgiveness is typically relevant when an event offends one's sensibilities enough to warrant a subjective negative emotional reaction. Thus, where forgiveness is relevant, "the more likely it is that the property [causing the offense] will be a projection."

Practically speaking, when something imposes enough tension to disturb the status quo and hence becomes an object of criticism, we find a projected element available for integration. Von Franz writes,

> To be precise, we could in practice speak of a projection only "when the need to dissolve the identity with the object has already arisen," or, in other words, when the identity begins to have a disturbing effect and exerts a negative influence on the adaptation to the outer world. At this point the identity of the inner image with the outer object becomes perceptible and the object of criticism, whether it be our own or that of other people.
>
> (Jung, 1921/1989, p. 457 [*CW* 6, para. 783])[23]

Jesus's metaphor of a speck in the eye thus artfully elicits the agitation of a "disturbing effect" experienced with a projection ripe for integration.

The speck, as an artifact of an un-integrated (projected) shadow element (the plank), being of the same element and differing only in size, can also reasonably be imagined as originating *from* the plank, the speck a direct result of the presence of the plank. Hence, if the plank is successfully removed—the "integration" of the projection is accomplished—"then the experience [of the speck] . . . is not repeated; if the content is not integrated, then the same or similar phenomena will occur in another context."[24] Yet as long as one is unaware of a projection, "the characteristic really does belong to the object" and can never truly be forgiven—only repeatedly denied, ignored, repressed, and resisted. When another situation or hook for the projection presents itself, the sensation of offense and pain will reoccur and the work of "forgiveness" would need to begin again. We could say that until one takes out the plank in one's own eye, splinters of the plank stubbornly remain in the eyes of others. Successful removal (integration) of one's own plank (shadow) consequently "removes" the speck in thy brother's eye. Seen in this context, shadow integration and forgiveness become *one and the same*.

A speck in the eye in the quite literal sense is experienced as painful, disturbing, foreign, and clearly undesirable. Similarly, in depth psychology we often find projection to reveal in the other disturbing, unwanted, painful shadow elements; the "speck" I see in my brother's eye would likely take the shape of that which I "fail to see" (deny, repress, or suppress) in my own eye in the form of *his* sin or shortcoming, something "in need" of being "looked at" or evaluated and consequently condemned or forgiven ("taken out"). While still in my line of vision, projection offers relief from the discomfort of the speck if it is seen in my brother instead—*he* must bear it, and my "help" in removing it for him thus validates its reality and source in *his* eye. Projection as Jesus describes it however reveals an astonishing difference with rather ominous implications; rather than a speck for a speck, it is a speck for a plank, a sliver for a beam: apparently I see only a *tiny fraction* of my own shadow in my brother! Following the idea of projection as a defense against the awareness of one's own shadow material, one would expect to see the speck in one's brother's eye that is actually overlooked in one's own. Yet as Jesus would have it, the shadow perceived externally is a mere shadow of a shadow, a tip of the iceberg—there is a *timber* in one's own eye! Jesus's comparison of the speck to the plank may speak to the phenomenon of how the unconscious shows itself to us; instead of an overwhelming confrontation of the ego with its colossal shadow, it is reflected back to the ego in tiny parts, ready for integration.[25] This also speaks to our relation with "the unconscious": instead of shining a light of awareness wildly into the overwhelming abyss of darkness, it is the other way around—we fetch and bring, piece by piece, as an *opus contra naturum*, slivers and specks of the vast unknown into the revealing light of consciousness.

Jesus's astonishing comparison also serves to heighten the urgency of tending to one's inner life. Giegerich remarks on the amplified intensity of unconscious shadow content:

> Where something is projected, we are already dwelling with this other. No one is closer to an inimical shadow and more personally affected by it than he who experiences it in projection upon somebody and is nagged by it constantly, even deep into his sleepless nights. [26]

Clearly, the part more urgently in need of tending is the log in one's own eye as opposed to the mere speck in the external other. Jesus thus explicitly asserts a crucial and required negation, a radical about-face inward turn and focus on interiority: "You hypocrite, first take the plank out of your eye, and then you will see clearly to remove the speck from your brother's eye" (Luke 6:42). As discussed in Chapter 4, forgiveness as a response to evil can serve to unwittingly validate and enforce the unconscious defense mechanism of projection. Forgiveness would make "real" the sin seen in thy brother insofar as it fails to turn inward and gaze upon the timber in thine own eye, which psychology claims gives rise to the speck in thy brother's.

While "taking the plank out of your own eye" seems straightforward in theory, the enormity of the amplified shadow from a speck to a plank reveals the near impossibility of the enterprise of shadow integration. Giegerich observes, "as soon as consciousness admits that it is in itself incompatible with itself, that it *is* what it absolutely does not want to be, it [ego-consciousness] will self-destruct."[27] A lifetime of effort and ego-dissolution may be required as the timber is integrated and sublated, speck by speck.

Jesus's use of the *eye* in the metaphor emphasizes the element of impaired "sight" that arises from projection; one's own unnoticed shadow (plank/log/beam) prevents accurate perception of the other. A person is unable to see the other as they truly are until they have dealt squarely with their own projections.[28] In fact, the implication given by a beam in the eye is surely complete and utter *blindness* to reality, to what is *actually* there. Projections thus profoundly interfere with correct vision or perception—one is unable to accurately "see" what one is doing. Jesus refers again to this inability to see when he says: "Father, forgive them, for they do not know what they are doing." In the English translation, the word "know" is taken from the original Greek οἶδα (transliteration *eídō*) which literally means "to *see* with *physical* eyes, as it naturally bridges to the *metaphorical* sense: *perceiving.*"[29] How can one see or know what one is doing in the face of projections? In both passages, forgiveness emerges as a response to distorted or impaired perception.

As noted, Jesus's exhortation concerning the speck and the beam occurs in the context of judgment, condemnation, and forgiveness, following these comments: "Do not judge, and you will not be judged. Do not condemn, and you will not be condemned. Forgive, and you will be forgiven. . . . For with the measure you use, it will be measured to you" (Luke 6:37–38). To the extent that the act of judging entails condemnation, ridicule, and criticism of others, and if such shadowy elements in others are in fact projections of one's *own* personality, Jesus's "directive" against judging others would seem less of a warning than an astute *psychological observation on the reflective nature of psyche*; from a psychological perspective, the hated aspect in the other *is* actually one's own, hence the judgment meted out lands squarely, albeit unconsciously, upon the self. In this way, "with the judgment you make you will be judged, and the measure you give will be the measure you get" (Matthew 7:2). This may also speak to what appears as redundant wording in the original Greek, translated as follows: "By what way indeed you criticize you will be criticized and by what standard you measure it will be measured again to you."[30] The word "again" at first seems superfluous but in fact may refer to yet another instance of judgment resulting from the act of criticizing another; the judgment against the other causes unconscious inner conflict, in that we "unhesitatingly condemn the object of offence, while all the time we are raging against an unconscious part of ourselves which is projected into the exasperating object."[31] In addition, there is the measure of psychological guilt that may arise from the false accusation of the other; not only is one guilty as the real culprit is understood to be the self, but guilty *again* for the mistaken attack upon one's brother. In passing judgment one then invariably and unconsciously carries an invisible burden of self-condemnation and guilt until the projection is recognized.

The Thought of the Heart

In his remarkable essay, *The Thought of the Heart*, Hillman describes three modes of responding unconsciously to the world, which he calls "disguises" of a heart "in exile" from its truth as thought.[32] The first mode depicts the passionate, heroic heart (which he calls the "Heart of the Lion" or *Coeur de Lion*), the second the scientific, positivistic heart ("Harvey's heart"), and the third the romantic, personal heart (the "Heart of Augustine"). These styles of heartfelt perceiving each serve to disguise or conceal the underlying mechanism of projection giving rise to each perspective; while each offers up seemingly genuine experiences in which the "thought of the heart" relates to the world, it relates in an unconscious manner, unaware of its origin *as thought*. These modes of perceiving Hillman aptly characterizes as "disguises" of the heart, as the owner is not aware that their contents are *thoughts*. Instead, they are mistaken for literal truth; from the perspective of the *Coeur de Lion*, the perils and suffering of the world need my participation, I *must act* to save them. For Harvey, the heart really *is* a pump and only a pump, despite the fact that one may die of a (merely subjective) broken heart. For Augustine, my heart *is* that place and the only place in which I find God.

While all three modes of being are unconscious and work from projection, of particular relevance to our discussion of forgiveness is the mode Hillman characterizes as the zealous, heroic heart (*Coeur de Lion*). The *Coeur de Lion* is that particular mode of relating that reacts most ardently in response to the agitation caused by others and the world; it is the heart of war. This heart *springs* us into action, it is the activist heart, driven by passion and desire (*himma*), fired by the alchemical sulphur that flares and erupts with fervor and zeal. Hillman says,

> Crucial to the heart of the lion is that it *believes*, and it believes that it does not think. So its thought appears in the world as project, desire, concern, mission. Thinking and doing together. This is the bold thought that takes us into battle.[33]

The outward focus of this heart "produces what Jung has called the 'dark body' at the core of ego–consciousness, its blindness to itself."[34] Because it sees only externally, it identifies with the world it beholds, its thought "completely coagulated into its objectifications."[35] Psychology calls this love in the heart of the lion *compulsive projection*. For Hillman, the task of consciousness here lies in recognizing

> the archetypal construct of its thought, that its actions, desires, and ardent beliefs are all imaginations—creations of the *himma*—and that what it experiences as life, love, and world is its own *enthymesis* [life force] presented outside as macrocosm.[36]

Because the heart of the lion merely acts out its urgencies, going directly, just like that, to the problems of the world to be solved, it lacks psychological conscience.[37] Reacting to things in the world as literal, it is given over to the concrete object before it, without wasting a thought on the *subject*, on what it itself as heroic problem-solving consciousness is doing (thus neglecting the "beam" in its own eye). Lion-hearted interaction with the world, while compelling and passionate, comes from a consciousness still blind to itself, unable yet to imagine the very soul of the world it is trying to save:

> the imagination captive in its sulphur that both burns and coagulates at the same instant, imagination held fused into its desire and its desire fused with its object. The *himma* blinded, unable to distinguish between feeling and image, image and object, object and subject, true imagining and illusion.[38]

Hearkening back to the religious zeal of the early Christian martyrs and theologians such as Irenaeus of Lyons, it seems likely that their religious conviction was born of the *Coeur de lion*, the anger and hysteria of the soldiers and throngs who put Jesus to death expressions of coagulated sulphur, eyes blinded by timber. While they *believe* with all their heart, the heart of the lion, *they do not see* that their "actions, desires, and ardent beliefs are all imaginations": *they do not know what they are doing.*

Yet according to Hillman, psyche needs the *Coeur de lion*, for "it is by means of the lion in the heart that we perceive and respond imaginally."[39] For Hillman, it is the mighty roar of the lion that shocks the still-born cubs into life; we *need* the heart to roar. The path therefore is not to kill, deny, or condemn the lion, but to wake it up to itself *as thought*. With this insight, it becomes consciously unified with itself; it *realizes* itself as the unity between thought and world, as the unification of the opposites. For this insight to dawn, Hillman describes how first the red lion heart must be alchemically whitened.

According to Hillman, "The phase called whitening in alchemy refers to the emergence of psychological consciousness, the ability to hear psychologically, and to perceive fantasy creating reality."[40] Whitening shepherds in psychological awareness and symbolic thinking to a heart that had previously been coagulated in literal and positivistic thinking, an "imagination held fused into its desire and its desire fused with its object." The alchemical operation of whitening

> raises the temperature to a white heat so as to destroy all coagulations in the intensity of the desire, so that what one desires no longer matters, even as it matters most, mattering now sublimed, translucent, all flame.[41]

The heart is whitened through its own humiliations, illusions, and failures.

> When the sulphur whitens within the heart, we feel at first discouraged . . . weakened. The heart now discovers its own inhibition and, driven in on itself, it feels both its desire and its inability, passion without seizure, compulsion and impotence together, "I want" and "I can't" at once.[42]

Giegerich notes the profound confrontation between "I want" and "I can't" as the foundation of dialectics. As we have seen, the infinite dimension of interiority, or the realm of soul, comes about through the absolute negation of externality, which in turn "is possible only through the negation or self-contradiction of a passionately attempted forward movement"; [43] *I want* and *I can't* at once. According to Giegerich, "The move into transcendence . . . is not a soaring higher and higher up beyond the earth and beyond the clouds into outer space. On the contrary, since it is negative (frustrated) movement, it stays put."[44] In "staying put," as it were, in a near-intolerable state, the heart alchemically "cooks in its own blood," as Hillman describes.[45] It is the whitening of hopelessness and despair, utter failure and frustration, devoid of possibility. Forgiveness can lead into this place of utter frustration, where one wants to forgive the other or oneself but finds one simply cannot; the "passionately attempted forward movement" of forgiveness is repeatedly self-contradicted by feelings of fresh rage, resentment, or despair, and forgiveness feels to be impossible. Repeated "failed" attempts at forgiveness thus induce a whitening effect on ego-consciousness in service to soul-making. For it is *only* under the circumstance where forgiveness is experienced as impossible, as Derrida (2007) insists, that *true* forgiveness emerges as a possibility.

Leaping after the Throw

While the traditional psychological task would be to recognize and integrate the projections of the *Coeur de Lion*, Hillman makes a significant detour in referring to Giegerich's unorthodox approach to working with projections.

Giegerich is critical of the general psychological concept of projection due to its inherent protection of the ego. Projection evokes the image of the subject ejecting an internal unconscious content out into the external world from a fixed place (one might imagine a person throwing a stone from the shore, or a spear into the forest) along with the therapeutic expectation of withdrawing the projection back inside of oneself. According to Giegerich, "What turns projection into a psychological problem is that the movement stops with the throw."[46] Such an aggressive-passive *stopping at the throw* is thought to be an abortive move by the ego in that one's focus is trained on the object itself, rather than on how the object is seen—on the entity rather than one's *relationship* to it. *The instinctual lunge after the projection is suppressed*, and the possible sloughing off of the ego by exposure to new territory is prevented, as is individuation. The ego remains intact, the alchemical whitening avoided. "The intent is always to achieve change, but to keep the subject as something fixed out of the process and to immunize him"[47] from transformation. In not "leaping after" the projected image, judgment, or dream material—but instead noticing it, feeling it, or giving creative expression to it by the ego complex—one avoids being transformed by it.

Yet isn't such "standing still" akin to Giegerich's requirement of "staying put," that very phenomenon which enables "the move into transcendence"? Here we have an example of the difference between the semantic or ego level of consciousness and the syntactic or soul level. From the ego perspective, withdrawing projections would involve thinking about, analyzing, noticing, or giving expression to the object of our projection from within the fortress of the ego complex, thus defending against the alchemical whitening or the "agonies involved"[48] in withdrawing projections. The soul perspective instead surrenders to the instinctual lunge forward, psychologically "leaping after" the projection into the world, freely taking in the new frontier opening up ahead. At the same time, this syntactical perspective would "stay put" in the alchemical acid bath of *feeling*; it would relentlessly undergo or go under the (often agonizing) *experience* of the sojourn, as the soul does not defend against feeling. In leaping after the throw, Giegerich claims, "projection . . . opens up my soul the whole world as its inner space; it procures for the soul an extendedness over the world so that it begins to carry its title *anima mundi* with full right."[49] From this perspective, one does not reclaim one's soul until having been transformed and whitened by the world one experiences in the very act of catching up with the projection.

For example, let us assume that one has been profoundly betrayed (this idea stands out in the story of the crucifixion, given Judas's betrayal and Peter's denial). From a practical perspective, a person working with the idea of betrayal as projection in light of the discussion above may need to surrender to an experience of devastating heartbreak that accompanies the betrayal by a loved one, such that the ego-truth of "betrayal" is exposed as the unexamined (unconscious) unmet demand for primal trust, the broken guarantee of perfect love, a violation of the demand to never be let down.[50] One may begin to journey down into places where one has been betrayed while in a position of utter dependency (as a child for example) and to explore the experiences of betrayal that live in oneself. One may see how one has likewise let *others* down, avoiding the domination of one's word to others, indulging willful disobedience and hubris, heartlessly betraying loved ones (beholding the beam in one's eye), yes, but also betraying one*self*, handing over and selling one's own soul. To go defenselessly into the *nekyia* of betrayal is to relentlessly expose oneself to the *experience* of betrayal, ultimately encountering its soul-truth, whereupon the devastating "treachery" is recognized as a soul movement in service to the soul's own homecoming. From an ego perspective, the heartrending cry of Jesus on the cross, "My God, my God, why hast thou forsaken me?" (Matthew 27:46; Mark 15:34) signifies a cruel God abandoning his Son. From a soul perspective, this "betrayal" signifies the final "emptying out" or *kenôsis* of Christ's divinity, his voluntary, unreserved, and utter humbling himself into mortal human being; it is the uroboric soul movement of God's "dying out of" matter and "dying into" Spirit and Love,[51] the soul's coming home to itself.

The withdrawal of projections would certainly have a transformational effect on interpersonal relationships. As von Franz observes:

> It happens again and again in psychological practice that when a person has been caught in blinding projections . . . and they are then withdrawn, in many cases this in no way annuls or sets aside the *relationship*. On the contrary, a genuine, "deeper" relation emerges, no longer rooted in egoistic moods, struggles, or illusions but rather in the feeling of being connected to one another via an absolute, objective principle.[52]

The "absolute, objective principle" von Franz is referring to is the objective psyche, soul, or the Self. Relationships based on the soul, rather than on subjective projection, "give rise to a feeling of immediate, timeless 'being together.' . . . In this world created by the Self we meet all those many to whom we belong, whose hearts we touch." It is here that, as Jung says, "there is no distance, but immediate presence."[53] When relating to others on this level, we may find ourselves aware of contingent synchronistic connections, not of our own choosing, whose presence we recognize as crucial to facilitating an expression of the soul or objective psyche *through* us.

Clarity of Perception and the Heart of Beauty

The whitening of the heart that Hillman describes is a form of purification, or *mundificatio*, as discussed in Chapter 4, and corresponds to the alchemical stage of silver—or *albedo*—marking a refined state of consciousness "that proceeds not from the soul as simply given but from the work done upon it."[54] In this transformed state, perception is no longer obscured by the disguises of the heart, which have been burned away. Writes Hillman, "Seeing, listening, attending all shift from the gross attachments of the nigredo to a new transparency and resonance. Things shine and speak. . . . They address the soul by showing forth their souls."[55] The degree of acuity given by the accomplished whitening is exquisite, where speech is "de-brided of literalisms"[56] and the world teems with the living soul Plato tells us is actually there. And this soul of the world, the *anima mundi*, is beautiful! Hillman writes:

> Beauty is the manifest *anima mundi* . . . and refers to appearances as such, created as they are, in the forms in which they are given, sense data, bare facts, Venus Nudata. Aphrodite's beauty refers to the luster of each particular event—its clarity, its particular brightness: that particular things appear at all and in the form in which they appear.[57]

The whitening of the heart ushers in a state of awareness in which beauty is recognized as *appearance itself*, enabling the beholder to "sense revelation in the immediate presentation of things as they are."[58] The implication is that absent the debris of projections, beauty as truth itself is revealed.

Beholding the world in this way occurs through *aisthesis*, the Greek word for perception or sensation, meaning

> at root a breathing in or taking in of the world, the gasp, "aha," the "uh" of the breath in wonder, shock, amazement, an aesthetic response to the image (*eidolon*) presented. In ancient Greek physiology and in biblical psychology the heart was the organ of sensation; it was also the place of imagination.[59]

In his wondrous description of a world ensouled, Hillman posits a revelatory state of consciousness akin to Corbin's[60] *imaginatio vera*—a state also similar to that given by the objective psyche or the Self as described by Jung and von Franz, in which projections are dissolved. In this state we would behold a thing as it is, as *it* shows *it*self, undistorted by projections, unhindered by a beam in one's line of vision.

The dissolution of projections invites a vision of stillness, a calm clarity of perception. In lieu of a reactive (projective) movement outward, one might imagine a complementary invitation into interiority, into the depths within. One is now open to *receiving*, to beholding and communing with others and the world from a transparent and undefended posture. We might imagine a vision unclouded by projections as Paul does in 1 Corinthians: "For now we see through a glass, darkly; but then face to face: now I know in part; but then shall I know even as also I am known" (1 Corinthians 13:12).

Such a vision shares many characteristics of the *mundus imaginalis* as related by Corbin. The imaginal world of Sufi mysticism is described as

> a place of union, of holy reciprocity, where divine, spiritual, and human love become one in the being of the lover. For love, after all, is the mode of knowledge whereby one being *knows* another. . . . Here, above all,

> is the place of resurrection, of presence, of the first encounter with the truth, where [one] awakens to [oneself] . . . meets [oneself] as if for the first time.[61]

In these imaginal worlds beyond projection, as Corbin describes, "There is only revelation. There can be only revelation."[62] In the spirit of Bion's idea of the mystical as "seeing things as they truly are—without disguise,"[63] we are entreated by Goodchild to "let the world, both real and subtle, and the Beloved that lies at its heart, reveal to [us] 'thine original face.'"[64]

This extraordinary mode of relating to the world is what Hillman describes as *the aesthetic response of the heart*—or the "heart of beauty" in contrast to the compulsive projection of the *Coeur de lion*—wherein beauty appears in and as the actual images themselves, sans projections, such that the very beholding of them, the "sniffing, gasping, breathing in of the world" enables the "transfiguration of matter" which "occurs through wonder."[65] It is the rapturous beholding of beauty in manifest images, the undefended taking in of an object, which activates *its* imagination "so that it shows its heart and reveals its soul."[66] Such "faithful attention to the imaginal world, this love which transforms mere images into presences . . . reveals the living being which they do naturally contain . . ."[67] According to Corbin, beauty *as such* is that great category which specifically refers to "the supreme theophany, divine self-revelation."[68]

The perception given by this mode of relating leads one out of the egoic captivity imposed by the disguises of the heart and into the realm of soul. "The soul is born in beauty and feeds on beauty, requires beauty for its life. . . . If beauty is not given full place in our work with psyche, then the soul's essential realization cannot occur."[69] The soul's essential realization signifies a *conscious thinking heart*, born in the presence of imaginal beauty given by the aesthetic apprehension of the *anima mundi.*

For Hillman, the aesthetic response provides a perspective exhibiting forgiveness as both cause and effect. According to Hillman,

> A new feeling of self-forgiveness and self-acceptance begins to spread and circulate. . . . Shadow aspects of the personality continue to play their burdensome roles but now within a larger tale, the myth of oneself. . . . My myth becomes my truth; my life symbolic and allegorical. Self-forgiveness, self-acceptance, self-love; more, one finds oneself sinful but not guilty, grateful for the sins one has and not another's, loving one's lot even to the point of desire to have and to be always in this vivid inner connection with one's own individual portion.[70]

This larger, integrated experience of oneself in the world is offered exclusively from the perspective of the purified (conscious) heart of beauty: "The *anima mundi* is simply not perceived if the organ of this perception remains unconscious."[71] Though Jesus entreats God to forgive the unconscious heart of his persecutors, such a heart is blinded by its own projections and unable to perceive the forgiven state; it stays unaware of its own already always forgiven-ness.

Forgiveness as Hospitality

In the prayer for forgiveness Jesus makes on the cross, the original Greek word used is ἄφες (transliteration *aphes*), which has the additional meaning of "to let be," "permit," "allow," or "suffer."[72] Thus, when Jesus says, "Father, forgive them," he is making the astonishing request to God to *allow* or *permit* the reality resulting from his crucifixion on account of the unconsciousness of his murderers. Jesus, as a symbol of the Self or God image, in effect performs psyche's prayer *to itself* to *make allowance* for acts of unconsciousness. In this sense, forgiveness may be imagined in the manner of *hospitality* toward the unconscious, making a place in consciousness for that which there is no place.

We might find a helpful model for forgiveness as hospitality in the Greek myth of Philemon and Baucis, a poor and elderly couple who generously provide hospitality to two weary travelers, realizing only later they are in fact Zeus and Hermes in disguise. "[O]ver all the land they wandered, begging for their food and bed; and of a thousand houses, all the doors were bolted and no kindness given."[73] The gods finally found refuge in the humble household of Philemon and Baucis, who bid the strangers welcome and went to great lengths to feed and entertain them with their meager provisions.

Ovid describes the scene in which the gods knock on the door of the elderly couple's home:

> Now when the two Gods, Jove and Mercury,
> had reached this cottage, and with bending necks
> had entered the low door, the old man bade
> them rest their wearied limbs, and set a bench,
> on which his good wife, Baucis, threw a cloth;
> and then with kindly bustle she stirred up
> glowing embers on the hearth, and then
> laid tinder, leaves and bark; and bending down
> breathed on them with her ancient breath until
> they kindled into flame. Then from the house
> she brought a store of faggots and small twigs,
> and broken branches, and above them swung
> a kettle, not too large for simple folk.
> And all this done, she stripped some cabbage leaves,
> which her good husband gathered for the meal.
>
> Then with a two-pronged fork the man let down
> a rusty side of bacon from aloft,
> cut a little portion from the chine;
> which had been cherished long. He softened it

in boiling water. All the while they tried
with cheerful conversation to beguile,
so none might notice a brief loss of time.

. . .

Now as the Gods reclined, the good old dame,
whose skirts were tucked up, moving carefully,
for so she tottered with her many years,
fetched a clean table for the ready meal—
but one leg of the table was too short,
and so she wedged it with a potsherd—so
made firm, she cleanly scoured it with fresh mint.

And here is set the double-tinted fruit
of chaste Minerva, and the tasty dish
of corner, autumn-picked and pickled; these
were served for relish; and the endive-green,
and radishes surrounding a large pot
of curdled milk; and eggs not overdone
but gently turned in glowing embers—all
served up in earthen dishes. Then sweet wine
served up in clay, so costly! all embossed,
and cups of beechwood smoothed with yellow wax.

So now they had short respite, till the fire
might yield the heated course.

Again they served
new wine, but mellow; and a second course:
sweet nuts, dried figs and wrinkled dates and plums,
and apples fragrant, in wide baskets heaped;
and, in a wreath of grapes from purple vines,
concealed almost, a glistening honey-comb;
and all these orchard dainties were enhanced
by willing service and congenial smiles.

But while they served, the wine-bowl often drained,
as often was replenished, though unfilled,
and Baucis and Philemon, full of fear,
as they observed the wine spontaneous well,
increasing when it should diminish, raised
their hands in supplication, and implored
indulgence for their simple home and fare.
And now, persuaded by this strange event
such visitors were deities unknown,
this aged couple, anxious to bestow
their most esteemed possession, hastily
began to chase the only goose they had—

> the faithful guardian of their little home—
> which they would kill and offer to the Gods.
> But swift of wing, at last it wearied them,
> and fled for refuge to the smiling Gods.[74]

Ovid describes in delightful detail the lengths to which the hosts go in offering hospitality to the strangers, and upon discovering their divinity due to the magically refilling wine jar, offer their goose, "their most esteemed possession." Citing the example of Philemon and Baucis, Giegerich writes of hospitality toward the gods as *an expression of loving*. The foundation of such loving is the generous provision of sanctuary to the divine, in whatever form is presented.

> Love makes the difference. . . . Love made it possible for the hosts to surrender and to splurge. By letting go, by freely sacrificing the goose to their guests, Philemon and Baucis fed the moment with love and with the rich fat and round wholeness of this bird.[75]

What if the weary travelers take the form of unwelcome strangers wandering in our internal landscape, as figures of our own unconscious shadow? Can our love extend to these? While the gods found refuge in Philemon and Baucis's hospitality, the much more common attitude of "No Entry" mimics the ego's hostility toward its shadowy projections, armed with defenses to protect itself from the unknown "beggars" of the unconscious. Jung poignantly describes such hostility:

> That I feed the hungry, that I forgive an insult, that I love my enemy in the name of Christ—all these are undoubtedly great virtues. What I do unto the least of my brethren, that I do unto Christ. But what if I should discover that the least among them all, the poorest of all the beggars, the most impudent of all the offenders, the very enemy himself—that these are within me, and that I myself stand in need of the alms of my own kindness, that I myself am the enemy who must be loved—what then? Then, as a rule, the whole truth of Christianity is reversed; there is then no longer any question of love or long suffering; we say to the brother within us "Raca," ["Revenge!"] and condemn and rage against ourselves. We hide him from the world; we refuse to admit ever having met this least among the lowly in ourselves. Had it been God himself who drew near to us in this despicable form, we should have denied him a thousand times before a single cock had crowed.[76]

Were not also the gods-in-disguise coldly denied "a thousand houses" before finally welcomed at the home of Philemon and Baucis? To say instead to the least of these within, not "Raca" but "Welcome" reflects true forgiveness as psychological hospitality. That it occurs one time in a thousand speaks to its extraordinary rarity.

Love, as it relates to the unwelcome presences of the personal unconscious, is also advocated by Hillman as "the cure" of the shadow's affliction:

> The cure of the shadow is a problem of love. How far can our love extend to the broken and ruined parts of ourselves, the disgusting and perverse? How much charity and compassion have we for our own weakness and sickness? How far can we build an inner society on the principle of love, allowing a place for everyone? And I use the term "cure of the shadow" to emphasize the importance of love. If . . . we approach ourselves to cure those fixed intractable congenital weaknesses of stubbornness and blindness, of meanness and cruelty, of sham and pomp, we come up against the need for a new way of being altogether, in which the ego must serve and listen to and cooperate with a host of shadowy unpleasant figures and discover an ability to love even the least of these traits.[77]

Love brought to our weaknesses relativizes the ego, making possible a position of generosity and hospitality. Hillman is here describing what forgiveness as hospitality means in the form of *self*-forgiveness. Forgiveness may also hold the possibility of reconnection with the soul insofar as our hospitality toward our shadow aspects results in the release of guilt, as illustrated in a patient's dream described by Whitmont:

> I was given an ugly filthy rag. At first I would not even touch it. But finally after long hesitation I accepted it. As soon as I touched it, it turned into a beautiful snow-white shining cloth.[78]

Whitmont notes that the nature of such a transformation is akin to

> the unfathomable mystery of *grace and redemption*, forever beyond our human grasp yet entering miraculously into our limited human lives. Symbolically, it is represented in the imagery of individuation, such as finding the elixir of life, drinking the draft of immortality. The holy marriage, the incarnation of the Holy Spirit, the birth of the Divine Child or the Redeemer all depict it.[79]

Forgiveness as hospitality would entail at attitude of "letting be, receiving hospitably"[80] *whatever it is* that presents itself, granting fantasy images "the dignity of an objective reality."[81] Such an attitude of radical hospitality is also present in the alchemical "mystical peregrination," which aim is to "understand all parts of the world, to achieve the greatest possible extension of consciousness."[82] Yet care must be taken not to reduce the notion to a mindless practice. Giegerich clarifies,

> Such hospitality is not literal hospitality—spending a lot on parties, having an open house for anybody; nor is it the Christian ethic of "love of

> thy neighbor." It is the devotion to the present and its hidden presence, its face and voice: it is the reception and the feeding of the image.[83]

Forgiveness as an expression of hospitality would thus oblige mindedness, openness, and attentiveness to the *present moment*, to whatever fantasy image, thought, or feeling reveals itself before us in its particularity. As Baucis and Philemon discovered, "it is hospitality to whatever present moment may knock on our door that allows this moment to reveal its divine radiance."[84]

While Jesus's entreaty for forgiveness as "allowing" is an expression of the most radical graciousness imaginable—he "permits" a place for unconsciousness in its most literal and deadly form—to be hospitable to the gods does not oblige us to enthusiastically say "yes!" to or "embrace" them:

> It has nothing to do with an ego action or attitude; what we think about them and whether we are for or against them is not all that important . . . they want something else, something at the same time more simple and more fundamental, more radical. *They want to be ontologically acknowledged and respected.*[85]

Indeed, Jesus's forgiveness does not deny nor alter the *facts* of literal reality; after all, "the stranger . . . is already inside the house."[86] Forgiveness as hospitality is a thoughtful expression of loving that "allows" for and acknowledges the existence of shadow elements, permitting them entry into conscious awareness, and if need be, bearing and suffering them as opposed to denying and turning them away.

If Jesus is seen not as a man but as a manifestation of pure consciousness, then his request for forgiveness on behalf of his murderers is not seen as so radical; it is rather the "suffering" and "allowing" of his crucifixion as an uroboric soul movement, the snake eating its own tail, in service of the soul releasing itself into an even deeper truth.

The Self and the Ego

The Self emerges in awareness often by way of the dissolution of the ego, announcing itself via the termination or "death" of one's self-image as projections are seen through and fade away. This experience is documented alchemically as the *nigredo*:

> The integration of contents that were always unconscious and projected involves a serious lesion of the ego. Alchemy expresses this through the symbols of death, mutilation, or poisoning.[87]

Similarly, von Franz describes a Turkish fairy tale in which the heroine, with the help of a magic pony—initially interpreted as her healthy instinct—manages to escape from an evil demon. "After the conquest of the demon, however, the little horse asks to be ritually slaughtered," writes von Franz. "The slaughter means an 'analysis' (dissolution) of instinct, which had hitherto functioned unconsciously, [and] the development of an inner readiness to accept the archetype of the Self."[88] The pony *requests* its own death at the hands of the self, signaling a conscious willingness to undergo what is necessary to convert consciousness at a structural level.

Likewise, the integration of projections involves a profound syntactical (structural) change or advance in consciousness. Such a change is

> very closely related to the phenomenon of deep moral change, of the Pauline *metanoia* (Galatians 6), of a mental and moral about face toward a new goal, which for the most part is experienced as coming from within. *Metanoia* is a change of character, even of mentality, through which the entire personality is renewed and altered in such a way that it is irreversible.[89]

A deep change resulting in an irreversible "mental and moral about face" is aligned with the phenomenal experience of true forgiveness. As we have seen, *metanoia* results from the accomplishment of *teshuva*, alchemical purification, absolute negation—and true forgiveness. All involve a "serious lesion" in the form of "dissolution," "annihilation," "dismemberment," "devouring," etc., of the originating ego-consciousness and a (re-)birth into a new state of awareness. This suggests the inaccessibility of true forgiveness to a still pristine and *uninitiated* consciousness. Similarly, the forged innocence of Hillman's heart of beauty emerges only in a consciousness that has achieved a "whitened" state, or alchemical *albedo*, after a brutal and annihilating psychological dark night of the soul. Jesus's most radical entreaty for forgiveness occurred during his crucifixion, a literal *nigredo*.

Jung interprets Jesus's crucifixion as a symbol of the dismemberment and death experienced by the ego as it is confronted by and held in excruciating tension between the opposing poles of the personality. According to Jung, the "great symbol" of Jesus's crucifixion between two thieves tells us that

> the progressive development and differentiation of consciousness leads to an ever more menacing awareness of the conflict and involves nothing less than a crucifixion of the ego, its agonizing suspension between two opposites.[90]

For Jung, the symbol of the crucifix is "a prototype and an 'eternal' truth" for one on the path of individuation:

> Nobody who finds himself on the road to wholeness [as opposed to perfection] can escape that characteristic suspension which is the meaning of crucifixion. For he will infallibly run into things that thwart and "cross" him: first, the thing he has no wish to be (the shadow); second,

> the thing he is not (the "other", the individual reality of the "You"); and third, his psychic non-ego (the collective unconscious). . . . This process underlies the whole *opus*.[91]

The meaning of the crucifixion for Jung thus signifies that of individuation, "the process underlying the whole opus," in which the ego must be crucified in the excruciating confrontation with one's own shadow as projections are acknowledged.

The Western Soul's *Opus*

For Giegerich as well, Jesus's life and crucifixion can be seen to symbolize the *magnum opus*, though not in the sense of a *person's* individuation. Rather they illustrate the fundamental dialectical process of the *soul's* logical unfolding and ultimately coming home to itself, "as the portrayal of the soul's *self-relation* and *self-unfolding*."[92] Here, the crucifixion symbolizes the final stages of Christ's *kenôsis*, signifying a process in which "Christ relentlessly gave up his divinity."[93] The arc of the process of the incarnation of God into man is described by the following biblical passage,[94] in which Jesus Christ,

> although he originally existed in the form of God,
> did not cling to his being-equal-to-God as his inalienable privilege,
> but emptied himself [of it] (*ekenôsen*, from which comes the term *kenôsis*),
> took the form of a slave, having been born like a man
> and living like a man, he humbled himself and was obedient to the point of death, indeed, [a criminal's] death on a cross.
>
> (Phil. 2:5–8)

Understood psychologically, the images we are given of Jesus's life and crucifixion reveal a manner of responding to "evil" dialectically, or from a soul perspective. According to Giegerich,

> these images portray a certain logic, the dialectical logic of how to relate to and overcome evil as well as the evils, the injustices and wrongs of the world: not by powerful conquest and subjugation, not by rejection and condemnation, but conversely by, with resistanceless sufferance, allowing them to *be*, indeed, even embracing them, and *ipso facto* unrelentingly exposing oneself to them, letting them permeate oneself. . . . [T]his is first of all a concept, an insight, a truth on a very deep and remote soul level. It is a *logic* to be comprehended, not a maxim to be acted out. It is the logic of Love.[95]

In this sense, the crucifixion represents less an annihilating pulling apart of horizontal opposites than a symbol of the *vertical* nature of the soul. "The Christian thought of 'incarnation' is vertical, the dynamic move of a consistent going under all the way to the bitter end."[96] Giegerich cites Jesus as one who "carries" and bears the world's griefs and sorrows.

> [Christ] bowed down so low that he was beneath the evil of the world and could shoulder it. This is clearly a vertical relation. The lamb is of course the image of absolute innocence, sinlessness. But this sinlessness does not shirk away from evil, projecting it out so that it receives a separate existence as Satan or the Antichrist. No, it gets involved with it, burdens itself with it, bears it. And the (criminal's) death on the Cross is the mode in which this idea of bowing beneath evil and shouldering it is "practically" performed, that is, how it becomes a reality.[97]

Giegerich makes a very interesting point in terms of projection, observing that Jesus does not project "evil" out "so that it receives a separate existence"; he does not position himself "horizontally" at odds with darkness as Jung interprets. Rather than shunning evil and striving for righteousness or perfection, Jesus actively engages with the shadow:

> The opposition of good and evil is . . . not a concern of Christ's preaching. On the contrary, he radically overcomes this harsh opposition. . . . "Son, be of good cheer, thy sins be forgiven thee" (Matthew 9:2). Christ has come to save the sinners, not the righteous. There will be more joy in heaven about one sinner who repents that about ninety-nine righteous ones.[98]

Repentance signals the integration of the shadow as opposed to the "righteous" person unconscious of or in denial of their shadow. We have seen the transformative effect of true repentance—alchemical *mundificatio, teshuva, absolute negation*—and its power to induce rebirth at the syntactic or structural level, bringing about an experience of innocence and freedom from sin. Thus this sinlessness "does not shirk away from evil, projecting it out. . . . No, it gets involved with it, burdens itself with it, bears it."[99]

Christ's sinlessness as such is a function not of his inherent divinity, but rather an *earned* status accomplished through his conscious negation of *this* world in lieu of his "true" kingdom, which is spiritual. Christ's sinlessness is

> the product of his logical act of negation of the devil's splendid offers and his realizing that "My kingdom is NOT of this world." Christ's purity and his being free of darkness are logically generated by his pushing off from "this world" by his refusal to fall for the tempting idea of success in the world. Christ chose the path of logical negativity.[100]

The "path of logical negativity" is a fundamental theme of Christianity as reflected in the following statements:

> Do good to them that hate you.
>
> (Matthew 5:44)

> For my strength is made perfect in weakness.
>
> (2 Cor. 12:9)

> If any man come to me, and hate not his father, and mother, and wife, and children, and brethren, and sisters, yea, and his own life also, he cannot be my disciple.
>
> (Luke 12:46)

> Love your enemies.
>
> (Luke 6:27)

These declarations are not logical on the level of *this* world; they make no sense within the substantial, material world, which meaning is contained solely within itself and is thus unable to acknowledge much less comprehend any other valid "world" in which "strength could be made perfect in weakness" or enemies could be loved. Yet despite this, their performance has a profound and transformative effect on the ego level *in* this world. Their presence or reality in the world tends to indicate a logical advance in consciousness. True forgiveness, in its rejection of ego concerns—justice, revenge, power—also follows the *path of logical negativity*, as it fundamentally negates the logic of the ego, reflecting instead the logic of the soul or Self, and is indicative of expanded awareness beyond the ego level.

Christ, as a manifestation of the Self, signifies Love (the ultimate reality of soul), the Self's ground of being as the process of the union of opposites. The Love offered by the Self cannot be threatened by *anything* on the semantic level (as no "thing" exists) and is immune to attack, as St. Paul reminds us:

> Nothing therefore can come between us and the love of Christ, even if we are troubled or worried, or being persecuted, or lacking food or clothes, or being threatened or even attacked. . . . For I am certain of this: neither death nor life, no angel, no prince, nothing that exists, nothing still to come, not any power, or height or depth, nor any created thing, can ever come between us and the love of God made visible in Christ.
>
> (Romans 8:35, 38–39)

Here we see again the "irrelevance" of forgiveness on the level of the Self, as no attack is "real" or possible or valid on that level, which is the non-substantial, infinite, and uroboric, unified realm of thought. Paul's rejoinder attempts to *extend* that reality to the semantic level, such that consciousness can begin to relate at the syntactic level while still existing on the semantic level, thus greatly expanding consciousness such that it can hold awareness of both the literal and symbolic levels of psyche.

But Paul does not just remind us of the presence of both—*he gives primacy to the syntactic level, to the absolute-negative logic of the soul.* This poses an enormous *threat* to consciousness on the semantic or literal level—which then is summoned by Christ (soul) to forgive the threat and subsequent attacks on the ego's reality by the absolutely negative soul.

This ultimately leads us back to the question of the meaning and role of forgiveness to psyche. On the level of soul, forgiveness *has* no meaning because there is nothing to forgive, no substantiality or content to be attacked or threatened. Forgiveness has meaning only on the semantic or ego level and in fact becomes relevant whenever the two levels threaten to come into contact. At the same time, forgiveness *spans* the vertical and horizontal divide of consciousness in that it is attendant when consciousness advances from the semantic to the syntactic level; when the reality of the soul is granted primacy over the reality of the ego, when the semantic level is recognized as secondary and the realization dawns that "*nothing that exists* . . . can ever come between us and the love of God," true forgiveness must naturally (logically) follow.

The Self as Pure Process

According to von Franz, "the Self appears as that aspect of the personality which puts an end to all projections."[101] This is due to the fact that when the "symbolical products" of the Self begin to arise from the unconscious, they no longer appear in personified form—that is, there are no *images* associated with the emergence of the Self. The Self *transcends* form altogether; it finds its reality in pure thought.[102] Thus the Self is experienced not in a substantial or positivistic way, but as the dialectical *process* of the unification of the opposites, whose unification would *dissolve* semantic content (instincts, fantasies, figures, ideas, opinions, one's self-definition, etc.). Giegerich clarifies and extends Jung's idea of the Self, describing it as a process:

> Because "Self" refers to the innermost subjectivity of the subject it cannot be represented. It cannot be symbolized. It can only be experienced, or to be more exact, it is in itself experience, the process of the union of opposites, the process of a logical, dialectical relation. Since it is experience (has the nature of a process of experience), it cannot be content, not a phenomenon, not something that we merely happen to be experiencing. The moment it became a content or image, it would cease to be the Self.[103]

The Self as *the process of the union of opposites* resides within a greatly expanded perspective availing the comprehension of one's reality as inclusive of *all that one is* and also of *all that one is not*—within the unified awareness of both states together.

Giegerich describes this complex dialectical relation of Self as "the process of the union of the opposites" in the following passage:

> The phrase "union of opposites" is an abbreviation. If one unfolds the complex logical relation implied by this abbreviation, one would have

> to say: the unity of the unity and the opposition of the opposites. I will take this statement apart into a sequence of several sentences. 1. I am not identical with myself, I am torn apart, I am my own opposite. I am a living contradiction. 2. Nevertheless, this Other who is my own opposite is nobody else than I myself. I am both myself and my opposite. In this sense I am united with my opposite. 3. I am the unity of the first statement about my being a contradiction and of the second statement about being united with my own Other. The realized Self is that status of consciousness that consciously exists as the complexity of this logical relation, but relation not in the sense of a static structure, but as the fluidity of a dialectical movement, as process and performance.[104]

To partake in an experience of the Self then is to recognize that there is no "other" of which one is not a part. It is an infinitely expansive yet intimately uroboric relation to oneself and the world. This idea is reflected in the teachings of the Barbelo Gnostics, in which a prophetess sees a great man (God) and hears him say:

> I am thou, and thou art I, and wherever thou art, there am I, and I am scattered in all things, and from wherever thou wilt thou canst gather me, but in gathering me thou gatherest thyself.[105]

With regard to forgiveness, the question would quickly arise as to "who" is forgiving "whom," and for what? An external "attack" by "another" cannot be comprehended on the level of the Self, which would experience itself as "the attacker," "the victim," *and* their unity, because

> the Self means that in myself and as myself I *am* both myself *and* my other. I am also the opposite of myself. There *must* not be a literal Other, if I am to become conscious of the fact that I am *myself* my other, *myself* my own opposite and thus divided from myself. And only if I have become conscious of myself as the irreconcilable opposition of myself and my Other, and at the same time conscious of the fact that this opposite Other is also *myself*, did the union of opposites occur and did I *ipso facto* advance to the status of Self.[106]

From the perspective of the Self, all activity would be perceived as a movement of the soul's further release into it*self*. If I am attacked by an "Other" who, under the auspices of the Self is none other than myself, then the need for forgiveness dissolves.

Because the Self is unrepresentable and cannot take the form of content, it comes into existence only to the extent that one can raise or expand one's own consciousness to the level of the Self, on which one experiences and has comprehended oneself as the complex movement of the dialectic [the unity of the unity and opposition of the opposites]. With this accomplishment, "we can understand what is meant when Jung said that the birth of the Self presupposes the death of the ego."[107] Von Franz notes that when contact with the Self begins, "the ego is then confronted with the necessity of sacrificing itself" and in fact, insight into the nature or essence of the Self

> is purchased only at the price of great suffering that wipes out the worldly prejudices and preoccupations of the ego, thereby forcing it into a change of attitude. . . . In the encounter with the Self there emerges a goal that points to the conclusive ending of all projections, namely, to death.[108]

We see again that an encounter with the Self brings about a *metanoia*, a transformation at the structural or syntactical level of consciousness. According to Giegerich,

> I am ego as long as I am defined as an existing being and consequently have as my prime interest my self-preservation—not only literal physical self-preservation, not only emotional self-preservation, but also logical self-preservation, i.e., the preservation of the very definition of me as existing entity or being. Becoming Self, by contrast, means that this definition sort of dives into, and drowns in, the logic of the play between the psychic opposites as not first and dominant reality.[109]

"Becoming Self" dislodges one's identification with the ego (as self-preservation) as "first and dominant reality," thus rendering the need for forgiveness unnecessary, neither here nor there, as the need for forgiveness emerges only to the extent that one perceives a threatening personal attack upon one's self (literal, emotional, or logical). "Becoming Self" means to dis-identify with the fixed and limited notion of one's self-definition and instead experience oneself as *process*, as the greatly expanded dialectical play that is the union of opposites, which by definition includes the very "other" who had been perceived as attacking the self. In this sense, the Self as the "process of the union of the opposites" mirrors forgiveness as *itself*, as *that very process* that reconciles and unites the opposites. Forgiveness/Self *is* the eternal ongoing dialectical logical mediating process on the level of soul that "makes peace between the enemies or elements, that they may love one another in a meet embrace,"[110] all the while "knowing" that the concept of "enemies" has no meaning at the level of the Self.

Forgiveness and the Soul

In our study of the early usage of forgiveness in the New Testament, the orientation has been for the most part from the human being's perspective; we have explored what forgiveness as the dissolution of projections might mean for our relationships to others and to the world. We have considered what it would mean *for us* to bring hospitality and generosity to our shadow aspects and to the fantasy images of the soul, no matter how unwelcome they may be. The alchemical processes believed to reflect the psychological processes of the maturation of the psyche were also grounded, for Jung, in the human being's personal journey of individuation. The assumption, naturally, is that the figure of Jesus, in his speaking about forgiveness, is talking to *us*, to our human egos. If we now take a precisely *psychological* perspective, our orientation pivots from horizontal—what forgiveness means for us—to vertical, or what forgiveness means in and of itself.

We now begin an exploration of the psychological nature of forgiveness with a dedicated focus on the soul's logical life. To understand the soul's relation to forgiveness, we need to gain a sense of the *teleology* of consciousness at large. What is the nature of the soul's work? In what ways does forgiveness matter to the soul, if at all? As we have seen, forgiveness has no meaning at the level of soul because there is no substantive thing or other to forgive; however, we may discover forgiveness's intrinsic meaning in the context of the soul's continuing unfolding.

What might the unfolding of the soul's life be? For Giegerich, the ongoing process of the integration and realization of Christ's kenôsis, signifying the soul's homecoming into its truth, or to know itself again directly as absolute negativity—as Spirit and Love—is the Western soul's *opus magnum*.[111] This ongoing process of integration and realization can be observed to follow a particular uroboric movement that makes itself apparent in the history of consciousness, one symbol of which is the great mythic river Okeanos.

The *Telos* of the Soul

The myth of Father Okeanos, signifying the great self-generative river at the outermost edge of the world from which springs all life and to which all life flows, "the mythic image of *interiority as such*, of *inner infinity*,"[112] provides an image of the soul "coming home to" or released into itself. Okeanos, "as movement that streams back into itself and thus is circular, uroboric, *self-reflective* and *self-referential*, it *is* self" and "its source is at the same time its mouth . . . its beginning is its end and vice versa."[113] "Forgive and you shall be forgiven," points to the uroboric, self-generative and self-reflective nature of forgiveness, implicating it as a soul movement.

The soul's "homecoming" is described in multiple historical movements by Giegerich, with the modern age expressing the fifth and final movement, wherein:

> The soul wants to become explicitly apparent and be objectively known *as* what it is—absolute negativity and interiority. The interiority that formerly, in myth, had been displayed and acted out as the soulful character of the world out there is now itself to be interiorized into itself.[114]

Describing the *initial* and early historical movements of the soul, Giegerich imagines a shift from the original stage—that of fully-contained and absolutely self-enclosed circular movement—to the second as an attempt of the soul to break free and "to release itself from the ideal sphere into otherness and to enter the real world, the world of nature."[115] This second type of soul movement

> is what in psychology is called projection, though of course not projection as people's doing, but as projections by Okeanos, the all surrounding soul, itself. It is the dressing up of nature as a "cosmos," an ordered world of beauty and divine dignity.[116]

The soul-projection of the natural world, "cloaked in mythical garments,"[117] thus comes into being as a movement of the soul: "[W]hat is in fact the self-depiction of the inner nature and logic of the soul appears as (as if it indeed were) the real outer world itself, nature, the cosmos—the veil of Maya according to Brahmanism."[118]

The third soul movement involves the participation of human beings through sacrifice and rituals, in particular,

> incisive, invasive acts performed by man with which he cuts in to and imparts himself on, the natural course of events. The prototype of this act may be Kronos's outrageous disruption of the eternal *gamos* of the World Parents, by castrating Father Heaven with his sickle and stemming him high up.[119]

As explored in Chapter 2, all sacrificial slaughterings "as diverse as their particular character and meanings may be, contain as one of the aspects that they reenact this violent deed,"[120] the murder of the father. While the first soul movement displays Okeanos as the self-contained uroboric circle or the soul, soul as pure thought, "self-moving, self forming activity," [121] the second movement extends it into the mythic world as a whole. In this third movement, the soul's further emergence depends upon "man's self-risk through coming forward, facing nature, willfully de-ciding (from Latin *caedere*, to kill) and thus also exposing himself."[122] Sacrifice thus signifies the birth of the soul into the consciousness of man.

The fourth movement of the soul is expressed as *initiation*, or "the entrance into a new logical status of consciousness,"[123] entailing the integration of the *meaning of the soul* gained from the prior stages into *individual consciousness*. Initiation allows that which was at first externalized—expressed by the need of the soul to "sink itself into the medium of the natural"[124]—to "come home to consciousness and through this homecoming be filled with fresh lifeblood."[125] The human ego-personality emerges in this stage and is able to interiorize the soul truths it has gained through its initiation or direct exposure to them, holding these truths as personal treasures.

It is the fifth and final movement of the soul, what Giegerich calls the alchemy of history, which reflects the goal of the alchemical opus, or the soul's homecoming. The final stage is the ultimate *opus contra naturam*; it requires the *release* of all semantic contents of consciousness and the decomposition of the external world as such. For man, this includes not only the natural world, which is finally itself in peril, but "all his ideologies, ideals and values, and later the substantiality of the notion of 'conscious subject' itself including its newly acquired inflated sense of importance as 'an individual' and 'a personality'"[126]—all would be dissolved and released as a movement of the soul coming home to itself.

Forgiveness as release (*apolyete*) may be seen to correlate to this final soul movement, the ultimate *opus contra naturam*. For what most often is the object of forgiveness but the offending by another of one's ideologies, ideals, and values, and the individual as a personality? To forgive is thus to consciously recognize and acknowledge the meaninglessness and soullessness of these semantic contents of consciousness, to abandon their worth, and in so doing, release and relinquish their substantiality and value as positivistic realities. Forgiving signifies a resonance between the *opus parvum*[127] and *opus magnum*. As the literal, substantial world is negated and dissolved—reflecting the relentless interiorization of the positivity of the empirical experience that occurs through the process of absolute negation—its underlying truth is revealed.

What then will the soul discover about itself when it is finally and fully released into its truth? Giegerich imagines the soul would ultimately recognize itself as Love:

> If the process of the negative interiorization into itself would have been completed, "the soul" would probably have become apparent as being Love (with a capital L). Love would be nothing else but Okeanos from which we started out, but Okeanos finally fully interiorized into itself and thus come home to itself after its former exile in the imagination's sensory world. . . . [I]nfinite Love as objectively existing Concept (the self-comprehension of the mind), Love as absolute logical negativity, fluidity, interiority, Love as "self," inner infinity.[128]

Forgiveness can be seen here to indeed serve a truly psychological function: facilitating the release of the soul into itself so that it may know itself again directly as "absolute logical negativity, fluidity, interiority," or Love.

Notes

1. C. Knapp, *The Classical World* (Philadelphia: Classical Association of the Atlantic States, 1918), 12.
2. Jeanette Bicknell, "The Individuality in the Deed: Hegel on Forgiveness and Reconciliation," *Bulletin of the Hegel Society of Great Britain*, 37/38 (1998): 77–78.

3. Bicknell, "The Individuality in the Deed," 77–78.
4. Jennifer Wright Knust, "Jesus' Conditional Forgiveness," in C.L. Griswold & D. Konstan (Eds.), *Ancient Forgiveness: Classical, Judaic, and Christian* (Cambridge: Cambridge University Press, 2012), 176–194.
5. Knust, "Jesus' Conditional Forgiveness," 138.
6. Knust, "Jesus' Conditional Forgiveness," 177.
7. Knust, "Jesus' Conditional Forgiveness," 177.
8. Knust, "Jesus' Conditional Forgiveness," 180.
9. Knust, "Jesus' Conditional Forgiveness," 184.
10. Knust, "Jesus' Conditional Forgiveness,"194.
11. Knust, "Jesus' Conditional Forgiveness,"194.
12. Wolfgang Giegerich, *What Is Soul?* (New Orleans, LA: Spring Journal, Inc., 2012).
13. In a rather awkward (and humorous) error, the 1972 edition of Edinger's book contains the word "bother" instead of "brother" in the citation from Matthew in E.F. Edinger, *Ego and archetype* (Boston: Shambhala, 1972), p. 133.
14. http://www.biblos.com/luke/6–37.htm.
15. Hannah Arendt, *The Human Condition* (1st ed.) (Chicago: University of Chicago Press, 1998), 236.
16. Lucy Allais, "Wiping the Slate Clean: The Heart of Forgiveness," *Philosophy & Public Affairs*, 36, no. 1 (2008): 67–68.
17. Arendt, *The Human Condition*, 236, emphasis added.
18. Wolfgang Giegerich, "Jung's Thought of the Self in the Light of Its Underlying Experiences," in *The Neurosis of Psychology* (Vol. 1, pp. 171–190) (New Orleans, LA: Spring Journal Books, 2005), 187.
19. Wolfgang Giegerich, "God Must Not Die!," *Spring Journal*, 84 (2010): 15.
20. C.G. Jung, "General Aspects of Dream Psychology," 264 [CW 8, para. 507].
21. Marie Louise von Franz, *Projection and Re-Collection in Jungian Psychology* (London: Open Court, 1980), 28.
22. C.G. Jung *General Aspects of Dream Psychology*, 272 [*CW* 8, para. 519].
23. von Franz, *Projection and Re-Collection*, 9.
24. von Franz, *Projection and Re-Collection*, 11.
25. von Franz, *Projection and Re-Collection.*
26. Wolfgang Giegerich, "The Leap after the Throw," in *The Neurosis of Psychology* (Vol. 1, pp. 69–96) (New Orleans, LA: Spring Journal Books, 2005), 84.
27. Wolfgang Giegerich, "First Shadow then Anima," in *Soul Violence* (Vol 3, pp. 77–11) (New Orleans, LA: Spring Journal Books, 2008), 98.
28. von Franz, *Projection and Re-Collection.*
29. http://biblesuite.com/greek/1492.htm.
30. http://biblos.com/matthew/7–2.htm.
31. Jung "General Aspects of Dream Psychology," 271 [*CW* 8, para. 516].
32. James Hillman, *The Thought of the Heart and the Soul of the World* (New York: Spring Publications, 1979/1992). Hillman was inspired by Henri Corbin's depiction of the thought of the heart as the source of *imaginatio vera.*
33. Hillman, *The Thought of the Heart*, 11.
34. Hillman, *The Thought of the Heart*, 12.
35. Hillman, *The Thought of the Heart*, 12.
36. Hillman, *The thought of the heart*, 13
37. Giegerich, *What Is Soul?*
38. Hillman, *The Thought of the Heart*, 70.
39. Hillman, *The Thought of the Heart*, 74.
40. James Hillman, *Alchemical Psychology: The Uniform Edition of the Writings of James Hillman* (Vol. 1) (Putnam, CT: Spring Publications, 2010), 158.
41. Hillman, *The Thought of the Heart*, 70.

42. Hillman, *The Thought of the Heart*, 71.
43. Wolfgang Giegerich, David L. Miller, & Greg Mogenson, *Dialectics & Analytical Psychology: The El Capitan Canyon Seminar* (New Orleans, LA: Spring Journal, Inc., 2005), 16.
44. Giegerich et al., *Dialectics & Analytical Psychology*, 16.
45. Hillman, *The Thought of the Heart*, 70.
46. Giegerich, "The Leap after the Throw," 89.
47. Giegerich, "The Leap after the Throw," 82.
48. Tom Cheetham, *Green Man, Earth Angel: The Prophetic Tradition and the Battle for the Soul of the World* (New York: State University of New York Press, 2004), 66.
49. Giegerich, "The Leap after the Throw," 84.
50. James Hillman, ed., *Senex and Puer: Uniform Edition of the Writings of James Hillman* (Vol. 3, 1st ed.) (Putnam, CT: Spring Publications, 2005).
51. Giegerich, "God Must Not Die!," 11–71.
52. von Franz, *Projection and Re-collection*, 174.
53. C.G. Jung, *Letters* (Vol. 1) ed. by G. Adler, trans. by R.F.C. Hull (Princeton, NJ: Princeton University Press, 1973), 298.
54. Hillman, *Alchemical Psychology*, 158.
55. Hillman, *Alchemical Psychology*, 158.
56. Hillman, *Alchemical Psychology*, 151.
57. Hillman, *The Thought of the Heart*, 43.
58. Hillman, *The Thought of the Heart*, 42.
59. James Hillman, "Anima Mundi: The Return of the Soul to the World," in *The Thought of the Heart and the Soul of the World* (pp. 88–130) (New York: Spring Publications, 1992) (Original work published 1982), 107.
60. Henry Corbin, *The Man of Light in Iranian Sufism* (New York: Omega Publications, 1994).
61. Henry Corbin, *The Voyage and the Messenger: Iran and Philosophy* (Berkeley, CA: North Atlantic Books, 1998), xx.
62. Corbin, *The Voyage and the Messenger: Iran and Philosophy*, xxxii. With regard to revelation, Hillman notes the difference between a psychology that has consciousness as its aim as opposed to therapy as the love of soul. In the first, the instruction is to "Know Thyself," which, while clearly a worthy goal, focuses on the intellect, thus protecting the ego and concealing its pathology from outer scrutiny. In the second, however, the instruction becomes "'Reveal Thyself', which, as Hillman observes, "is the same as the commandment to love, since nowhere are we more revealed than in our loving." Again we are reminded of the connection between the apprehension of true reality, in which defenses, obstruction, and protections are laid aside, and the presence of love. The revelatory *metanoia* that dissolves barriers impeding the apprehension of the real we may thus call *forgiveness*: "Look gently on your brother, and behold the world in which perception of your hate has been transformed into a world of love." (*A Course in Miracles*, 1976/2007, p. 552, Ch 26-V-14-5).
63. James Grotstein, "Bion's 'Transformation in 'O'" and the Concept of the 'Transcendent Position,'" (1997). http://www.sicap.it/~merciai/bion/papers/grots.htm.
64. Veronica Goodchild, *Eros and Chaos* (Lake Worth, FL: Nicholas Hays, Inc., 2001), 212.
65. Hillman, *The Thought of the Heart*, 47.
66. Hillman, *The Thought of the Heart*, 47.
67. James Hillman, *A Blue Fire* (New York: Harper & Row, 1989), 85.
68. Corbin, *The Man of Light in Iranian Sufism*, 103.
69. Hillman, *The Thought of the Heart*, 39–40.

70. Hillman *A Blue Fire*, 85.
71. Hillman, *The Thought of the Heart*, 108.
72. http://biblesuite.com/greek/863.htm.
73. Ovid, Book VI, 647–650.
74. Ovid, Book VI, 612–727.
75. Wolfgang Giegerich, "Hospitality Towards the Gods," in *The Neurosis of Psychology* (Vol. 1, pp. 197–218) (New Orleans, LA: Spring Journal Books, 2005), 202.
76. C.G. Jung, "Psychotherapists or the Clergy," in R.F.C. Hull (Trans.), *The collected works of C.G. Jung* (Vol. 11, 2nd ed, pp. 488–347). Princeton, NJ: Princeton University Press, 1977) (Original work published 1932), 339 [*CW* 11, para. 520].
77. James Hillman, "The Cure of the Shadow," in C. Zweig & J. Abrams (Eds.), *Meeting the Shadow* (pp. 242–243) (New York: Penguin Group (USA) Inc, 1991).
78. E.C. Whitmont, *The Symbolic Quest* (Princeton, NJ: Princeton University Press, 1991) (Original work published 1969), 96.
79. Whitmont *The Symbolic Quest*, 96.
80. Giegerich, "Hospitality Towards the Gods," 216.
81. Giegerich, "Hospitality Towards the Gods," 217.
82. Jung, *Mysterium*, 215 [*CW* 14, para. 284].
83. Giegerich, "Hospitality Towards the Gods," 203.
84. Giegerich, "Hospitality Towards the Gods," 204.
85. Giegerich, "Hospitality Towards the Gods," 217.
86. Giegerich, "Hospitality Towards the Gods,", 216.
87. Jung, "The Psychology of the Transference," 264 [*CW* 16, para. 472].
88. von Franz, *Projection and Re-Collection,* 161.
89. von Franz, *Projection and Re-Collection*, 161.
90. C.G. Jung, "Christ, a Symbol of the Self," in R.F.C. Hull (Trans.), *The collected works of C.G. Jung* (Vol. 9ii, 2nd ed, pp. 36–71). Princeton, NJ: Princeton University Press, 1979) (Original work published 1951), 44 [CW 9ii, para. 79].
91. Jung, "The Psychology of the Transference," 262 [*CW* 16, paras. 470–471].
92. Wolfgang Giegerich, "God Must Not Die!" *Spring Journal*, 84 (Fall, 2010): 11–71, 32.
93. Giegerich, "God Must Not Die!", 21.
94. Giegerich, "God Must Not Die!", p. 21.
95. Giegerich, "God Must Not Die!", 43–44.
96. Giegerich, "God Must Not Die!", 43.
97. Giegerich, "God Must Not Die!", 43.
98. Giegerich, "God Must Not Die!", 25.
99. Giegerich, "God Must Not Die!", 43.
100. Giegerich, "God Must Not Die!", 46.
101. von Franz, *Projection and Re-Collection*, 160.
102. Wolfgang Giegerich, "Jung's *Thought* of the Self in the Light of Its Underlying Experience," in *The Neurosis of Psychology* (Vol. 1, pp. 171–189) (New Orleans, LA: Spring Journal Books, 2005) (Original work published in 2001).
103. Giegerich, "Jung's *Thought* of the Self," 182.
104. Giegerich, "Jung's *Thought* of the Self," 183.
105. as cited in von Franz, *Projection and Re-Collection*, p. 171.
106. Giegerich, "Jung's *Thought* of the Self," 182–183.
107. Giegerich, "Jung's *Thought* of the Self," 183.
108. von Franz, *Projection and Re-Collection*, 158.
109. Giegerich, "Jung's *Thought* of the Self," 184–185.
110. "Tractatus aureus," *Theatrum Chemicum*, IV, 691.

111. Giegerich, "God Must Not Die!", 57.
112. Wolfgang Giegerich, "The Movement of the Soul," in *The Soul Always Thinks* (Vol. IV, pp. 307–323) (New Orleans, LA: Spring Journal, Inc., 2010) (Original work published in 2005), 312.
113. Giegerich, "The Movement of the Soul," 308.
114. Giegerich, "The Movement of the Soul," 319.
115. Giegerich, "The Movement of the Soul," 311.
116. Giegerich, "The Movement of the Soul," 312.
117. Giegerich, "The Movement of the Soul," 312.
118. Giegerich, "The Movement of the Soul," 313.
119. Giegerich, "The Movement of the Soul," 314.
120. Giegerich, "The Movement of the Soul," 314.
121. James Hillman, *Anima: An Anatomy of a Personified Notion* (New York: Spring, 1985), 146.
122. Giegerich, "The Movement of the Soul," 314.
123. Wolfgang Giegerich, *The Soul's Logical Life* (Frankfurt: Peter Lang, GmbH, 2008), 25.
124. Giegerich, "The Movement of the Soul," 349.
125. Giegerich, "The Movement of the Soul," 349.
126. Giegerich, "The Movement of the Soul," 321.
127. The *opus parvum* signifies one's personal evolution of consciousness, or the "little work" of individuation in contrast to the great work of the soul, or *opus magnum*.
128. Giegerich, "The Movement of the Soul," 323.

6 The Logic of Forgiveness

Is Forgiveness Psychological?

We have seen how the phenomenon of true forgiveness brings about profound *psychological* transformation. It would appear strange, then, that the matter of forgiveness has been largely neglected by depth psychology. Freud and Jung did not write about the topic, nor did any other major authorities in the field.[1] Whereas in recent years research and literature in mainstream psychology on the phenomenon of forgiveness has expanded dramatically (in addition to a plethora of self-help books and seminars on the topic), its omission as a serious topic of depth psychological study is curious. As we have seen, forgiveness would seem a contradiction, a "madness of the impossible," because, simply put, it both posits and absolves an offense; sin and innocence are mutually constituted—a logical impossibility. Here we are reminded of Jung's transcendent function, which, in holding the tension of two opposites, bestows a *reconciling* symbol.[2] James Hillman describes the alchemical process of "silvering," where, from an innocent white, through a grueling and putrefying *nigredo* process, we witness the emergence of a second, purer white—a paradox of a *forged innocence*.[3] Indeed, the underlying structure of forgiveness reveals a complexity and character remarkably suited for depth psychological study.

The omission of the concept of forgiveness as a serious topic of depth psychological study may have its basis in the idea that forgiveness does not *belong* in psychology. Given the moral/ethical character of forgiveness and the emphasis of forgiveness in Christianity and other faiths, it is typically seen as more appropriately addressed by religious communities, pastoral psychology, philosophy, and political theory, than depth psychology. Psychoanalytic literature deems forgiving to be generally suspect due to its tendency to unwittingly serve as a repressive defensive structure against conflict; forgiveness is here reduced to an implied masochistic reaction formation. The clear *interpersonal* and *behavioral* nature of forgiveness also puts it squarely outside the bounds of depth psychological study.[4] These reasons support the claim that the notion of forgiveness is unpsychological (i.e., forgiveness does not belong to psychology).

Indeed, how could forgiveness, which in its very *definition* would require a perpetrating "other" as its object, have a genuine place in psychology proper, at the objective level of soul that knows no betraying other, but only itself? For psychology, the soul is uroboric, its logical life existing as *self*-expression, *self*-representation, *self*-portrayal.[5] In psychology, there *is* no external other. As Giegerich observes:

> Anger, fury, the wish for revenge or compensation, etc. are unpsychological, namely (if I may say so) "sociological." These emotions establish and uphold the fantasy of the externality of *interpersonal* transactions between people (or between "life/fate/God" and me). But there is no 'between' between me and my pain. It is utterly mine or rather me. *I* hurt. Where the pain or wound came from is psychologically absolutely irrelevant. What was done to me by others I have to psychically make my very own, part of my self . . ., and without grudge or resentment at that. [Giegerich here adds a footnote: "This is also why forgiving is psychologically so important. It is not only morally or religiously important. It also helps me to be freed from the constraints of my complex."] I have to embrace it as my very own pain, injury, or loss and these as my new inalienable reality. No otherness. This is the only way I can become free again. Otherwise I will stay caught in the resentment against what happened to me, that is, caught in a *complex*. The flow of life will then be arrested, get stuck (in this area). I have to learn to live with my wounds and deficiencies, to integrate them into my self-definition.[6]

Giegerich deems retributive emotions as "unpsychological" because they are based in a perspective that insists on the "fantasy of the externality of *interpersonal* transactions" in lieu of the *psychological* truth that there really is no *literal* other present in the psyche. Psychologically, the "other" exists as self-generated *self-representation*. The wish for vengeance exists as an unpsychological projection of one's *own* pain.

Giegerich's footnote on the importance of forgiveness highlights forgiving as helpful not only for moral or religious reasons, but for the psychological benefit of freedom from the constraints imposed by neurotic complexes. When the "flow of life" is arrested or stuck, we find ourselves "caught in a *complex*," trapped in a *neurotic* perspective in which the offense is inflated and granted "special" status above other events, "plucked," so to speak, out of the normal flow of life and time, reinstalled in the present moment, and enlarged to enormous proportions. To attempt "forgiveness" when caught in a complex is ineffective until the offense or offending other is "seen through" and recognized as a complex. Forgiveness would then mean the *recognition* of the fundamental nature of psyche as *self*-relation, which would thus "free" one from the domination and enslavement by a perpetrating external world.

It is crucial here to read Giegerich's footnoted comment as strictly *descriptive* as opposed to *prescriptive*; it is not that one *should* embrace pain and suffering as one's own, or that one *should* forgive. Acceptance and forgiveness are rather a condition of psychological freedom. To read Giegerich prescriptively (whether he intends it or not) has us fall into the trap of the "psychic" or ego realm, where forgiving takes on a "project" nature and reifies the semantic level (i.e., maintains a focus on personal wounds inflicted by an external other, be it another person, life, fate, or God). To prescribe forgiving is ineffective at any rate, as the ego cannot *accomplish* true forgiving.[7] No one doubts the ego can certainly *encounter* forgiveness, but the event serves only as an *indicator* of a transformation of consciousness at the objective or logical level. Psychological forgiveness, we could say, is accomplished only at the level of the objective psyche or soul. Giegerich's "version" of forgiving, if read *prescriptively*, is itself "unpsychological" and accurately relegated to the status of a footnote.[8]

We are confronted here with the underlying *logical* problem of forgiveness as a psychological phenomenon. The very notion of forgiveness is characterized by a yawning chasm between two selves, the victim and the offender, I and Thou.[9] Forgiveness's inherent stipulation of an offending other (without whom there would be no-one and nothing to forgive) exposes it as a feature of modernity,[10] an indicator that "the logic of otherness rules."[11] Modern consciousness, having "been born out of" or emerged from a relatively blissful and innocent sense of embeddeness in and containment by the *anima mundi* in former times, now experiences itself as alienated from the natural world.[12] It strives desperately for meaning and a sense of belonging, encountering people and the world as no longer part of itself but as wholly "other." Giegerich observes:

> In modernity, especially since Feuerbach, the otherness of the Other has become irreducible. I and Thou (just think of Martin Buber or Emmanuel Levinas) stand vis-à-vis each other in mediation-less opposition. In the human sphere, this opposition shows concretely . . . in the unbridgeable difference between guilty perpetrator and innocent victim. "Victimization" and the corresponding notion of "traumatization" is a *logical* problem, an index of the fact that otherness rules, and thus clearly a problem and distinguishing mark of modernity.[13]

Forgiveness, in requiring the condition of otherness for its very existence, is a testament to and a symptom of this problem, *posing* as its solution. Forgiveness would seek to bridge the chasm that it itself posited, but is itself evidence of humankind's modern condition of *otherness*. In its perpetual attempt to cross the (uncrossable) chasm between victim and perpetrator, the promise of forgiveness only serves to reinforce the divide on the semantic and horizontally spacial level of the *psychic*, utterly unable to approach the vertical dimension of the uroboric, self-referential *psychological*. The hope of forgiveness inadvertently and retroactively instantiates a concretized *psychological difference* in the form of "unbridgeable difference between innocent victim and guilty perpetrator." This unbridgeable perpetrator-victim dynamic is the "concrete" or "acted out" manifestation of the psychological reality of modern consciousness. To grasp this is to comprehend and accept the *logical necessity* of the modern construct of the "unbridgeable difference between guilty perpetrator and innocent victim" in the practical sphere as the mere *acting out* of the soul's logic (otherness of the Other)—thus resulting in no *human* need (or ability) to resist or obliterate the construct[14] (i.e., to forgive).

Giegerich's characterization of the relation in modernity between perpetrator and victim as "unbridgeable" acknowledges the inherent *contradiction* of attempted reconciliation between the two. The perspective that gives rise to "otherness" is the *same* perspective that gives rise to the ego; from this side, there *is* no bridge to the other.[15] Neither is there a larger notion of soul, nor thus of the psychological difference. Here forgiveness is trapped in the psychic realm where its inherent *dialectical* aspect is misrecognized as mere paradox.

The Contradiction of True Forgiveness

The contradiction of forgiving extends to its very definition. Let us revisit Lucy Allais's observation that the attempt to cease "to hold an action against someone while continuing to regard it as wrong and as attributed to the perpetrator in the way which is necessary for there to be something to forgive" lacks coherence. "Forgiving seems to mean ceasing to blame," she continues, "but if blaming means holding the perpetrator responsible, then forgiveness requires *not* ceasing to blame, or else there will be nothing to forgive."[16] The "gracious" utterance *I forgive you* at once reifies the offense and asserts guilt while intending both "wiped clean" through the act of forgiveness.[17] This contradiction renders forgiving devoid of logic (i.e., "impossible" to the rational mind), effectively sawing off the very branch it rests upon.[18] The concept of forgiveness is not *rational* at the ordinary, everyday level of discourse or thought, on which level it is logically impossible—a fact that generally fails to discourage the inflated ego from thinking it *can* forgive (or vice versa, withhold forgiving).

To wiggle out of this contradiction, the ego co-opts it by inserting a trade: forgiveness in exchange for a reestablishment of the status quo, often under the cover of the "noble or spiritual" aims of "atonement or redemption, reconciliation, [or] salvation." Whenever forgiveness is used for the purpose of reestablishing a normality, "then the 'forgiveness' is not pure—nor is its concept."[19] Derrida is critical of the application of forgiveness to accomplish particular ends, for in the effort to correct, reconcile, repair, normalize—in fact, in the attempt to achieve any aim whatsoever—forgiveness is hijacked by the ego and cannot be considered "pure" or psychological.[20] This critique extends even to the granting of forgiveness in response to the plea, "forgive me," for then forgiveness is not *freely* given but rather serves as an economic exchange for "the repentance attesting at once to the consciousness of the fault, the transformation of the guilty, and the at least implicit obligation to do everything to avoid the return of evil."[21] Forgiveness offered under such conditions is reduced to a trade, undermining the possibility of "pure forgiveness," which Derrida argues is "unconditional, gracious, infinite, aneconomic forgiveness granted to the *guilty as guilty*, without counterpart, even to those who do not repent or ask forgiveness."[22]

Such pure forgiveness is wonderfully psychological and in stark contrast to the more limited, commonplace, "everyday" grade of forgiveness as defined by many psychologists and philosophers. These two versions are not only different, but diametrically opposed, defined by what the other is *not*. The commonsense notion, motivated by a myriad of fantasies such as repaired interpersonal relations, moral confidence, reduced conflict, spiritual salvation, internal peace, and greater power, inspired by remuneration or a contrite apology from the offender, and emboldened by assurances of the absence of future transgressions, occurs on the semantic level and is intelligible to the ego. But this normal, commonsense definition is absolutely rejected by Derrida, and rightly so as we have seen if the inner contradiction of forgiveness is taken to its proper conclusion in thought. "Forgiveness is not, it *should not be*, normal, normative, normalising. It should remain exceptional and extraordinary, in the face of the impossible: as if it interrupted the ordinary course of temporality."[23] In negating the meaning, usefulness, and intelligibility of forgiveness, Derrida thinkingly articulates forgiveness's own internal logic, allowing it to come home to itself as a rupturing, syntactic phenomenon, operative only on the vertical level of soul.[24] Such forgiveness is indeed exceptional, a "miracle." After all, Derrida asks, "what would be a forgiveness that forgave only the forgivable?"[25]

Derrida asserts the "impossibility" of forgiveness, noting its emergence only in the face of the unforgivable. If the contradiction inherent in forgiveness is *acknowledged and confronted* (rather than overridden, avoided, or ignored), we are deposited up against solid rock, so to speak, with no way out—in the same spot Giegerich characterizes as a way *in*, an entrance into the soul's interiority. If we can "hold our place in the absolute contradiction of dead end and continued faithfulness to our purpose . . . the experienced stone wall interiorizes our progressive movement into itself so that it becomes an in itself recursive progression."[26] Here the apparent impasse of forgiveness may become instead a place of passing from the semantic level—where forgiveness posits external, literal wounding, the perpetrator/victim dynamic, and the irreducible otherness of the other—into the sphere of logical negativity, or the exceptional, extraordinary, *impossible* realm of the soul.

Subjectivity and Forgiveness

Before we attempt to follow the dialectial interiorizing movement of forgiveness, let us explore the nature of consciousness capable of granting it. Forgiveness is inherently *relational*. If we are to understand the role of forgiveness on the psychological level of soul consciousness, we must consider the soul's relation to *itself*.

Regarding the relationship of consciousness to itself, Hegel writes, "Self-consciousness exists in and for itself when and by the fact that, it so exists for another; that is, it exists only in being acknowledged."[27] Only in its being *acknowledged* by the other does the unity of itself in its otherness become explicit for consciousness. Here we see that the very existence of consciousness (its objective phenomenological display) also requires recognition *by* consciousness (in the form of subjective receptivity and appreciation). Giegerich elaborates on the nature of the relationship of consciousness to itself in the "two foldness of what we call soul":[28]

> [T]he soul is the-uroboric-unity and difference of (a) its own truths and (b) its own potential to perceive, appreciate, reflect and enact those truths, a unity and difference, moreover, that in Neoplatonic thinking has been expressed in the image of the correspondence of eye and sun, of seeing and shining, we could say: as the internal dialectic of *light*.

One can easily imagine here the subjective "eye" of the analyst perceiving, appreciating, and reflecting the objective "sun" or "soul truths" of the patient. And the experience can be healing, extraordinary, and powerful. Even so, this appreciation occurs on the semantic ego level; consciousness does not transgress into the logic of syntax *until the notion of subject and object are left behind altogether*; until the soul apperceives *itself* in the other self-consciousness, and is itself so recognized by the other as one and the same. Here we are again approaching the crystal clear realm of projectionless consciousness akin to the *imaginatio vera* of Sufi mysticism,

> the mode of knowledge whereby one being *knows* another. . . . Here, above all, is the place of . . . the first encounter with the truth, where [one] awakens to [oneself] . . . meets [oneself] as if for the first time.[29]

Such consciousness is the achievement of the modern soul's birth out of itself[30] into its modern form of subjectivity, or "that which *knows*, as the *organ* of truth (its own truth) and as the soul-*making* subject (in the sense of the object that makes that which merely *is* true also *become* true, which is a movement from the implicit to the explicit)."[31]

The consciousness of the soul-making subject is capable of "hosting" or presencing the soul, so to speak. Because human consciousness is the place in and through which soul can realize itself,[32] in psychology the form of subjectivity as the soul-making subject is the "being" of the psychologist, or what Giegerich calls "the psychological I" (as precisely distinct from ego-consciousness). Such psychological consciousness is "absolved" of ego-personality, unclouded by the distractions of personal agendas or idiosyncrasies. The moments of subjective perception, reflection, and appreciation by the psychological I in recognition as soul events themselves retroactively *become* objective moments by nature of their having been recognized as such by the psychological I. It is in this way the psychologist, as the soul-*making* subject, transcends the psychological difference between ego and soul, for as long as soul-making happens. It is also apparent that the process of forgiveness, as the release of semantic content (the ego-personality) and hospitality to the soul, is a precondition for psychological consciousness to arise.

The Ego and the Psychological I

It is worth briefly exploring the relationship between the ego and the 'psychological I' or soul consciousness in the context of forgiveness. As we have seen, the ego has no access to true forgiveness but only a neurotic form it uses or withholds for its own benefit. The ego and psychological consciousness are similarly mutually exclusive. Let us recall *the psychological difference*, or that difference between soul and not-soul, syntax and semantics, which, if made conscious, allows for true psychology to happen. While the psychological difference distinguishes between soul and ego, it would be misleading to equate soul with merely "not-ego."[33] Giegerich writes,

> It is inherent in the very nature of the ego or (modern) empirical man that he stands with his back turned to the soul. It is an illusion that there could possibly be a *Relation between the Ego and the Unconscious*, if we take "the unconscious" as Jung's covert term for the soul and not merely for the ego's own repressed or ignored contents. It is more than folly. It is a sowing of a terrible confusion, a leveling of the psychological difference. The moment there would indeed be such a relation, the ego would have ceased being ego. . . . If the soul is not-ego, as we know from Jung, the negation here is not an indifferent one simply meaning "something else than," as in the statement that a bed is not a door and not a dog. It is the active negation of on principle or by definition refusing a relation and thus: impossibility of a connection.[34]

The soul "actively negates" and "refuses a relation" to the modern ego, by logical definition, providing the context in which the psychological I "has to be as the negation of the ego, and the psychologist . . . has to speak as one who has long died as ego-personality." But what is meant by "ego-personality"? What exactly is it that must "die" or be negated for the condition of psychological consciousness—and by extension, true forgiveness—to arise?

Freud described the ego as first and foremost a sense-perceiving "bodily ego." In addition, the ego is that psychic element that mediates between the unconscious id and superego, "like a man on horseback, who has to hold in check the superior strength of the horse."[35] To these aspects we can add the apparent appropriation of the modern soul's achievement of subjectivity; the apprehending, witnessing, self-determining seat of consciousness—the Subject as "I." However, this subject as I is within itself the dialectical unity and difference between itself as "the subject of true knowing, the organ of truth and of the syntactical or logical form on the one hand," and as that function oriented toward survival and self-preservation, in other words, the pragmatic, technical I on the other.[36] The dialectical unity of consciousness that is aware of itself *as* this living contradiction constitutes psychological consciousness.

Psychologically speaking, the "ego" arises as a one-sided or undialectical form of consciousness, wherein one or more aspects become concretized or substantiated. For example, when the pragmatic or protective aspect solidifies into a persistent structure of primitive defense mechanisms, or when the self-determining aspect of the modern soul is taken literally, sharpening into a determined will for power and control.

In understanding the relation between ego and soul, we might imagine individual consciousness as an instrument in an orchestra, a violin for example. As a mere instrument, it has no logical access to the composer, conductor, musician, or any *music* that is not played by its own strings. All that is "real" for itself and the world is its own pure, performative function as a particular means of soulful expression. Anything else is irrelevant. Yet now, in modernity, the violin finds itself born out of its former status as embedded symphonic instrument; it is now not only able to play its own sounds, but to *hear and appreciate the symphony, at once recognizing its participation in and contribution to it*. If this astonishing phenomenon of subjectivity "sticks" to the instrument, or somehow leaves a residue, the instrument may mistake itself as the *source* of the music rather than its *medium*, insisting on *itself* as composer, conductor, and musician, and the modern ego is born! Modern soul consciousness, in its extraordinarily powerful bloom of subjectivity, spills over into semantic form, where it is substantiated, particularized, and imbued with countless fixed and false identities, veering away from its logical form as pure self-expression and self-awareness. We are left with the semantic fallout or afterimage of the soul's syntactical birth out of itself into subjectivity; the ego as debris, as a multitude of regressive *instantiations* of subjective "I."

Returning to our example of the instrument, one might be tempted here to envision the "egoic" violin self-inflated to the caliber of a Stradivarius. Yet *any* degree of "excess" subjectivity that has become substantiated or "hardened" into a familiar and comfortable *sense of oneself* can be a psychological problem. Giegerich writes,

> The sick soul, the neurotic soul, that spitefully refuses to go along with its own movement and its experience of truth, but wants to be in control

> of this movement and the truth is the substantiated "the ego." In neurosis the soul's own form of I or subjectivity goes to the head of the soul. It is taken completely literally and is acted out in the positivity of the psyche.[37]

In appropriating and literalizing the syntactic qualities of subjective consciousness, the modern ego is effectively utilized by the sick soul to continually block and undermine the soul's own truth. Just as the violin as "composer" is a logical impossibility, so too is the ego as "real" logically impossible, existing merely as one of countless projected instances of the neurotic soul's *mise-en-scène*—albeit exquisite in its apparent reality. I *seem* absolutely real to myself! And yet, there can be no place in the soul of the Real for that familiar sense of self (i.e., who I "know" myself to be), no existing relationship, no abiding containment. This is because when I (as psychologist) "enter the retort" with whatever subject matter is at hand (problem, dream, text, fantasy image, situation, experience, etc.) and cross the threshold into the infinite and unknown terrain of interiority, the familiar sense of self functions as a block to consciousness; the ego is an external contaminant to the extent that idiosyncratic or recognizable personality consists of coagulated features of consciousness.[38] The "music" loses access to pure and unfettered self-expression. What is needed for psychology is *mindedness* (not "my" mind), the psychological I (not "me"). Psychologically, the ego *qua* ego is not only irrelevant but functions as an obstacle to consciousness.

In psychotherapy, if the psychological difference between ego and soul is not continuously and relentlessly discerned by the analyst, the false "sense of oneself" is protected, *especially if it seems able to distinguish itself from "ego."* The problem we face here is that *any* substantiated self—even the part that "tries" to distinguish itself from one's ego, the aware personality that individuates, contributes, matters, is somehow mystically "meant," real, or cherished—is *itself* ego, is the *substantiated neurotic soul*. "When the ego [in its blindness] stumbles over something, even if it should in fact be the soul, it only finds more 'ego,' but not soul."[39] Distinguishing oneself from the ego is a simple negation on the semantic level. The negation of the negation—which would mean the negation of the familiar *sense* of self altogether—is a true going under, akin to the purifying process of *mundificatio*, and is understandably resisted or, by the same token, attempted, as an ego project with great effort.[40] Here we see that *forgiveness is not only applicable to "sin" but to the very construct of the ego itself.*

The Source of True Forgiveness

The conscious practice of forgiveness is problematic because it tends to ignore what Giegerich defines as the "psychological difference," or "the difference between soul and human being."[41] To ignore the psychological difference would be to collapse personal interiority and absolute interiority, or ego and soul, resulting in tremendous inflation in which the ego takes on the burdens of the psyche such that "now *I* have to develop and mature";[42] *I* must become Hero, Savior, Wise Sage; *I* must forgive.

The conscious (ego) endeavor of forgiveness follows the neurotic inability to tolerate ambiguity and hence is compelled to "*do* something" in order to relieve unbearable tension. Yet in its "doing" and initiating, awareness now tends to the explicit phenomenon and the soul is experienced as having "departed" into interiority. Even in holding an awareness of the non-ego dimension of forgiveness, the very *act* of saying "*I* forgive *you*" *ipso facto* collapses ego and soul, giving rise to a perspective in which "the non-ego can . . . be annexed by the ego."[43] With the offer of forgiveness, the neurotic ego elicits the contradictory nature of soul in its positivized or appearing form, wherein the "paradoxical concept of *a soul without soul dignity*"[44] forces itself upon us—attempted "forgiveness" in its lesser form, "performed" by the ego, and susceptible to ego purposes.

True forgiveness, or forgiveness as a function of interiority or the soul, is not immediately accessible to the ego, as it lies not in the material realm of performance (doing) or substantiality (images) but in thought:

> The *soul* of and in the Real, the *Mercurius* "imprisoned in the matter" of our reality, the *logical form* animating our real world, are logically or syntactically negative (the negation of the semantic as such). They can only be thought.[45]

Thus we discover forgiveness as thought, not action; concept, not "doing." Hillman writes, "I cannot directly forgive, I can only ask, or pray, that these sins be forgiven."[46] He does not ask for an *act* of forgiveness, but that these sins *be forgiven*; forgiveness not as performance on the semantic level, but as the already always given syntactic ground of being itself.

True forgiveness constitutes a *vertical* appeal—"Father, forgive them"—sourced from within the interiority of soul *from within* itself. By calling out, "Father, forgive them," Jesus appeals for forgiveness to a *non-ego source* and maintains the psychological difference, so to speak. Jesus does not forgive his attackers directly because *he can't*—true forgiveness, as a thought of soul, cannot *be performed* at the semantic or ego level (interestingly, Jesus is not described as "performing" forgiveness in the scriptures, forgiving no one directly). Jesus, as a manifestation of the Self, accordingly appeals to itself ("Father," soul, Self) directly for an act of forgiveness, since it is on the level of soul that true forgiveness, as logical negativity, can actually *be* performed.

Yet Jesus also seems to encourage forgiveness be "performed" on the semantic level with his many exhortations to forgive (Mark 11:25; Matthew 6:14, 18:11, 18:35; Luke 11:4, 17:3, etc.). This may speak to the ego's role in true forgiveness as not necessarily its source, but certainly as a "willing participant" or enabling agent.[47] While the ego cannot "will" forgiveness, it must be willing, open to being affected by the experiences in the inverted world of the soul. Giegerich[48] describes a (non-ego) soul experience, *upon the ego*, of integrating a projection below:

> Catching up with what has been projected far out into space or into the future does not imply a journey to it at all. It implies conversely that the intuited reality affects you while you are staying right here; that it "dawns" on you, "comes home" to you, reconstitutes your own mind. *My* catching up with *it* means *its* imperceptibly catching up with *me*, but as if from behind or *from within* myself. It means my being contaminated with or infected by it. This is what is meant by "absolute-negative interiorization." It means being reached and moved by it (like by an object loved), in contrast to being physically pushed or pulled or manipulated. It is like being overcome by an insight. There is absolutely no violence in this being moved or overwhelmed by what is catching up with consciousness, nor in the subject's catching up with it: my intently, but passively looking and looking at the projected image *is* its coming home to me and surprising me one day from within as my own *way* of thinking.[49]

This beautiful passage calls to mind a description on the phenomenology of forgiveness wherein one is often "taken by surprise," that it "comes out of nowhere",[50] and that resolution,

> in the form of forgiveness, appears to come to us in an unexpected context, often at an unexpected moment. And yet, as one is surprised by the resolution, it becomes apparent that at some level it was sought—one was willing to forgive and was open to this possibility. It seems that this willingness, even if the person never consciously thought of forgiveness, is crucial for forgiving to occur.[51]

The ego's role in true forgiveness is willing but passive, surrendering to a vertical bowing down underneath and bearing of the longing for forgiveness, reflected in Hillman's humble entreaty, "I can only ask, or pray, that these sins be forgiven."

Neurotic Forgiveness

Derrida established for us two "versions" of forgiveness; the "commonplace" version is utilized for economic aims, while the "pure" version of forgiveness maintains its contradictory, dialectical, unconditional nature, which qualifies as "psychological" or true forgiveness. As we have seen, a standard dictionary definition of "forgive" reads simply, to "absolve or to acquit, pardon, release,"[52] and is consistent with true forgiving. In particular, the abstract notions of *absolution* and *release* inherent in this definition of forgiveness are essential properties of *absolute-negative interiorization*, or the dialectical act of negation which opens up the space of logical negativity, or soul.[53] However, it is common for psychologists and others to redefine forgiveness to meet practical and/or social demands and in so doing, forsake its profoundly psychological aspect. For example, a prominent psychologist in the field of forgiveness studies, Robert Enright, dramatically revises the simple dictionary definition to the following:

> Forgiveness is the willingness to abandon one's right to resentment, negative judgment, and indifferent behavior toward one who unjustly injured us, while fostering the undeserved qualities of compassion, generosity and even love toward him or her.[54]

Forgiveness redefined in this way allows the forgiver to avoid the absolution demanded by pure forgiveness, opting instead for a simple (or undialectical) negation: one's "right to resentment" is merely suspended, the love remains "undeserved," and a literal offense is explicitly posited and reified (in contrast to the abstract definition in which any offense remains implicit). This definition stays on the *psychic* or semantic side of the psychological difference; the semantics are negated, but the syntax or logic that gives rise to the victim/perpetrator dynamic is not left behind (i.e., it is similar to merely rearranging the deck chairs on the Titanic).

Such a limited definition is also *neurotic*, as it relates to the injury as externally caused and unjustified. Giegerich notes, "A neurotic way of erecting and celebrating . . . one's absolute invulnerability and unwoundedness is by blaming others for one's wounds . . ."[55] As we recall, psychologically, wounds are exclusively one's own, "they are not caused, there is no cause. Any cause is outside the range of [one's] psychological sphere."[56] In maintaining the offender as its object, forgiveness singles out and traps the offense out of the flow of time like a fly frozen in amber. This is precisely what happens with neurosis. Giegerich writes:

> Neurosis begins when a disruption takes place. The stream of events is stopped, the flow of time is arrested. How does this happen? The one disappointing event or condition is singled out, wrenched from, and protected against, the natural process that ultimately would inevitably end in forgetfulness, and is raised to ultimate importance. The one event is frozen, fixated and thereby made to last. It is held on to beyond its time.[57]

A definition of forgiveness that smuggles in the right "to resentment, negative judgment and indifferent behavior" and characterizes qualities of compassion, generosity, and love as "undeserved" unwittingly protects and prevents the offender (and offense) from undergoing the naturally occurring alchemical (psychological) process of time itself. We could even say the neurotic soul, or that element of consciousness that stubbornly insists upon its own untruth, strategically *utilizes* psychic forgiveness to avoid undergoing the process of *actual* forgiveness. Returning to the original abstract definition of forgiveness, we can see that to truly forgive would require not a mere *simple* negation of the offense in question, but its *absolute* negation; only then would the offending event be *absolved* of its semantic content and *released* back into the flow of time, thereby exposing it to the natural process resulting in "forgetfulness."[58] The limited form of forgiveness described above would seem preferable to the neurotic soul, which by definition stubbornly denies the osmotic character of time and insists upon a positive semantic presence in defiance of the soul's absolutely negative *modern* reality as pure subjectivity, or consciousness.[59] Genuine forgiveness would be unthinkable to the neurotic soul precisely because it would absolve or emancipate it from its identity with the Absolute.[60] By withholding *true* forgiveness, the neurotic soul stubbornly prevents the offense from allowing it to come home to itself as absolute negativity, as truth. Instead, the offense remains categorically characterized as "that which shall not be!"[61]—"frozen, fixated, and made to last."

Psychological Forgiveness

Returning to the New Testament, where forgiving is first referenced historically in earnest,[62] recall Jesus's astonishing claim: "Forgive, and you will be forgiven" (Luke 6:37). Jesus's use of forgiveness here negates the semantic reality not merely of the sin in question, but of *otherness itself*, instead affirming the uroboric nature of relating to another, as one's *own* other. "Forgive, and you will be forgiven"—if understood as an *observation* in addition (or alternative) to a dictate—is consistent with the psychological law of *comprehensive subjectivity* in which "consciousness has its own otherness no longer out there in some Other, but in itself as its own ontological self-contradictoriness: integrated into its very Being, into its Concept."[63] This form of forgiveness explicitly overcomes of the neurotic form of forgiving, which posits, and then directs itself toward, an external other.

As we have seen in Chapter 5, in Christ's petition on the cross, "Father, forgive them," we hear the extraordinary entreaty to God to *allow* or *permit* the event of the crucifixion—God's own death.[64] Christ's injunction to "forgive" the crucifixion can be seen psychologically as a plea from the soul *to itself* to "suffer" this event, its own absolute negative-interiorization, allowing it to go under into itself, dissolving into "spirit." Forgiveness can be seen here as supporting the movement of the soul's emancipation from itself as substance and its return to itself in truth as Spirit.[65] Giegerich writes, "The dying on the Cross IS the absolute *kenosis*, the going under, the resistanceless bowing down under evil, and this IS nothing else but a spelling out of what Love is. And it is *in itself* and *as such* absolute forgiveness."[66]

The combination of "releasing" and "allowing" as seen in the New Testament reflects the important dialectical notion of *sublation*. According to Hegel,

> To sublate [*aufheben*] has a twofold meaning in the language: on the one hand it means to preserve, to maintain, and equally it also means to cause to cease, to put an end to. . . . Thus, what is sublated is at the same time preserved; it has only lost its immediacy but is not on that account annihilated.[67]

For Hegel, the death of Jesus on the cross resulted in God's ultimate "sublation" in the Holy Spirit (this includes sublation of both God's human *and* transcendent form). Sublation, however, is "not directly the sublation of otherness, its return into the same, its recuperation by the One."[68] This is evident in Jesus's observation "Forgive and you shall be forgiven," where forgiving yield's not merely a self-same reflexive act, but rather accomplishes an *advance* in consciousness in which a prior state has been overcome or sublated.[69]

With sublation, the dialectical process provides a crucial alternative manner of "holding" reality that reaches beyond other modes, such as denying, forgetting, recalling, or retaining. Where neurotic forgiveness stops short with an undialectical negation, positing the semantic offense as imminent empirical fact, psychological forgiveness recognizes the new logical status of the offense and the logic that gave rise to it as *sublated*, no longer explicit or immediate. It is "released" from immediacy and also "permitted" its existence insofar as it is "not annihilated." In this way forgiveness maintains the psychological difference, engendering a perspective in which the "sin" is seen in a way that is different truly in itself, "that as one and the same is at the same time posited and negated."[70]

Jesus's use of forgiveness is dialectical or psychological and illustrates its non-ego or objective form, in contrast to the sharply restricted form of forgiveness found in modern ego discourse - a neurotic redefinition that deprives forgiveness of its psychological character, as Derrida has shown us. To better understand the underlying *logic* of the unrestricted form of forgiveness discussed above, let us utilize the dialectical methodology afforded by psychology defined as the discipline of interiority,[71] through which we can methodologically think forgiveness forward, negatively interiorizing and fully releasing forgiveness into its truth as a psychological notion.

Interiorizing Forgiveness into Itself

As we have seen, forgiveness's primary problems emerge as a contradictory positing of the literal offense and the victim/perpetrator dynamic. Our *prima materia* is just this unpsychological nature of forgiveness: its assertion of semantic reality and otherness. And it is this error *itself* that opens up the space to overcome the error.[72] Consistent with psychology as the discipline of interiority, "the dialectic proceeds via the self-application of the notion or category that happens to be at stake in each case,"[73] in this case the notion of forgiveness. For to merely apply the notion, forgiveness, to an object (the sin or sinner), we have seen thus far results in only a simple negation, an "acting out" of the concept insofar as an "attempt" to forgive is undertaken. "But [the concept] must also be *er-innert* [interiorized], come home to itself. Physician, heal thyself, take your own medicine. The concept must not remain aloof, itself exempt from and above the sphere of its jurisdiction."[74]

Applying forgiveness to itself (i.e., "forgiving" the notion of forgiveness) would entail both (1) *releasing* the notion from itself, "letting go" of the very construct of otherness, such that the logic that posited the sin and its perpetrator/victim dynamic is itself *released*, absolved from its intentionality and semantic meaning *and* (2) permitting, allowing, and suffering the construct of otherness and the event arising from it to *exist* in its true—or sublated, and no longer imminent—form. The dialectic reveals forgiveness as a fundamentally psychological process that absolutely negates what the soul itself posited, what it itself produced, opening the way to a psychological perspective by methodologically "forgetting" the semantic content of the "sin," thus making possible a structural or syntactical perspective. In this way, forgiveness *transgresses* the psychological difference not only horizontally—through a mere simple negation of the offense—but *vertically*, by leaving behind the logic giving rise to the very concept of otherness ("innocent victim and guilty perpetrator") and revealing a consciousness that recognizes itself *as* and *in* itself *both* victim *and* sinner *and* their difference at once. "The other becomes psychological only when it ceases to have the form of 'other' and is recognized as having the form of self."[75] The recognition of consciousness existing *as* this contradiction is equivalent to the state of "forgiveness" in which the logic of otherness has been overcome.

Forgiveness is astonishing because it is an inherently dialectical negating process that both presupposes the fundamental unpsychological errors of semantic reality and otherness *and* exists as the process of overcoming them. The inner dialectic of forgiveness "destroys its own premises within itself. . . . It implies a sublimation or *sublation* of the logical form or status in which the message first occurred."[76] While true forgiveness lives at the level of thought or logos, at the same time, forgiveness has no meaning on that level because there is literally nothing to forgive, no substantiality or content to be attacked or threatened. At the *objective* level of consciousness, there is no "perpetrating other" or semantic offense in the sphere of absolute negativity, therefore nothing for "the soul" to forgive, other than itself. Forgiveness is utilized by, yet irrelevant to, soul and renders itself obsolete upon reaching its goal.

Excursion on Redemption

"To redeem the past and to transform every 'It was!' into an 'I wanted it thus!'—that alone do I call redemption!"—Zarathustra[77]

Redemption is often understood in connection with forgiveness; after all, would not the "sinner" find herself "redeemed" in the forgiver's eyes? For Nietzsche's Zarathustra, however, the *only* avenue of redemption is "the transformation of every 'It was!' into an 'I wanted it thus!'" We are reminded of Freud's statement, "Where it was, there I shall be,"[78] in reference to the progression of the psyche from unconscious or implicit "it" or id to conscious or explicit *I*, aware of itself as creator.[79] What is the nature of such a transformation? Would forgiveness be comparable?[80]

For Nietzsche, the originating condition from which the will must be redeemed is its unwillingness to accept its inability to change the past, acted out as the 'spirit of revenge'[81] in humankind. Insofar as true forgiveness dissolves the desire for revenge, both redemption *and* forgiveness would occur on the occasion that every "It was!" is transformed into an "I wanted it thus!" Nietzsche's transformational notion of redemption, as explored below, reveals the common underlying ego-mechanism responsible for ordinary redemption and forgiveness.

At first glance, the bald attempt to 'transform' every "It was" into an "I wanted it thus!" may appear as an ego program that aims to avoid the domination of life by retroactively reversing the ego's relation to the world from passive victim of its effects—muttering a helpless, "It was"—to its very *cause:* "I wanted it thus!" Through this displacement of power, the egoic subject is "redeemed" through "buying back" or regaining its dignity and former position of domination over life.[82] This clever manipulation of power from the object (the past) to the subject (the ego) mimics the assumption of power gained by the magnanimous 'forgiving' ego, which similarly uses forgiveness to refashion the past more to its liking. The shift of power in both cases stays on the semantic level—no structural or logical change takes place—and therefore the change cannot claim the title of true "transformation." Redemption and forgiveness here both stay on the level intelligible to the ego and remain merely "neurotic," not psychological or transformative.

A closer reading of Zarathustra's commentary on redemption offers a more psychological perspective. Nietzsche's redemption focuses squarely on the transformation of *the will*, or ego-consciousness. The will, while "the liberator and bringer of joy," still finds itself imprisoned.

> Willing liberates: but what is it that fastens in fetters even the liberator? 'It was': that is what the will's teeth-gnashing and most lonely affliction is called. Powerless against that which has been done, the will is an angry spectator of all things past.[83]

Here, the will is "imprisoned" not because of guilt, shame, or moral exile from sin. Instead, the will is jailed by something even more fundamental—its own rage at its impotence and inability to alter the past. "The will cannot will backwards; that it cannot break time and time's desire—that is the will's most lonely affliction."[84] Here we might imagine the will's longing for power not merely over the present and future, but inflated to include *all* of time. Because it cannot have the past, "time" itself occurs as a hated Other from which the will sets itself apart and irrevocably against. Nietzsche continues:

> Willing liberates: what does willing itself devise to free itself from its affliction and to mock at its dungeon? . . . It is sullenly wrathful that time does not run back; "That which was"—that is what the stone which it cannot roll away is called. And so, out of wrath and ill-temper, the will rolls stones about and takes revenge upon him who does not, like it, feel wrath and ill-temper. Thus the will, the liberator, becomes a malefactor: and upon all that can suffer it takes revenge for its inability to go backwards. This, yes, this alone is *revenge* itself: the will's antipathy towards time and time's "It was".[85]

Like an enraged child having a temper tantrum, *revenge* is the thwarted will's answer to its affliction caused by its "antipathy towards time." This rage bleeds then into a generalized "spirit of revenge," the will's projection of fury at its powerlessness to move the stone called "It was." The insolent will acts out its vengeance covertly in the more "acceptable" form of *punishment*: "'Punishment' is what revenge calls itself: it feigns a good conscience for itself with a lie."[86] Even the 'honorable' notion of Justice is merely the extended fallout of the enraged will's scheme of "madness."[87]

> "Alas, the stone 'It was' cannot be rolled away: all punishment, too, must be eternal!" Thus madness preached. "No deed can be annihilated: how could a deed be undone through punishment? That existence too must be an eternally-recurring deed and guilt, this, this is what is eternal in the punishment 'existence'![88]

True forgiveness has no role in the divergent will's scheme, which must enforce the endless issuance of punishment in concert with an infinite cycle of deed and guilt, thereby assuring immortality for itself. All this a function of the will's obstinate insistence on asserting power where it has none—in the past.

Zarathustra continues, "Except the will at last redeem itself and willing become not-willing—: but you, my brothers, know this fable-song of madness!"[89] Here we discover the will's ultimate redemption corresponding to its being *absolutely negated*, that "willing *become* not-willing." This "fable-song of madness!" describes the *dialectical* moment in which the divergent will goes under into its opposite, "*not-willing*," or *that which willing wills* (its own other, or the object of willing) and encompasses both, resulting in the absolute negation of willing: *creating*.

> I led you away from these fable-songs when I taught you: "The will is a creator." All "It was" is a fragment, a riddle, a dreadful chance—until the creative will says to it: "But I willed it thus![90]

Referring to our discussion above on subjectivization, or the play of psychological consciousness in the symbol of the relation between the subjective "eye" and the objective "sun," we can well imagine "All 'It was'" being a mere fragment, empty debris, until the eye of subjectivity discerns and recognizes it*self* in 'It was,' thereby retroactively "creating" it as a moment of Truth as it acknowledges its self-authorship: "I willed it thus!" [91]

This dialectical moment of redemption demonstrates concrete universality—*when the knowing subject loses its external position and itself becomes caught up in the movement of its content.*[92] The knowing subject here is the absolutely negated will, which willingly enters into the movement of its particular content—the past—and *recognizes* its creation. *It was* becomes *I willed it thus*.

Nietzsche weaves a remarkably succinct and psychologically plausible commentary on the ego's construct of justice and punishment as a cover for raw *revenge*, the abreactive form of the will's near intolerable frustration and rage when confronted with its impotence regarding the past. His theory explaining the cycle of guilt and punishment as sourced by an angry, teeth-gnashing will differs from Freud's, where the primary source of guilt and subsequent need for atonement is caused by the ego's murderous wish to kill the Father. In both cases, however, we find rage toward an other that cannot be controlled (time and God) and the insistence upon an *alternate* narrative of reality in which the ego's will reigns, and where its rage can be acted with vengeful force in the morality play called *justice*.

The psychological key to Nietzsche's redemption is the inversion required by the transformation from "It was" to "I willed it thus!" in which the ego finds itself absolutely negated, its alternate illusory universe dissolved and seen through as its own defiant willing is compelled to join with the creative will of life itself. The transformation of redemption requires the will to *forgive* time and time's immovable stone called "That which was." The paradox here is the ultimate absence of the personal will altogether; insofar as an experience of true redemption occurs, one will *find* oneself in a transformed position, will *comprehend* "I wanted it thus!" to be *the truth of one's life*. Or here we may also say, the condition of the soul is redemption.

Nietzsche's redemption is a *conscious* form of forgiveness. As creative willing, it knows what it is doing, it understands "who" it is. It does not withhold punishment out of "kindness" or generosity or goodness—rather it sees through to what punishment actually is—that it is a denial of the truth, or an acting out of its own untruth. Likewise, true forgiveness forgives not out of goodness but out of fidelity to the soul's truth.

Sacrifice, Forgiveness, and *Entlassen*

Forgiveness would appear to entail true *sacrifice* insofar as it results in the fundamental giving up of the right to make another wrong (along with the resulting blame, anger, resentment, pain, etc.) and a relinquishing of the wish to change the past. The idea of sacrifice, in order to *be* sacrifice, must exist outside the realm of economy of exchange. Otherwise it becomes a sacrifice of something in order to get something else (an intern sacrifices his pay in order to gain experience), or a loss of something that was never wanted in the first place (in the way of donating unwanted or unneeded items or shedding limiting behaviors or lifestyles), thus gaining more autonomy for the person and not a true sacrifice. True sacrifice must involve a *real* loss, and one for which *one does not expect anything in return*. Even the neurotic sacrifice, as awful as it is for the sufferer, elicits the delight of the neurotic soul and as such is not true sacrifice.[93] In one light, we might see sacrifice as a gift, "a pure act if given with no return."[94] The philosopher Jean-Luc Marion states: "Sacrifice gives the gift back to givenness, from which it comes, by returning it to the very return that originally constitutes it. Sacrifice does not leave the gift, but dwells in it totally."[95] Sacrifice must mean the pure act of giving—with no return—and thus is *not* sacrifice, even though it must be. Therefore true sacrifice is *impossible*. And yet true forgiveness entails fundamental sacrifice.

Following the philosopher Frank Ruda, we would turn to Hegel, who states: "To know one's limit, is to know how to sacrifice."[96] What does this mean? "Knowing one's limit" is akin to absolute knowing for Hegel. Absolute knowing is an impossible knowledge because it knows its own limit and that its truth rests upon inherent instability or contingency. Absolute knowing therefore knows that it cannot know everything and is thus impossible, just as sacrifice is.[97] We might also say that for the psychologist, "to know one's limit" is to comprehend oneself as *existing contradiction*, as the unity of the difference between the soul as subject and organ of truth on the one hand and the finite ego on the other. To know one's limit means to know that, "I am only that!"—the comprehending, appreciating, conscious "instrument" through which the soul expresses and recognizes itself.

Hegel continues,

> This sacrifice is the externalization in which Spirit displays the process of its becoming Spirit in the form of *free contingent happening*, intuiting its pure Self as Time outside of it, and equally its Being as Space. This last becoming of Spirit, *Nature*, is its living immediate Becoming; Nature, the externalized Spirit, is in its existence nothing but this eternal externalization of its *continuing existence* and the movement which reinstates the *Subject*.[98]

This "externalization" that is sacrifice and in which Spirit unreservedly surrenders into the process of its becoming Spirit—and through such movement reinstates the Subject—is the uroboric play of the soul's own witnessing of itself, of its own unfolding. And the mind and being of the psychologist, to the extent that one's consciousness *becomes* the Subject proper, is the ground out of which this display may arise—and only in its arising does one become the Subject proper.

Spirit becomes what it is where there is what one might call with Alain Badiou *subjectivization*, or the act of becoming an objective subject (what we have above called soul-making or the being of the psychological I).[99] The act of becoming an objective subject is the act of becoming a psychologist; one is now able to *receive and recognize* a soul event, similar to what Badiou calls "an Event of Truth."[100] Such an event represents that which is outside ontology, belonging to a wholly different dimension—that, precisely, of *non*-Being. "The Event is the Truth of the situation, that which renders visible/readable what the 'official' state of the situation had to 'repress,' but it is also always localized, that is, the Truth is always the Truth of a specific situation."[101] This fits with the reality of a soul event, which has eachness character (i.e., it is associated with a particular phenomenon wedded to its historical context). Ruda calls being able to receive a Truth Event "becoming a subject proper." Such becoming corresponds to the being of the psychologist who "becomes" the place for soul as Subject to make an appearance.[102]

Subjectivization, or becoming a subject able to receive and recognize an event of truth, can only happen when there is externalization.[103] What does this mean? The word Hegel uses for 'externalization' in German is "Entlassen," which has multiple meanings, including *to let something go* (for example, one can say that one "entlässt" one's child into the world), to *relieve something of its function* (for example, to dismiss someone from a job), and also *the act of letting things be*. We can see clearly here the connection of *entlassen* with sacrifice—and forgiveness! Giegerich reminds us of this when he writes, "We have to learn to suffer our hands to be empty, in the fullest sense of the word suffer. No image. No symbols. No meaning. No gods: No religion. For is it not the empty hand, and the empty hand alone, that can be filled?"[104]

Capturing the contradiction and impossibility inherent in subjectivization, Ruda states,

> only by fully sacrificing, i.e. *entlassen [forgiving]* what I am, by fully subscribing to the idea that I have nothing in my power, one can generate the condition [for receiving a Truth event] . . . To say it another way, as long as one thinks that there is something internal that should be treated as if it is unsacrificeable, there never will be emancipation. [Ultimately] One needs to assume that one cannot sacrifice and this is the greatest sacrifice. This is a sacrifice [the truth] demands. Its mode is what Hegel calls *Entlassen [forgiving]* and its slogans may be: act as if you are not free; act as if you are dead. [105]

To "act as if one is not free" means to give up any recourse of personal will (i.e., to surrender into the truth of redemption). To "act as if one is dead" has everything in common with Giegerich's observation of the sacrificial ego "death" required for psychological consciousness. The degree of sacrifice Hegel implies with *entlassen* could be compared to what the ego experiences when confronted with the need to sacrifice the wholeness and harmony of the highest principle itself. Giegerich writes, "If this *exclusive* goodness and consequently the entire highest principle as it had been understood have to be sacrificed, this requires the *katastrophê*, the going under, of the anthropological ego."[106] Similarly, from the point of view of the ego, the "task of psychology is nothing less than to saw off the branch one is sitting on, so that one loses one's firm hold and plunges into the bottomless depth of the 'between' space where there are no straight lines and no fixed points." *Ent-lassen, or psychological forgiveness*, means the absolute negation of the false ego and a release of the self into its true identity: the conscious recipient of soul events.

The Logic of Love

"In the negation of the negation," Slavoj Zizek explains, "the subject includes itself in the process, taking into account how the process it is observing affects its own position." He writes, "[The] properly Hegelian 'negation of negation' . . . resides in the decisive shift from the *distortion of a notion* to *a distortion constitutive of this notion*, that is, to this notion as a distortion-in-itself."[107] Similar to an alchemical death through yellowing, "the vessel itself is drawn into the process. . . . The vessel, too, is subjected to the corruption ."[108] True forgiveness includes not merely the object, the offense, but the subject, the "vessel itself." In other words, where true or absolute forgiveness is concerned, the posited error or "sin" undergoes a radical translocation from the object to the subject—it is not *what* or *who* I am seeing that is the problem, but *my* seeing *per se*. *And* the problem I see is *necessary to exist* so that I may *see* that I am the problem: "for only what is explicit for consciousness can also be explicitly overcome."[109] The negation of the negation involves a shift in methodological approach from *seeking* to *seeing*. True forgiveness allows the corrupted vessel to be infused with and penetrated by the shadow element or "sin" it had been protecting itself against. A fully integrated consciousness would then recognize the self-contradiction it exists *as*—or the unity of its unity and (former) difference.[110]

On a human level, to forgive would mean to "reach the truth in its own conceptual element"[111]—in other words, to cross the "unbridgeable difference" from horizontal to vertical logic, from semantics to syntax. The seeming "impossibility" of forgiveness lies in its ability to span this infinite divide. Zizek writes, "[T]he transubstantiation of the subject from a 'concrete' self immersed in its life world into the subject of pure thought [requires undergoing] . . . a process of 'abstraction' which has to be accomplished in the individual's 'concrete' experience, and which as such involves the supreme pain of renunciation."[112] On a human level, forgiveness can be likened to the alchemical acid bath of "silvering" and "yellowing"[113] as Hillman describes, the excruciating purification process of *mundificatio* as depicted in the *Rosarium Philosophorum* woodcuts, or the Judaic notion of *Teshuvah*, in which one dies to oneself and is reborn a "new person." All such processes entail the releasing of one's archetypal "mythical garments," letting go of being identical with the "God-man in the shape of a servant,"[114] suffering the substantial absence of the Absolute, permitting the reality that "'I am *only* that!', neither servant-shape, nor God-man."[115]

True forgiveness functions as a dialectical logic as it relates to and overcomes injustice, the wrongs of the world, and even evil itself. One does not overcome these antagonisms. Giegerich writes,

> by powerful conquest and subjugation, not by rejection and condemnation, but conversely by, with resistanceless sufferance, allowing them to *be*, indeed, even embracing them, and *ipso facto* unrelentingly exposing oneself to them, letting them permeate oneself . . . [T]his is first of all a concept, an insight, a truth on a very deep and remote soul level. It is a *logic* to be comprehended, not a maxim to be acted out. It is the logic of Love.[116]

The "logic of Love" here shares the dialectical logic of forgiveness; a "going under," a "resistanceless bowing down under evil"—this is "*in itself* and *as such* absolute forgiveness."[117] Reflected on the psychic level, such Love takes on an unconditioned, radical, and even "impossible" form.[118] While Love, as the soul's direct knowing of itself, is not in need of forgiveness, the precondition of Love *is* forgiveness as that very bridge that spans the unbridgeable difference between guilty perpetrator and innocent victim, between semantics and syntax, between I and Thou.[119]

Clinical Implications: Betrayal

Before examining the phenomenon of true forgiveness as it may occur in a clinical setting, I will add the caveat that the following exercise is not intended to be a "guide" or instructional aid in forgiving, as such an intention would utterly defeat the purpose and likely obstruct true forgiveness from actually occurring. It is merely offered as one of infinitely many possibilities of the unfolding of the forgiveness process as a referent for the clinician wishing to work with her or his patient *psychologically*.

A common clinical situation in which the concept of forgiveness arises is that of infidelity. Let us consider, for example, an innocent husband feeling rejected, humiliated, and betrayed by a cheating partner. The husband wishes to "forgive" his wife and restore trust.[120]

In his excellent essay, *Betrayal*, James Hillman follows the evolution of consciousness from primal trust to its inevitable betrayal, and then (hopefully) to forgiveness. (Hillman does not define forgiveness, however, but notes that it does not come from the ego.) Hillman asserts that forgiveness marks an advance of consciousness following betrayal and poignantly observes that betrayal only occurs in those most intimate relationships where primal trust is possible. "You cannot have trust without the possibility of betrayal," he claims. "It is the wife who betrays her husband, and the husband who cheats his wife; partners and friends deceive, the mistress uses her lover for power, the analyst discloses his patient's secrets, the father lets his son fall. The promise made is not kept, the word given is broken, trust becomes treachery."[121] Indeed, for their treachery, Adam and Eve were expelled from the paradise of primordial unity with God. Hillman makes a powerful case that a profound experience of betrayal initiates us into new consciousness. He writes,

> it may be expected that primal trust will be broken if relationships are to advance; and, moreover, that the primal trust will not just be outgrown. There will be a crisis, a break characterized by betrayal, which according to the tale is the *sine qua non* for the expulsion from Eden into the "real" world of human consciousness and responsibility.[122]

Hillman's characterization of betrayal is important because it distinguishes the *psychological difference* between one's own personal experience of betrayal and the purpose of betrayal for the soul; the husband begins to see for the *soul's own forward movement* the necessity of betrayal *per se*. His wife's treachery no longer belongs exclusively to her, the humiliating cuckoldry no longer so terribly personal for him. Such a move may serve to free the husband from pain and humiliation, help him mature, and even restore the relationship. The husband may even feel an experience of *forgiveness* toward his wife (although for Hillman, because "forgiveness by the one probably requires atonement by the other,"[123] forgiveness can be held hostage by the other, so to speak).

According to Hillman,

> The unfolding through the various stages from trust through betrayal to forgiveness presents a movement of consciousness. . . . For all its negativity, betrayal is yet an advance over primal trust because it leads to the "death" of the puer through the anima experience of suffering. This may then lead, if not blocked by the negative vicissitudes of revenge, denial, cynicism, self betrayal and paranoid defenses, to a firmer fatherhood where the betrayed can in turn betray others less unconsciously, implying an integration of a man's untrustworthy nature. The final integration of the experience may result in forgiveness by the betrayed, atonement by the betrayer, and a reconciliation—not necessarily with each other—but a reconciliation by each to the event.[124]

Forgiveness marks an advance in consciousness—a hard-fought recognition of the necessity of betrayal as the price of life itself—and depends upon the essential achievement of integration. An *integration of a man's own untrustworthy nature* reflects an ability to "betray others less unconsciously," and the "*final integration of the experience* may result in forgiveness by the betrayed, atonement by the betrayer, and a reconciliation . . . by each to the event."[125] Here integration implies an absence of unconsciousness—previously cast out shadow elements are "taken back," so to speak, and properly recognized as belonging to "a man's own untrustworthy nature." "Final integration of the experience" could be likened to *releasing* the experience of betrayal back into the flow of time, liberating it from a neurotic need to single it out and inflate it to enormous, painful proportions.

However, for Hillman, integration refers to *one's own* consciousness—I must develop *my own* anima, integrate *my own* brutality. The concern is on the person, not the soul. His conceptualization appeals to those working with interpersonal forgiveness, but it is not a psychological conceptualization (and again, may serve to defer true forgiveness). Psychological forgiveness, as a soul process, is indifferent to a person's individuation or identity and in fact requires the ego's absolute negation. It is not the person's personality that is to be integrated, but their greater consciousness to the extent that it reflects the objective psyche's (which already *is* "integrated").

For Hillman, betrayal—though seen through and acknowledged as a soul necessity—is still merely displaced from the subjective to the objective sphere. Its burden has simply been offset, the notion of betrayal not fully interiorized into itself.[126] The integration he speaks of does not truly leave the realm of ego-personality. It is still "a man's own" integration and thus leaves consciousness intact (while relatively less burdened). To fully integrate the shadow at a soul level would mean undergoing an absolute negation of one's sense of oneself, yielding to the ego's *utter dismemberment*—including one's firm identity as a "man," a "father," or "son," etc. One cannot have it both ways. There is no bridge from ego to soul.

Psychologically speaking, not only would the betrayed husband release the structure of his consciousness that dwells in the idea of a primal "union with God"; he is obliged to release the logic that gives rise to otherness itself. His self-relation must be absolutely negated. Otherwise, he will likely experience betrayal by his wife again and again (or the fear of it). With Hillman's program of forgiveness, the husband is "saved" from having to undergo what his wife's betrayal demands from him psychologically. Until the logic that gives rise to the notion of betrayal itself is overcome, true forgiveness has yet to occur. The psychological difference is not transgressed.

Where psychological forgiveness entails absolute negation, the traditional call of forgiveness expects a simple negation (i.e., the subject would hope to observe a change in the object—its disintegration, its passage into its opposite). In our example, the cheating spouse would be expected to repent, crumble, and pass into her opposite (a faithful wife), upon which event forgiveness would be granted. Conventional forgiving tends to focus on the *object* of forgiveness and wait upon its simple negation.

However, as noted earlier, "in the negation of negation, the subject includes itself in the process, taking into account how the process it is observing affects its own position." Similar to an alchemical death through yellowing, "the vessel itself is drawn into the process. . . . The vessel, too, is subjected to the corruption."[127] True forgiveness includes not merely the object, but the subject, the "vessel itself." In our husband's case, he himself as the "vessel" and his notion of marriage *as such* (and its status as "broken") must undergo the "corruption" process. As noted above, this can be a very difficult and dismembering process, likely resulting in the disintegration and shattering of the husband's notion of marriage altogether; the construct of marriage itself would be negated and *seen through* (e.g., as containing vestiges of "ownership" of the other, assuming exclusive rights to the other's internal desires, demanding absolute psychic fidelity, etc.). The husband may undergo an experience of profound negation, including the renunciation of his identity *as* "husband." As in betrayal, the husband may come to recognize his partner's actions as not strictly related to his own subjectivity, but rather as a movement related to consciousness at large—possibly a reflection of the inadequacy of an unreflected construct of marriage to authentically contain the modern psyche.

Undergoing the "supreme pain of renunciation" of the semantic content of his identity *as* husband makes possible an expanded horizon of relatedness (i.e., marriage) to include within it that which before would have been impossible and unthinkable—an "adulterous wife"—and love her *as she is*, insofar as his own self-definition as husband or partner is radically opened up and transcended. What began as the *distortion* of a notion. (i.e., "a broken marriage") is decisively shifted to a distortion *constitutive of the notion* of marriage—that is, the subjectively held previous notion of *marriage as such* as *broken*. The landscape of psychological forgiveness reveals a new perspective of the antagonism or offense—the psychological or soul perspective of the event and the experience of *comprehensive subjectivity*, in which the husband may see the *logical* necessity of infidelity, wherein the notion of marriage is deepened to contain the unity of the unity of marriage (as fidelity) on one side and its opposite (infidelity) on the other. The formerly "forgiving husband" is thus able to know his partner profoundly in her truth, a logical truth that *includes* both "cheating"[128] partner *and* devoted spouse and the infinity between; this is the logical self-contradictory unity of "forgiven-ness," a new consciousness of which he is a part.

An initial conception of a "betraying other" betrays its own denial of a betraying *self*; its shadow element is split off and projected. The process of true forgiveness is one of profound *integration*, allowing the mind's own penetration and "corruption" by the very "sin" it had been defending against, coming home to the truth of its reality as existing self-contradiction—the unity of its unity and (former) difference—or love. This process is beautifully laid out in Giegerich's essay, "First Shadow, Then Anima"[129] and faithfully documents, as it were, the soul's journey of forgiveness.

Making Way for Soul

In the consulting room, forgiveness may appear as a worthy project taken on by patients and encouraged by therapists for numerous reasons. As discussed above, however, when forgiveness is *intentionally* undertaken, it by definition becomes an ego scheme. That being said, the genuine pull *toward* forgiveness may reflect a growing awareness of the "gap" of the psychological difference, or between one's particular consciousness and abstract soul's. Soul, paradoxically, "*'appears' (actualizes itself) as the experience of negativity, of the inadequacy-to-itself, of a particular identity.*"[130] This "inadequacy-to-itself" of one's particular identity, if acute, can serve to corrode the ego structure and make way for soul, resulting in the organic emergence of forgiveness.

From a phenomenological perspective, while true forgiveness by definition overcomes otherness, it does so on a *logical* level; forgiving does not necessarily "fix," "repair," or reconcile the relationship to its former status on a semantic level. From Zizek we read:

> [When] Hegel introduces the notion of reconciliation as the way to resolve the deadlock of the Beautiful Soul, his term designates the acceptance of the chaos and injustice of the world as immanent to the Beautiful Soul which deplores it, the Beautiful Soul's acceptance of the fact that it participates in the reality it criticizes and judges, not any kind of magical transformation of this reality.[131]

While forgiveness *is* a transformation of *consciousness*, nothing actually *happens*; it is not an "experience." "The change from one stage or logical status of consciousness is something very real . . . but it cannot be an experience inasmuch as it is something syntactical and not something semantic, something psychological and not something psychic."[132] We must remember that forgiveness is the recognition of "a concept, an insight, a truth on a very deep and remote soul level." Forgiveness would make way for that which remains when the soul is absolved from empirical semantic reality, released into its truth as absolute negativity, as pure consciousness; forgiveness thereby makes possible the soul's direct knowing of itself as Love.[133] True forgiveness is thus the *recognition of a conceptual truth*, a logical shift in perspective, however profound.

Forgiveness in the way described here applies to psychology at large—it is meant to describe the activity of the soul toward itself—and the human person actively involved would be the psychologist (or anyone thinking psychologically) insofar as the soul achieves its actuality in human consciousness. And when a person finds herself freed from a neurosis, she may find she has forgiven (and been forgiven).

Reflection

> The holiest of all the spots on earth is where an ancient hatred has become a present love.[134]

In concluding this depth psychological study on forgiveness, I would like to revisit the particular image that inspired it. In my imagination, the fantasy described in Chapter 1 has not changed; the "holy spot" a grassy, flat area, on a small hill, or in a meadow, the two people approaching one another, arms outstretched, still anticipating a deeply longed-for embrace. Their identities—enemy kings who have laid down their arms and come to make peace after centuries of war, or two siblings who have been estranged for years, finally ready to love again—remain the same. For me, the image remains a symbol of the miraculous reunion of souls who, until the moment of communion, had been lost to one another. Now, however, our "miracle" gives way to understanding as we realize their communion is a soul event of *recognition*. "Here is revealed an entirely new state of relating which had formerly been unimaginable to consciousness." This too, resonates; true forgiveness signifies an advance in consciousness that was not conceivable to its previous state, an advance allowing the soul's recognition of itself in the other, overcoming what had formerly been an unbridgeable difference. The passage concludes,

> In the mystical transformation from hatred to love, an image of the soul's redemption is revealed. Such a profound shift in perspective, which we call *forgiveness*, reveals the enormous power and possibility of psyche and reflects psychological transformation of the highest order.

The "mystical" nature of the transformation from hatred to love signifies the ego's relative role in true forgiveness, which it has no power to effect but merely would *undergo* to the extent that it is willing to go under and surrender its external, semantic reality as secondary to that of interiority or the inner infinity of soul.

From our human perspective, this process of forgiveness occurs as a function of what Jung calls individuation, which includes the shedding of the self's inflated identification with unconscious archetypal influences, the integration of the shadow so that it is no longer unconsciously projected—therein revealing the *imaginatio vera*, the breathtaking beauty of the manifest *anima mundi*. The truth of one's identity finally dawns, not as ego-personality, but as Self, as the reconciliatory dialectical process of the unity of the unity and the opposition of the opposites, thereby revealing one's own "holy" ground of being as Love. Such a shift in perception surely reveals "the enormous power and possibility of psyche and reflects psychological transformation of the highest order."

For the soul itself, the process of true forgiveness prepares our finite human consciousness as the receptive stage upon which "the process of knowing spirit's essence takes place and that the divine self-consciousness thus arises. Out of the foaming ferment of finitude, spirit rises up fragrantly."[135] Giegerich concurs, writing

> [A]s the place in and through which [soul] can realize itself, we are . . . needed, even indispensable for it, and if we let it find its "eternal recreation" and fulfillment, then even we may, through our participation in it, also find our deepest satisfaction, because in the deepest sense we exist not as organism, but as soul.[136]

Zizek affirms this (contradictory) identity between finite consciousness and the infinity of soul, writing that Hegel's absolutely negative Spirit "is a virtual entity [that] exists only insofar as subjects act as if it exists. . . . [I]t is the substance of the individuals *who recognize themselves in it*, the ground of their entire existence."[137] That subjects must consciously "recognize themselves in it" requires a radical redefinition of the self, accomplished through the taking leave of everything that one is, going all the way to an *absolute* negation: subjectivization. Here it is not the *ego* that forgives, but the structure giving rise to the ego as such is released (*entlassen)—forgiven!*—creating a clearing for that space out of which "spirit rises up fragrantly." For, if "in the deepest sense we exist not as organism, but as soul," the *true* relation between self, each another, and soul is not one to the other, but one and the same.

Notes

1. As noted by T.M. Grant, *Forgiveness in Psychoanalysis*. Unpublished manuscript (1987) and Melvin R. Lansky, "The Impossibility of Forgiveness: Shame Fantasies as Instigators of Vengefulness in Euripides' Medea," *Journal of the American Psychoanalytic Association*, 53, no. 2 (June 1, 2005): 437–464. Hillman has written about forgiveness, albeit sparingly. On the one hand he is suspicious of it, noting that the ancient gods wished their wrath to be remembered, not forgiven, yet on the other he intuited that forgiveness "does not come from the ego" Hillman, however, did not examine forgiveness psychologically, but took it at face value as a "given" so to speak. See James Hillman, *Senex and Puer: Uniform Edition of the Writings of James Hillman* (Vol. 3, 1st ed.) (Putnam, CT: Spring Publications, 2005).
2. C.G. Jung, "The Transcendent Function," in *The Collected Works of C.G. Jung*, trans. by R.F.C. Hull (Vol. 8, 2nd ed.) (Princeton, NJ: Princeton University Press, 1981) (Original work published in 1916), 67–91.
3. James Hillman, "The Yellowing of the Work," in *Alchemical Psychology: Uniform Edition* (Vol. 5, 1st ed.) (Putnam, CT: Spring Publications, 2010), 204–230.
4. L. Horwitz, "The Capacity to Forgive: Intrapsychic and Developmental Perspectives.—PubMed—NCBI," (2005). http://www.ncbi.nlm.nih.gov/pubmed/16045162.
5. Wolfgang Giegerich, *What Is Soul?* (New Orleans, LA: Spring Journal, Inc., 2012), 44.
6. Giegerich, *What is Soul?*, 246–247.
7. From Hillman, "We must be quite clear that forgiveness is no easy matter. If the ego has been wronged, the ego cannot forgive just because it 'should,' notwithstanding the wider context of love and destiny. The ego is kept vital by its *amour-propre*, its pride and honor. Even where one wants to forgive, one finds one simply can't, because forgiveness doesn't come from the ego." Hillman, *Senex and Puer*, 209.
8. It is interesting to note that for Giegerich, forgiveness as a humanistic concept posits a "not-yet-ness" insofar as one's salvation or freedom exists in the future dependent upon its achievement. Of such forgiveness, he writes, "What is in its sites is correction, development, the substitution of one 'wrong' behavior for another 'mature' one; for example: Where there was resentment, there love and kindness shall be." Wolfgang Giegerich, *The Neurosis of Psychology (Collected English Papers, Vol. I)* (New Orleans, LA: Spring Journal, Inc., 2005), 109.

Here Giegerich criticizes the use of forgiveness as a tool for self-improvement or betterment of sorts.

9. Though rarely is the perpetrator imagined as a "Thou" but instead reduced to an object, an "it."
10. The notion of personal forgiveness was not practiced in early Western culture and only introduced with Christianity. In Greek and Roman antiquity, the act of "forgiveness" typically referred to the king's prerogative to pardon captured soldiers for political reasons. In early Judaism, forgiveness was reserved for one's relationship with Yahweh, and forgiveness offered to others was mediated by that relationship. See Jennifer M. Sandoval, "Forgiveness and the Soul: A Depth Psychological Perspective on Forgiveness" (Pacifica Graduate Institute, 2013). http://gradworks.umi.com/35/61/3561083.html.
11. Giegerich, *What Is Soul?*, 246.
12. Wolfgang Giegerich, "The End of Meaning and the Birth of Man: An Essay about the State Reached in the History of Consciousness and an Analysis of C.G. Jung's Psychology Project," in *The Soul Always Thinks (Collected English Papers, Vol. IV)* (New Orleans, LA: Spring Journal, Inc., 2010), 235–236.
13. Giegerich, *What Is Soul?*, 282.
14. A campaign to "Make Love, Not War," for example, that fails to recognize the inherent character of modern war as an "acting out" of the prevailing logic of the soul (or more accurately, the *neurotic* soul), would likely be an ineffective campaign. While, as already noted, with Freud, Jung lamented, "'*Homo homini lupus'* [man is to man a wolf] is a sad, yet eternal truism," the recognition of its source as an "acting out" of the modern problem of otherness at the level of soul is Giegerich's. While wars are a feature of humanity throughout history, in premodern culture it is safe to assume that instinctive "eye for an eye" retributive justice (or worse) was the rule, in contrast to the neurotic perpetrator/victimization dynamic ubiquitous in modernity.
15. Giegerich also writes, "What in this description sounds totally negative and is also experienced negatively, namely as painful alienation and soullessness, from a soul point of view, however, has to be conceived as a step forward in the history of the soul. It means that man has become born man and come of age. He is no longer contained in the womb of Mother Nature as her child. Psychologically, he now has to live all on his own account, and with a metaphor of Jung's, has to sew his garment himself (cf. *CW* 9i, § 27) on his own responsibility and risk. The mythic garments that preciously had always already been provided for him with unquestionable authority have dropped from him like a snake's old shed skin. Nature and the world have become obsolete (of course only psychologically, not pragmatically). The soul has overcome the world and thus come home to itself." In Giegerich, *What Is Soul?*, 285.
16. Lucy Allais, "Wiping the Slate Clean: The Heart of Forgiveness," *Philosophy & Public Affairs*, 36, no. 1 (January 2008): 33–68, doi:10.1111/j.1088-4963.2008.00123.x, 32.
17. In addition, the offending act is often inextricably bound to the other such that their identity takes on the status of "offender."
18. Allais's way of "making sense" of the contradiction is to separate the doer from the deed (or avoid the tendency to "collapse" the offense with the offender), recognizing the inevitable fallibility of human beings. "Without changing our beliefs in the culpability and wrongness of another's actions, we can come to have an attitude towards her that sees her as better than her wrong actions indicate her to be, and thus can move forward in a relationship that is not bound by past wrongdoing" (Allais, "Wiping the Slate Clean," 68). In my view this tactic avoids the contradiction inherent in forgiveness, thus not acknowledging its *logical impossibility* in the ego realm.

19. Derrida, *On Cosmopolitanism and Forgiveness*, 31–32.
20. The ego's appropriation of forgiveness to dominate the other or to display moral superiority has been noted by Kenneth Wapnick in *Love Does Not Condemn: The World, the Flesh, and the Devil according to Platonism, Christianity, Gnosticism, and "A Course in Miracles"* (Roscoe, NY: Foundation for A Course In Miracles, 1989) and *Forgiveness and Jesus* (Roscoe, NY: Foundation for A Course in Miracles, 1998) and others. For Derrida, pure forgiveness would make no use of power. "What I dream of," he writes, "what I try to think as the 'purity' of a forgiveness worthy of its name, would be a forgiveness without power: unconditional but without sovereignty" (*On Cosmopolitanism and Forgiveness*, 59).
21. Derrida, *On Cosmopolitanism and Forgiveness*, 34.
22. Derrida, *On Cosmopolitanism and Forgiveness*, 34.
23. Derrida, *On Cosmopolitanism and Forgiveness*, 31–32.
24. Derrida is here describing forgiveness's logical truth as an interiorized soul movement. In the context of the psychological difference, we could even say the characterization as "exceptional," "extraordinary," "in the face of the impossible," and rupturing "the ordinary course of temporality" is a vivid phenomenal portrayal of the absolutely negative *soul* aspect of virtually *any* phenomenon when held up against its unreflected, semantic instantiation.
25. Derrida, *On Cosmopolitanism and Forgiveness*, 36.
26. Giegerich, *Soul always Thinks*, 172.
27. G.W.F. Hegel & J.N. Findlay, *Phenomenology of Spirit*, trans. by A.V. Miller (Revised ed.) (Oxford: Oxford University Press, 1977), paras 175, 178.
28. Giegerich, *What Is Soul?*, 257.
29. Henry Corbin, *The Voyage and the Messenger: Iran and Philosophy* (Berkeley, CA: North Atlantic Books, 1998), xx.
30. See Wolfgang Giegerich, "End of Meaning," in *The Soul Always Thinks (Collected English Papers, Vol. IV*, pp 189–283) (New Orleans, LA: Spring Journal, Inc., 2010).
31. Giegerich, *What Is Soul?*, 298.
32. For Hegel, "it is in the *finite consciousness* that the process of knowing spirit's essence takes place and that the divine self-consciousness thus arises. Out of the foaming ferment of finitude, spirit rises up fragrantly." See G.W.F. Hegel, *Lectures on the Philosophy of Religion* (Vol. III), 233.
33. This, even given the distinction Jung makes in a letter to Charteris when he writes, "To hell with the Ego-world! Listen to the voice of *daimonion*. It has a say now, not you" (C.G. Jung, *Letters* 2, p. 532, 9 Jan 1960).
34. Giegerich, *What Is Soul?*, 129–130.
35. Sigmund Freud, *The Ego and the Id* (New York: W.W. Norton & Company, 1923/1990), 15.
36. Giegerich, *What Is Soul?*, 298.
37. Giegerich, *What Is Soul?*, 298.
38. An essential guiding principle of psychology as stated by Jung is, "Above all, don't let anything from outside, that does not belong, get into it, for the fantasy image has 'everything it needs' [*omne quo indiget*] within itself." (C.G. Jung, *Collected Works, Vol. 14*, para. 749).
39. Giegerich, *What Is Soul?*, 130.
40. See Giegerich, *What Is Soul?*, 294–298. While it would seem that this absolute negation would "destroy" the ego, there really is no ego to destroy or sacrifice at the soul level. An absolute negation is thus not an attack on the ego. It is, however, the recognition that the soul is "the active negation of on principle or by definition refusing a relation [to the ego] and thus: impossibility of a connection."

While the soul still occurs as "departed" for the psychological I, it is utterly "nonexistent" for the ego, as is true forgiveness.

41. Wolfgang Giegerich, "The Present as Dimension of the Soul," in *The Neurosis of Psychology* (Vol. 1, pp. 104–117). (New Orleans, LA: Spring Journal Books, 2005) (Original work published 1977), 111.
42. Giegerich, "The Present as Dimension of the Soul," 111.
43. Giegerich, "The Present as Dimension of the Soul," 112.
44. Giegerich, *What Is Soul?*, 163.
45. Giegerich, *What Is Soul?*, 150.
46. Hillman, "Betrayal," 209.
47. Paul Gabrinetti, personal communication.
48. Wolfgang Giegerich, *The Soul's Logical Life* (Frankfurt: Peter Lang, GmbH, 2008) (Original work published 1998).
49. Giegerich, Giegerich, *The Soul's Logical Life*, 147.
50. Steen Halling, Michael Leifer, & Jan O. Rowe. "Emergence of the Dialogal Approach: Forgiving Another," in Constance T. Fischer (Ed.), *Qualitative Research Methods for Psychologist: Introduction through Empirical Studies* (pp. 247–277) (San Diego, CA: Elsevier Academic Press, 2006), 256.
51. Halling et al., *Qualitative Research Methods for Psychologist: Introduction through Empirical Studies*, 257.
52. Forgive, *Roget's II: The New Thesaurus* (Cleveland, OH: Wiley Publishing, 2010).
53. *Absolution* and *release* also correspond to alchemical processes that attempted to free the Mercurial spirit from matter (i.e., *putrefactio, mundificatio, solutio*).
54. Robert Enright & The Human Development Study Group. "The Moral Development of Forgiveness," *Handbook of Moral Behavior and Development*, ed. by W. Kurtines and J. Gewirtz (Hillsdale, NJ: Erlbaum, 1991), 123.
55. Wolfgang Giegerich, *Neurosis: The Logic of a Metaphysical Illness* (New Orleans, LA: Spring Journal, Inc., 2013), 387.
56. Giegerich, *Neurosis*, 280.
57. Giegerich, *Neurosis*, 280.
58. "Forgetfulness" here does not mean the event is obliterated. The event occurred (as all historical events do) and is recognized as historically necessary; it is therefore *logically* remembered. However its *semantic reality* no longer invades and violates the present moment and is thus phenomenologically experienced as "forgotten."
59. For Giegerich, a neurosis has no redeeming qualities for the person who suffers it. At the objective level, however, neuroses are seen to be the soul's way of making what had been unconscious *explicitly conscious* through the painful "working off" of earlier fragments or statuses of consciousness. See Chapter 4 in Giegerich, *What is Soul?*
60. Giegerich defines neurosis as a "metaphysical illness" in which the neurotic unconsciously insists on attempting to simulate the lost experience of the Absolute (or God) via the neurotic symptom. See Giegerich, *Neurosis*.
61. Giegerich, *Neurosis*, 280.
62. As discussed in Chapter 1, in ancient Greek culture, the concept functioned primarily as a political tool of rulers in wartime to demonstrate power by granting clemency (or not) to prisoners of war. In early Judaic culture, the notion of forgiveness greatly expanded and was a primary element conditioning one's spiritual relationship with G-d—and was only relevant within that context. Not until Christianity was forgiveness generally construed as relevant to interpersonal relations.
63. Wolfgang Giegerich, 2008, 106.

64. That the object of forgiveness is "them" may foreshadow the imminent *sublation* of the substantial figure of the transcendent God in Jesus into the transubstantiated form of the Holy Spirit, which exists only *as* the virtual presupposition of the activity of finite individuals, in other words, the actions of men. See S. Zizek & J. Milbank, *The Monstrosity of Christ* (Cambridge, MA: MIT Press, 2009), 61.
65. However, not spirit as preexisting "substance." According to Zizek, Hegel's Spirit "is a virtual entity [that] exists only insofar as subjects act as if it exists. . . . it is the substance of the individuals *who recognize themselves in it*, the ground of their entire existence . . . [T]he only thing that really exists are these individuals and their activity, so this substance is actual only insofar as individuals believe in it and act accordingly." From Slavoj Zizek, *God in Pain*, 171.
66. Wolfgang Giegerich, "God Must Not Die!" *Spring Journal*, 84 (Fall 2010): 11–71, 49.
67. Georg Wilhelm Friedrich Hegel, *Hegel's Science of Logic* (Later Printing ed.) (Amherst, NY: Prometheus Books, 1991), 107.
68. Zizek and Gunjevic, *God in Pain*, 172.
69. Otherwise one would merely say, "Forgive, and you will be forgiving."
70. Giegerich, *What Is Soul?*, 81.
71. The dialectical process explicitly reveals soul as the process of reflection *into itself,* thus continually revealing itself as the infinite "bottomlessness of its own ever-negated base, absolute negativity, 'the soul'" in Wolfgang Giegerich, David Miller, & Greg Mogenson, *Dialectics & Analytical Psychology: The El Capitan Canyon Seminar* (New Orleans, LA: Spring Journal, Inc., 2005), 103.
72. Slavoj Žižek, *Less Than Nothing: Hegel and the Shadow of Dialectical Materialism* (London; Brooklyn, NY: Verso Books, 2012).
73. Giegerich, *Dialectics & Analytical Psychology*, 17.
74. Giegerich, *Dialectics & Analytical Psychology*, 17.
75. Wolfgang Giegerich, *Soul Violence (Collected English Papers, Vol III)* (New Orleans, LA: Spring Journal, Inc, 2008), 106.
76. Giegerich, *The Soul's Logical Life*, 261.
77. Friedrich Nietzsche, *Nietzsche: Thus Spoke Zarathustra*, ed. by Robert Pippin, trans. by Adrian Del Caro (Cambridge: Cambridge University Press, 2006), 110–111.
78. Ian Parker, *Psychoanalytic Culture: Psychoanalytic Discourse in Western Society* (New York: Sage,1997), 198.
79. For soul, extended to the awareness of itself as the unity of created and creator with their difference.
80. The corresponding adjustment of Zarathustra's quote, "To redeem the past and to transform every 'It was!' into an 'I *didn't* want it thus, but I shall wipe the slate clean!'" does not quite hold up, revealing forgiveness (as typically defined) to be a psychologically *inferior* concept, unable to reach the depths of transformation of redemption asserted by Nietzsche.
81. Ted Sadler, *Nietzsche: Truth and Redemption: Critique of the Postmodernist Nietzsche* (London: Bloomsbury Publishing, 2000), 148.
82. The notion of redemption is *active*: "redeem" stems from the Latin *redimere*, from *re(d)-* 'back' + *emere* 'buy.' It is *intentional*, it aims to *buy back* one's former state or property. To forgive, on the other hand, derives directly: 'for' and 'give'. So quite literally, 'for' + 'give' is the reverse, the very opposite of 'back' + 'buy' and to this aim, the logic of true forgiveness refers to the opposite yet complementary movement of Nietzsche's "redemption"—it is its own other and co-constitutive soul movement.
83. Nietzsche, *Thus Spoke Zarathustra*, 110.

84. Nietzsche, *Thus Spoke Zarathustra*, 110.
85. Nietzsche, *Thus Spoke Zarathustra*, 110.
86. Nietzsche, *Thus Spoke Zarathustra*, 111.
87. "And that law of time, that time must devour her children, is justice itself": thus madness preached. "Things are ordered morally according to justice and punishment. Oh, where is redemption from the stream of things and from the punishment 'existence'?" Thus madness preached. "Can there be redemption when there is eternal justice?" (Nietzsche, *Thus Spoke Zarathustra*, 111).
88. Nietzsche, *Thus Spoke Zarathustra*, 111.
89. Nietzsche, *Thus Spoke Zarathustra*, 111.
90. Nietzsche, *Thus Spoke Zarathustra*, 111.
91. Nietzsche's redemption follows the transformation of consciousness from substance to subject described by Giegerich: "Expressed in Hegel's language, what at first was grasped and expressed only as *Substance* [a perceived or envisioned imaginal content, which, as perceived or envisioned, was so-to-speak vis-a-vis the perceiving person] would also be grasped and expressed as *Subject*, namely as one's own thinking, one's own actual and living thought. As such it could turn into what Hegel terms the Notion *(der Begriff)*." Giegerich, Soul's Logical Life, 48.
92. Žižek, *Less Than Nothing*, 360.
93. For Giegerich, the neurotic suffers terribly at the expense of the neurotic soul, which delights in her misery. However, for the neurosis to dissolve, the neurotic must acknowledge her willing participation, however distant that willingness may seem to her consciousness.
94. Ruda, "Entlassen," 122.
95. In Ruda, "Entlassen," 122.
96. Hegel, *Phenomenology of Spirit*, para. 492.
97. Ruda, "Entlassen," 125.
98. Hegel, *Phenomenology of Spirit*, para. 492.
99. Oftentimes we use the term "soul-making," which has the helpful connotation that active "work" on our part is required, but has the unhelpful implication that it requires our active involvement, that soul "needs" us in order to be made—which shoves us right back into an ego-oriented, personalistic perspective (in other words, not you or I in particular, but human consciousness in general, and if it's not us, it will be somebody else). The reason the comparison of soul-making to receiving an event of Truth is helpful is because all the subject can do to receive an event of Truth is to *prepare* to receive it—and it will either come or it won't. The preparation to receive also correlates to the preparation Giegerich describes as taking up the mask of the psychologist or the psychological I. In addition, one is only a subject able to receive an event upon receipt of the Event. Again we have the correlation to the notion that one can only reach soul if one is already there to begin with.
100. In addition to the consciousness of the Psychological I, an example of subjectivization might be the description of "true prayer" as "only a true prayer if it is already God who through one's human praying is speaking the prayer to God, in other words, *not* the human person per se—not the ego" (Giegerich, *What Is Soul?*, 125). Here we might say that true prayer was made possible through the subjectivization of the worshiper, whose status *as* subject was reinstated through the event of true prayer.
101. http://www.lacan.com/zizek-badiou.htm.
102. Critical theorists identify three ways to *betray* an event of Truth: (I) The first is a simple disavowal, with a corresponding attempt to follow old patterns as if nothing had happened, as if it were just a minor disturbance (an example for us would be the denial of soul in psychology altogether); (2) the second betrayal

is the false imitation of the event of Truth (i.e., new-age re-enactment of an ancient mythological ritual as a pseudo-event); and (3) a direct positivization or ontologization of the Truth event, with its reduction to a new positive order of Being (i.e., the ego's program of individuation and establishing a connection with soul, or with the wholesale reduction of psychology as the discipline of interiority to a branch of depth psychology called "PDI").

103. Ruda, "Entlassen," 126.
104. Wolfgang Giegerich, "Rupture, or: Psychology and Religion," in *The Neurosis of Psychology* (Collected English Papers, Vol. I, p. 231) (New Orleans, LA: Spring Journal, Inc., 2005).
105. Ruda, "Entlassen," 127–128.
106. Wolfgang Giegerich, "First Shadow, then Anima, or The Advent of the Guest," in *Soul Violence* (Collected English Papers, Vol. III, pp. 77–109) (New Orleans, LA: Spring Journal, Inc., 2008), 104.
107. Žižek, *Less Than Nothing*, 298.
108. Giegerich, *The Soul's Logical Life*, 194.
109. Giegerich, *Neurosis*, 351.
110. This process is beautifully laid out in Giegerich's essay, "First Shadow, then Anima," and faithfully documents, as it were, the soul's journey of forgiveness.
111. Žižek, *Less Than Nothing*, 111.
112. Žižek, *Less Than Nothing*, 111.
113. Giegerich writes, "A real death through yellowing and a yellowing that 'applies to psychology itself' would . . . refer to that process through which, in alchemical imagery, the vessel itself is drawn into the process; it can no longer preserve its intactness as container vis-à-vis the prima material and the corrupting process that the matter undergoes. The vessel, too, is subjected to the corruption" (Giegerich, *The Soul's Logical Life*, 194).
114. Giegerich, *Neurosis*, 344.
115. Giegerich, *Neurosis*, 344.
116. Giegerich, "God Must Not Die!," 43–44.
117. Giegerich, *Spring # 84 A Journal of Archetype and Culture*, 49.
118. As reflected in the seemingly monumentally impossible entreaty, "Love your enemies."
119. Insofar as it exercises the dialectical logic of absolute negation and sublation, insofar as it transgresses the psychological difference to "reach the truth in its own conceptual element" or absolute negativity, Psychology as the Discipline of Interiority is fundamentally a psychology of forgiveness.
120. I am using the terms "husband" and "wife" merely for clarity, but obviously the idea applies to same-sex couples and/or any relationships where betrayal may occur.
121. James Hillman, "Betrayal," in *Senex and Puer* (1st ed., Vol. 3, pp. 193–213) (Putnam, CT: Spring Publications, 2005) (Original work published 1964), 196.
122. Hillman, "Betrayal," 196–197.
123. Hillman, "Betrayal," 211.
124. Hillman, "Betrayal," 212.
125. Hillman, "Betrayal," 212.
126. I would venture to guess that for Hillman, the experience of profound betrayal can cause a *real* expansion of consciousness to occur (in other words, the experience of betrayal supports individuation). For Giegerich, a person's traumatic experience of betrayal is merely a simulation, a neurotic attempt to re-experience the Absolute in the form of a theatrical "expulsion from the garden."
127. Giegerich, *The Soul's Logical Life*, 194.
128. Semantically, the betrayal would exist as it actually *is*—a sublated moment in the history of the marriage.

129. Wolfgang Giegerich, *Soul Violence* (New Orleans, LA: Spring Journal Books, 1988).
130. Žižek, *Less Than Nothing*, 362. Žižek describes this in terms of an appearance of "abstract universality," which I liken to objective consciousness (soul).
131. Žižek, *Less Than Nothing*, 478.
132. Giegerich, "God Must Not Die!," 54.
133. The relentless interiorization of the positivity of the semantic level that occurs through the process of absolute negation would reveal this underlying logic (i.e., "the soul") would "probably . . . become apparent as being Love (with a capital L) . . . [I]nfinite Love as objectively existing Concept (the self-comprehension of the mind), Love as absolute logical negativity, fluidity, interiority, Love as "self," inner infinity." Giegerich, "The Movement of the Soul," in *Soul always Thinks*, 323.
134. *A Course in Miracles*, 1976/2007, p. 562, Ch 26-IX-6-1.
135. G.W.F. Hegel, *Lectures on the History of Philosophy*, E.S. Haldane and Frances H. Simson (Trans.) (Vol. III Medieval and Modern Philosophy) (Lincoln, NE: University of Nebraska Press, 1995), 233.
136. See Wolfgang Giegerich's, "'*Geist*' Or: What Gives Jungian Psychology Its Absolute Uniqueness and Is the Source of Its True Life," in J. Sandoval & J. Knapp (Eds.), *Psychology as the Discipline of Interiority: 'The Psychological Difference' in the Work of Wolfgang Giegerich* (London: Routledge, 2016), 17–42.
137. Slavoj Zizek & Boris Gunjevic, *God in Pain: Inversions of Apocalypse*, trans. by Ellen Elias-Bursac (New York: Seven Stories Press, 2012), 171.

Index